State of Affairs

The Science–Theology Controversy

RICHARD J. COLEMAN

CASCADE *Books* • Eugene, Oregon

STATE OF AFFAIRS
The Science–Theology Controversy

Copyright © 2014 Richard J. Coleman. All rights reserved. Except for brief quotations in critical publications or reviews, no part of this book may be reproduced in any manner without prior written permission from the publisher. Write: Permissions, Wipf and Stock Publishers, 199 W. 8th Ave., Suite 3, Eugene, OR 97401.

Cascade Books
An Imprint of Wipf and Stock Publishers
199 W. 8th Ave., Suite 3
Eugene, OR 97401

www.wipfandstock.com

ISBN 13: 978-1-62564-701-6

Cataloguing-in-Publication data:

Coleman, Richard J.

State of affairs : the science–theology controversy / Richard J. Coleman.

xii + 272 pp. ; 23 cm. Includes bibliographical references and indexes.

ISBN 13: 978-1-62564-701-6

1. Religion and Science. 2. Knowledge, Theory of. I. Title.

BL240.2 .C255 2014

Manufactured in the U.S.A.   10/20/2014

This book is rightfully dedicated to my father, James M. Coleman, a graduate of Rensselar Polytechnic Institute, an engineer all his life. My father lived his life in the truths of his Christian faith and the principles of science. While he never found it necessary to explain himself, I have, and found myself writing this book.

Contents

Preface   ix

1   The Contemporary Scene   1

     The New Atheism
     Liberal Protestant Theology
     The Evangelical Turnaround
     The Roman Catholic Tradition
     Bothersome Questions

2   Irreconcilable Differences   30

     Rereading History
     A History of Irreconcilable Differences
     A Clash of Methodologies
     Conclusion

3   The New Rapprochement with Science   70

     Amicable Separation
     Antecedents
     The New Rapprochement

4   Lingering Questions and Some Tentative Conclusions   110

     Lingering Questions
     Some Tentative Conclusions

5   The Distinctiveness that Is Science   142

     The Measure of All Things
     Radical Reductionism
     To Think Mathematically
     Tinker, Inventor, and Engineer

I ask whether theology has been bent out of shape by chasing science's methodological success. Has she lost her distinctive voice? And can she establish a place at the table of secular issues of importance without a firm grip on what she does best, or what makes her methodology distinctive and legitimate?

What disquiets me is the possibility that Christian theology may have sacrificed a critical distance because she speaks a peculiar word arising from a faith in a peculiar subject. One has to wonder if liberal Christian theology has been so eager to disown the conflict syndrome of the past that it shies away from engagements that are not aimed at reconciliation.

I also pursue the thesis that in the attempt to find common ground between theology and science in a postmodern context, the new rapprochement has bowdlerized long-standing and substantial differences between the two disciplines in order to pursue a course of consonance. Drawing out this somewhat arguable conclusion, we will examine the thesis that in the last century, but particularly since the introduction of process theology, Christian theologians have been trying to reestablish theology's stature as a credible source of authentic and valuable knowledge by adopting a scientific mentality.

Lastly is the question concerning how we move the conversation to a new level if the participants are satisfied with maintaining the status quo. Notwithstanding the various research projects and exchanges that continue to take place, the lack of debate about fundamental differences regarding governing interests and methodological approaches prevents a deeper kind of exchange.

This, then, is not a book that seeks to advance the exchange between science and theology beyond a critical examination of the exchange itself. What you will not find is a review of familiar arguments that may have run their course. I have no desire to add to the long list of books that examine their history of mutual support, explore further the best model for dialogue, extend specific points of interfacing, or paint a promising picture.

The book's focus is the new rapprochement with science, and necessarily so because it constitutes a foundation from which we cannot retreat. One observation, though, is immediately worth mentioning. Over the years the conversation between the two disciplines has been muddied unnecessarily by pairing science with religion and by casting the opposition to be science versus Christian faith. Religion and science do belong to different realms of inquiry for all the usual reasons. Religion and faith are diffuse, undisciplined, and highly personal. On the other hand, science and theology are appropriate dialogical partners because both represent well-established disciplines along with the structure and professionalism required of them.

With this in mind, I will clear away the debris and focus on the issues, as I believe they should be defined.

The outline of the book is straightforward, though it is helpful to see how the main arguments unfold. The first chapter is historical in nature because a rereading of the history of science and theology with an eye on irreconcilable differences is necessary for the project at hand. The second chapter charts the development of the new rapprochement with science from its antecedents to a description of its principal arguments. The third chapter is more philosophical and theological in nature by following through with questions lingering from the first two chapters about specific suppositions that are normally taken for granted. Chapters four and five constitute a unit since they attempt to identify the integrity of science and theology, and this is done to further elucidate what constitutes a realistic expectation for future interdisciplinary intercourse. Chapter six is the last step in bringing together the pieces in order to suggest what needs to be done to move forward in the years ahead.

Hopefully this book will satisfy two readerships. The first are those who are finding their way through a century or more of intentional interfacing between those who have felt the tug to explore where their interests converge, or where they inevitably clash, or where they just go their separate ways. Second is a readership already engaged in cross-disciplinary conversations. They are in position to critique my evaluation and add their experience toward exploring new possibilities.

On a personal note, this is the book I should have written first. In two previous books I have been suggesting but not developing a thesis regarding the interplay between theology and science. In *Competing Truths* (2001) I recast the history of their relationship as one of sibling rivals. This is not only a different interpretation of their history together but also a different assessment of how they are presently positioned. If one were to characterize their relationship as sibling rivals during the seventeenth to nineteenth centuries, the twentieth century was a "cold war" of siblings preoccupied with establishing and defending their own domains. One way to view the publication of *Eden's Garden: Rethinking Sin and Evil in an Age of Scientific Promise* (2006) is to see it as a case study of what a rivalrous engagement would look like regarding a specific issue, namely sin and evil. Here again I broached the subject of how theology and science might understand their role as working toward the common good by counterbalancing each other. And again I argued for the integrity of each discipline as doing what the other discipline is not equipped or prepared to do. Let the two disciplines continue dialoguing together as intellectual rivals, and find mutuality where they can. Let there be more collaboration at the practical level concerning the pressing social and political issues of our times. But until now I did not tackle the issue of rapprochement directly.

Throughout the book I have tried to be as reader friendly as possible. Where a citation is straightforward it is included in the text with a full reference in the Selected Bibliography. When a citation is unwieldy and is enhanced with further comment, a footnote is found at the bottom of the page. Any references not found in the Selected Bibliography, because they are secondary, are fully cited the first time they are used but not in the Selected Bibliography.

1

The Contemporary Scene

THE TIME HAS COME to examine the state of affairs between science and theology with a degree of candor heretofore lacking. The last sixty years have witnessed a virtual explosion of interest in how modern science and traditional Christianity intersect. Standing as we do in the twenty-first century, we can declare that the classical warfare between theology and science is a leftover from a bygone era. At the same time a new atheism has arrived with its biting criticism of all things religious. And while the combative nature of this new atheism has stolen the headlines, just as the ongoing controversy about intelligent design has muddied the water, we are feeling the ground beneath our feet shifting with the emergence of new disciplines, such as evolutionary biology and evolutionary anthropology. The results of ground-breaking research into the origins of religion, morality, and human nature greatly enrich and expand the conversation as we have known it. In addition, there is an unexpected turn of events among Evangelicals who desire to hew out their own reconciliation with science. Replacing the negative attitude toward empiricism as undermining Christian faith is a positive effort to accommodate science and incorporate empirical evidence, even when it cuts across the grain of traditional beliefs. As these forces converge, the time is right to examine the state of affairs between science and theology as it now unfolds, and to render a critical but friendly assessment of where we are and how we might move forward.

We should be forewarned that we probably hold a variety of misconceptions about the nature of that "warfare."[1] A closer examination of the

---

1. See the variety of essays from a variety of disciplines (sociology, history, science, theology) in Harold W. Attridge, ed., *The Religion and Science Debate: Why Does It Continue?* (New Haven, CT: Yale University Press, 2009).

American scene reveals a more complex picture and the most egregious fault is the neglect of what I choose to call the new rapprochement (NR) between science and theology. By their creative and positive approach toward empiricism, we rightly associated Alfred North Whitehead and Teilhard de Chardin with charting a new course. As their influence waned another generation of scientist-theologians associated with Ian Barbour, Arthur Peacock, and John Polkinghorne moved to the fore in the 1950s and '60s. Succeeding them is a new generation of scholars who represent a broad spectrum of disciplines and who write, as I do, from within a long-standing theological tradition that has nothing to fear from a scientific perspective; a tradition that has been wrestling with, challenged by, and learning from science. Their model of rapprochement is now an established fact of life in our colleges and universities, seminaries, and publications.

The American landscape is unique for a number of reasons, no less than the fact that theology and science have coexisted in a contentious manner that is not necessarily true for Europe. The very diversity of religious denominations and sects compounds the problem of relying on generalities. An accurate assessment requires us to take into account a diversity of perspectives. At the very least they include Protestant, Evangelical, and Roman Catholic. In addition, because it has attracted so much public attention, the emergence of a new atheism must be mentioned, and this is where I start.

The New Atheism

There are ubiquitous signs that the gloves are finally coming off between the new atheists and the established apologists for Christian faith. A forum held in November of 2006 at the Salk Institute for Biological Studies in La Jolla, California, turned into an opportunity to tell it like it is. With an attendance of well-known scientists, along with fewer defenders of the faith, and even fewer believing scientists, religion took a beating. One speaker after another called on fellow scientists to openly challenge the irrationality of religious belief. Steven Weinberg, who famously finished his 1977 book on cosmology, *The First Three Minutes*, with the words that "the more the universe seems comprehensible, the more it also seems pointless," went a step further, saying, "Anything that we scientists can do to weaken the hold of religion should be done and may in the end be our greatest contribution to civilization."[2]

One reason for this abrupt change is not difficult to discern. Since September 11, 2001 and the terrorism that followed, religion has been scrutinized like never before. Apart from the political ramifications, the American public was stunned by the idea that such atrocities could be motivated by religious ideals. I remember very well the evening National Public Radio aired a program that debated whether religion, overall, did more good or more harm. It wasn't just Islam that found it necessary to defend itself; Christianity also found itself so compelled.

Not only is religion being measured and found wanting, a strategy is being employed to make believers look foolish and dangerous, and the scalpel being used is religion's failure to measure up to the standards of scientific inquiry. In *The End of Faith*, Sam Harris finds new ways to provoke the religiously minded. "Religious beliefs," he writes, "are simply beyond the scope of rational discourse."[3] Thus he strikes a common note. A postmodern atheism not only wants the gloves to come off, it wants to portray religion as unhealthy, irrational, delusional, and predatory. One could read the new atheism as a postmodern update of David Hume's project of a natural history of religion or even William James's study of religion as a variety of mystical experiences. But there is a difference because James belonged to a tradition epitomized in the Gifford Lectures and dedicated to interdisciplinary discourse.[4] The new atheism, on the other hand, wants to use science against religion as evidenced by such books as *God: The Failed Hypothesis, How Science Shows that God Does Not Exist* by Victor Stenger, or the offering of literary critic and intellectual contrarian Christopher Hitchens, *God is Not Great: How Religion Poisons Everything*. With an evangelical faith of their own, these contemporary atheists/agnostics clearly believe faith in God is an evolutionary adaptation that has outlived its usefulness. Thus, added to the stock arguments about religion being a human projection (Feuerbach) of some inner emotional need (Freud) is the implication that religion emanates from a childish lack of courage to see life and the world as it actually is.

---

2. George Johnson, "A Free-for All on Science and Religion," *New York Times*, November 21, 2006.

3. Sam Harris, *The End of Faith* (New York: W. W. Norton, 2005), 13.

4. For an insightful account of the Gifford Lectures see Witham, *The Measure of God*.

No survey of the contemporary scene would be complete without mentioning two highly respected scientists who also write for the general public. Daniel C. Dennett, the American-born cognitive scientist, is well known for a number of best-selling books that are both very lucid and controversial. The publications of *Darwin's Dangerous Idea* (1996) and *Breaking the Spell: Religion as a Natural Phenomenon* (2007) stand as bookends to a consistent argument. Charles Darwin's dangerous idea was natural selection but that in itself was not the tipping point. From the day of its publication in 1859, *On the Origin of the Species By Means of Natural Selection* raised the possibility that nature's design is simply the outcome of a natural process of selecting the fittest species. Quite intentionally, in order to avoid a distracting ruckus, if not outright rejection of this theory of evolution, Darwin did not press the implications of descent by natural selection. Dennett, though, relishes the task of showing that no intelligent designer is needed in order to explain how life began and how it evolved. Darwin was himself a self-confessed agnostic, unsure about the existence of a benevolent, omnipotent God or what role God plays in creating the universe. In his own words Darwin writes, "I gradually came to disbelieve in Christianity as a divine revelation. . . . Thus disbelief crept over me at a very slow rate, but was at last complete."[5] Dennett, on the other hand, forthrightly eliminates any reliance on a preexisting Mind or "skyhook" explanations used to grasp the seemingly unexplainable. In *Breaking the Spell* Dennett takes the next logical step, at least from his perspective, and urges "a forthright, scientific, no-holds-barred investigation of religion as one natural phenomenon among many."[6] Religion then is its own dangerous idea, for it provides nothing that is particularly unique or valuable.

Casting an even wider purview, historian of science David Hull clarifies the resultant collapse of four towering constructs supporting a theistic world view: the primacy of the *inductive method* along with the value of intuition and inspiration; the presence of unobservable *occult qualities*, such as Aristotle's four humors, vital forces, and even Newton's action at a distance (until proven after his death); *teleology* or the belief that things in the natural world "seek" to attain their given *purpose*; and

---

5. *The Autobiography of Charles Darwin*, 72. See also the introduction by David Quammen, who nicely summarizes Darwin's belief or lack of it, *Charles Darwin On the Origins of Species, The Illustrated Edition* (New York: Sterling, 2008), viii.

6. Daniel C. Dennett, *Breaking the Spell: Religion as a Natural Phenomenon* (New York: Viking, 2006), 17.

faith in the existence of ideal types or *essences*, which are static, immutable, and divinely created. Together these paradigms constituted a world view that science dismantled, slowly but steadily eliminating God as a casual explanation.[7]

Evolutionary biologist par excellence Edward O. Wilson has his own bookend publications that frame the issue as he sees it. Beginning with *Sociobiology: The New Synthesis* (1975) and amplified in *Consilience: The Unity of Knowledge* (1998), Wilson extols the virtues of scientific knowledge.[8] There is nothing conciliatory in his proposal since consilience has the goal of transforming as much philosophy and theology as possible into science.[9] Even when it comes to ultimate questions, science should rule since "theology, which long claimed the subject for itself, has done badly."[10] Wilson's elevation of science to the queen of all knowledge is echoed by Sam Harris, who has no use for religion because it does not measure up to the rigor of natural science, and Peter Singer, along with Paul Bloom, who believes we would be better served by objective normative truths.[11] What all of these writers have in common is little or no awareness of a Christian theological tradition that has been informed and shaped by modern science, that is, the NR described in this book, and the even longer tradition of a self-critiquing faith (see below).

The emergence of a few prominent voices who take religion to task for being juvenile, foolish, and irresponsible does not mean that they are have nothing valid to say, but for one important reason they miss their mark. They criticize religion for being unscientific, that is, religious belief lacks empirical standards and therefore cannot be counted as a source of legitimate knowledge. Apologists for Christianity routinely deflect this criticism by pointing out that religion and science address very different questions and serve very different purposes. Not incidentally, more than one prominent scientist has made the very same argument. Albert Einstein, no less, is remembered for his statement that connects science and religion when they each play out their defined role: "Science without religion is lame, religion without science is blind." The same sentiment was

---

7. Hull, *Darwin and His Critics*, Part I.

8. Wilson reiterates the same attitude concerning the superiority of science in his more recent *The Social Conquest of Earth*, 292-95.

9. Edward O. Wilson, *Consilience* (New York: Vintage, 1998), 12.

10. Ibid., 294.

11. Peter Singer, *The Expanding Circle* (Princeton, NJ: Princeton University Press, 2011) and Paul Bloom, *Descartes' Baby* (New York: Basic, 2004).

expressed by a more contemporary scientists of enormous stature, Freeman Dyson, in his acceptance speech as recipient of the 2000 Templeton Prize for Progress in Religion. "Science and religion are two windows that people look through, trying to understand the big universe outside, trying to understand why we are here. The two windows give different views, but they look out at the same universe. Both views are one-sided, neither is complete. Both leave out essential features of the real world. And both are worthy of respect."[12]

Adding confusion across the spectrum is the careless pairing of religion with science rather than theology with science. By taking the former route, all sorts of accusations can be made since by its very nature religion is not driven by a search for objective, normative truths. Religion bashing is relatively easy compared to a disciplined conversation between informed scientists and informed theologians, informed that is by both disciplines simultaneously. It is curiously telling that the new atheists prefer to engage a religion that is little more than a literal reading of its sacred texts. How convenient to ignore the substantial engagement between theology and science that accompanied the emergence of a modern science, not to mention the most recent engagement of a postmodern theology with a postmodern science (see chapter 2). What the new atheists do accurately reflect is the secularization of modern thought and life. The noted Canadian philosopher Charles Taylor depicts the story line of secularization in this way:

> Once human beings took their norms, their goods, their standards of ultimate value from an authority outside themselves; from God, or the gods, or the nature of Being or the cosmos. But then they came to see that these higher authorities were their own fictions, and they realized that they had to establish their norms and values for themselves, on their own authority.[13]

Secularization and modern science are, to be sure, major hurdles for religious beliefs, but the questions they pose must be addressed by the reasoned thought processes of individuals equipped to think both theologically and scientifically.

While newspaper headlines are adequate for capturing the public's attention, they obscure what is actually happening and what really

---

12. Freeman Dyson, "Progress in Religion" (Templeton Prize for Progress in Religion acceptance speech, Washington National Cathedral, Washington, D.C., May 16, 2000).

13. Taylor, *A Secular Age*, 580.

matters. Unless you read past the headlines about Stephen Hawking's inference that the universe might not need a grand designer (*The Grand Design*, 2010), you are unaware of a disciplined approach to the kind of questions astronomers and physicists have been posing since Ptolemy and Copernicus, Newton and Descartes. Out of the limelight of newspaper headlines and the hyped controversy over intelligent design is a revolution in how scientists understand why religious belief is so fundamental and universal in the evolution of our species. In many ways the standard conceptions we have of human nature have been turned on their heads. The received idea that we are born a to be molded by culture or that we are born with overriding instincts for self-preservation is being overturned. Displacing "red in tooth and claw" depictions is a view of evolution benefited by altruism, cooperation, moral conscience, and belief in a supernatural being or beings. Hot off the presses are major titles, such as *The Age of Empathy* by the well-known primatologist Frans de Waal, *The Better Angels of Our Nature* by the influential Harvard Professor of Psychology Steven Pinker, *Why We Cooperate* by the esteemed evolutionary anthropologist Michael Tomasello, and *Born Believers* by Justin L. Barrett, a research associate at Oxford's Center for Anthropology. And in a major interdisciplinary contribution of three volumes, Maxine Sheets-Johnstone ranges across the humanities and sciences to offer an in-depth analysis of the most fundamental roots of thinking, power, and morality.[14]

Two lines of thinking have emerged to explain the origins of religious belief. The first seeks to find in our distant past the adaptive or survival reasons why it might be advantageous to believe in the supernatural. The focus here has been on altruism and cooperation because these two traits, even though they may be of little value to the individual, might well serve the survival of a group. A diversity of religious traits could have benefits for the survival of a community that is cohesive and fiercely loyal. David Sloan Wilson, an evolutionary biologist at the State University of New York at Binghamton, builds his case that religion is best understood as a living organism with complex adaptive features (*Darwin's Cathedral*, 2002). The cost of holding admittedly counterintuitive beliefs—that Mary is both a mother and a virgin and so forth—can be outweighed by the benefits of being part of a cohesive group that

---

14. Maxine Sheets-Johnstone, *The Roots of Thinking* (1990), *The Roots of Power* (1994), *The Roots of Morality* (2008). All University Park, PA: Penn State University Press.

out-competes the others. Who is to deny that a symbolic belief system that departs from factual reality may also enhance group fitness in the long run? (Remember Durkheim's claim that human social life is only possible when a system of symbolism is present.)

A second and growing trend among scientists is a view that religion emerged by accident. Here religion is seen as a by-product of biological adaptations gone awry. Displacing "God is Dead" headlines is the eye-catching question, "Is God an Accident?"[15] During the struggle to survive humans acquired the ability to distinguish the world of objects from the world of minds and learned the best way to respond to each. The latter required a higher level of sophistication and abstraction, including the reading of minds (the intentions of another person), the belief in spirits to explain certain phenomena, the doctrine of the soul as a solution to the problem of death, and belief in a benevolent God ready to hear and answer the prayers of those who have nowhere else to turn. The propensity to posit the existence of minds, our own and the omniscient, is the basis for belief in immaterial souls and a transcendent God. These universal themes of religion, Bloom argues, emerged as accidental by-products of our mental systems, and this leads him to conclude that religion and science will always clash.

Both lines of thinking, nevertheless, lead to the same conclusion that religion can be explained away. When Pascal Boyer writes about the human instincts that fashioned religious belief, he titles his book *Religion Explained* (2001). That in a nutshell is what the natural sciences intend to achieve: a naturalistic explanation of all things religious, utilizing a methodology that excludes supernatural explanations. Darwin, it could be said, was doing much the same thing by explaining the origin of religion and morality as noteworthy, though not necessarily as unique events in the evolutionary history of human life, but he stopped far short of the naturalistic explanation provided by the modern utilization of the tools of biology, genetics, evolutionary psychology, paleontology, anthropology, and primatology.[16] With good reason E. O. Wilson bluntly summarizes the situation in this way:

15. Bloom, "Is God an Accident?," *Atlantic Monthly*, 105–12. Cf. Rodney Stark and Roger Finke, *Acts of Faith: Explaining the Human Side of Religion* (Berkeley, CA: University of California Press, 2000); Scott Atran, *In Gods We Trust: The Evolutionary Landscape of Religion* (Oxford: Oxford University Press, 2002); and Justin Barrett, "Exploring the Natural Foundations of Religion," *Trends in Cognitive Science* 4 (January 2000) 29–34.

16. See Darwin's chapter 4 of *Origins of Species*.

The Armageddon in the conflict between science and religion (if I may be allowed so strong a metaphor) began in earnest during the late twentieth century. It is the attempt by scientists to explain religion to its foundations—not as an independent reality within which humanity struggles to find its place, not as obeisance to a divine Presence, but as a product of evolution by natural selection. At its source, the struggle is not between people but between world views.[17]

Liberal Protestant Theology

Since Luther's decision in 1517 to challenge the Pope and Catholic doctrine about a good many matters, protest has been in the blood of Protestants. On the negative side, Protestants have sacrificed unity for independence, resulting in the individual's right to protest and question, even to establish new denominations. On the positive side, a spirit of *ecclesia semper reformanda est* ("the church is always to be reformed") permitted and encouraged an open discussion regarding what is true and essential regarding Christian faith. And even though Protestants looked to the Bible as the final court of last resort (*sola scriptura*), even the Scriptures were subject to the most searching analysis. A century or more later my own ministerial education at Princeton Theological Seminary included a thorough reading of Albert Schweitzer (*The Historical Jesus*, 1910) and champion of form criticism Rudolf Bultmann (1884–1976) for they were considered to embody the very same tradition of critical thinking that inspired the Reformation. It is important, then, to think of liberal Protestantism (Reformation theology) as a self-critiquing expression of Christian faith. In a best-selling primer for Christians, professor Daniel Migliore of Princeton Seminary reminds us of the classical definition of theology as *fides quaerens intellectum* ("faith seeking understanding"—Anselm), and thus "theology is faith asking questions and struggling to find at least provisional answers to these questions."[18]

Liberal Protestants made their peace with science easily enough. When the scientific method began to require a weighing of the evidence, a critical mind-set explained why both clerics and laymen delighted in discovering for themselves the intelligent design of a world they had

---

17. Wilson, *Social Conquest*, 255.
18. Migliore, *Faith Seeking Understanding*, 2.

taken for granted. And there was little to fear about where the evidence would lead since it could only open a door to understanding the universe God created. Nevertheless, over time an unresolved tension persisted because scientific evidence could not always be interpreted as leading back to an omnipotent and omniscient Creator. As science proceeded to discover a universe of indifference and chance, open-minded believers did not abandon empiricism per se, for the methodology proved itself to be fruitful beyond all expectations. The answer seemed to be one of accommodation. Theologians would work on reinterpreting Scripture and the history of how we understand God. After all, it was not a history of interpretation and understanding set in stone. It was, as would always be the case, that the ineffable One should be understood developmentally, as humans themselves evolved. In a postmodern context one understands knowledge to be historically conditioned, and so the challenge for liberals is to honor faith and revelation as a way of knowing what transcends the boundaries of what is finite and observable.

Protestant liberal theology is distinguished by its use of the critical historical method. Coming to the fore in the middle of the eighteenth century and the nineteenth century with Jean-Jacques Rousseau, a liberal tradition flowered at the hands of Lessing, Kant, Herder, Novalis, Hegel, Schleiermacher, Feuerbach, Strauss, and Ritschl.[19] The engine driving this liberal tradition is a critical spirit regarding all matters of truth but especially the historical texts so important to Christianity. It is a mind-set of looking behind the obvious, behind the literal reading, into how the text was constructed, and what the text's history and origins were. One important consequence of the critical historical method was to shift the locus of faith away from the metaphysical categories of scholasticism to the personal, redemptive-history characteristic of Protestantism.[20] Theology became primarily exegesis, and historical exegesis at that, and this served to orient Protestant theology toward the Darwinian insight that everything has a developmental history.

It would be difficult to underestimate the importance of the link between appropriating a historical critical methodology and adopting a modern consciousness, for the outcome was to swing liberal

---

19. By no means the only valuable analysis of this period, Karl Barth, *Protestant Thought from Rousseau to Ritschl* (New York: Harper & Row, 1952) remains an outstanding contribution.

20. This is the conclusion of Gerhard Ebeling, "The Significance of the Critical Historical Method," 31–36.

Protestantism into the orbit of modern science. It becomes perfectly understandable why Protestant theology does not have a history of fighting against modern science when it was trying to be scientific itself. A decisively modern consciousness would include the historical character of human truth, the knower as a disengaged autonomous self, the standard of reasonable evidence, the rejection of supernatural explanations, the preference for induction over deduction, and, to quote Charles Taylor, the willingness to "resist the comforting illusions of earlier metaphysical and religious beliefs, in order to grasp the reality of an indifferent universe."[21] Nevertheless, Protestant theology found itself in the awkward position of striving to be empirically grounded while not exactly measuring up to the empirical standards demanded of a natural science, and this, in part, was a matter of making an intentional choice. There never has been a natural fit between the humanities and the physical sciences, and Protestantism, beginning with Luther, has been leery of conceding too much to the power of reason. Sociologist and theologian Jacques Ellul writes unsparingly, "My affirmation is that the rationality of technique and all human organization plunges us into a world of irrationality and that technical rationality is enclosed in a system of irrational forces."[22] And therein lies the conundrum of Protestant liberalism, namely, how to demonstrate a modern consciousness, including an uncompromising use of empirical evidence, while being faithful to its tradition of questioning all aspects of human aspiration to claim for ourselves an objective, untainted truth

The Evangelical Turnaround

The declaration that religion and science are no longer at war has been reiterated to the point of not only being trivial but obscurantist. The notion that religion and science are at war with each other stems in part from a book written by John William Draper in 1874, *History of the Conflict between Religion and Science*. The book was not so much a history as a crusade to liberate scientific rationalism from the grip of Christian dogma (Roman Catholic dogma in particular). In 1896 Andrew Dickson White, the president of Cornell University, published a more restrained offering, *History of the Warfare of Science with Theology in Christendom*.

---

21. Taylor, *A Secular Age*, 574.
22. Ellul, *The Technological Bluff*, 170.

While their motives for writing their books were quite different, they both derided the intrusion of religious beliefs into the work of scientific progress and projected a cultural war between revealed religion and scientific rationalism. Even then the unfortunate categorization of two enemies at war with each other was not an accurate depiction of the complexity of the views held by most clergy and professional scientists.[23] Some may think the "war" continues, fueled by a new form of conservatism verging on fundamentalism, and that this is what leads us to the contemporary debate between creationists and the scientific establishment.[24] And to the extent that one chooses to categorize this controversy as "war," it seems to be a dead end because neither side is likely to convert the other. Way too much ink and energy has been spent arguing about intelligent design, and it is quite possible that the fury and flurry around intelligent design has blinded us to the ground swell that is, and will be, the locus of what matters.

Whether evidenced by the cover story of *Christianity Today* ("The Search for the Historical Adam," June 22, 2011), the catchy title of Denis Lamoureux's *I Love Jesus and I Accept Evolution* (2009), the level of interest in local churches and at seminars and workshops offered at Evangelical colleges and seminaries, or a generation of students who want to know how to fit together an age of dinosaurs and the Adam and Eve story, a growing number of Evangelical Christians have turned the page, so to speak, and are requiring a new perspective. The *New York Times* best seller by Francis S. Collins, *The Language of God: A Scientist Presents Evidence for Belief* (2006), fits the bill in every way. In 2007 Collins took a crucial step in opening an avenue of dialogue among progressive Evangelicals by establishing a forum for exploring the belief in theistic evolution: the BioLogos Foundation (www.biologos.org). Francis Collins is by no means a name to pass over lightly. He was President's Obama's choice in 2009 to assume the directorship of the National Institutes of Health, America's largest biomedical research agency. He is also the same Francis Collins who stood beside President Carter in 2000, along with his rival, Craig Venter, in the race to announce to the world a working draft of the human genome. What is remarkable and heartening is that here is

---

23. Complexity is the theme of articles collected by Lindberg and Numbers, *When Science*. For the reference to Draper and White, see Livingstone, "Re-placing Darwinism," 192–94.

24. See Kenneth R. Miller, *Only a Theory: Evolution and the Battle for America's Soul* (New York: Viking, 2008).

a renowned scientist and a confessing Evangelical Christian demonstrating that the two realms of Christian faith and science can be reconciled in a practical way.

As the editor of *Perspectives on Science and Christian Faith*, the journal of the American Scientific Affiliation, an organization of Evangelical scientists and individuals committed "to investigat[ing] any area related to Christian faith and science," Arie Leegwater relates his own "hard lesson." In his introductory editorial for an issue devoted to the historical Adam, genomics, and evolutionary science, Professor Leegwater recounts his experience of walking through the new David H. Koch Hall of Human Origins at the Smithsonian Museum of Natural History in Washington, D.C. "One is taken on a journey of over seven million years," he writes, "and I found myself rethinking some of my long-cherished positions." [25]

For those who teach science and are well acquainted with the rubrics of science, such as members of the American Scientific Affiliation, the process of rethinking is not so earthshaking. It would be misleading, however, to jump to the conclusion that reconciling traditional Christian beliefs and science means the same thing for everyone. Even when defending inerrancy or verbal inspiration is no longer the primary issue, the historicity of the Bible remains a contentious issue (see below). But it seems that those already trained as scientists see a bigger picture, which overrides an "intense battle between believing science and believing Scripture."[26]

Recently, the historicity of Adam and Eve has come to the forefront, revealing how divided Evangelicals remain. There are several ways to interpret the Genesis account, and each reveals a fault line. God directly created Adam and Eve, the historical parents of the human race. And it is this individual (Adam) that Luke refers to in recounting the ancestry of Jesus reported in chapter 3 of his Gospel. It is the same Adam St. Paul refers to in Romans 5 as the way sin entered the world and spread to all humans. Such an interpretation leaves little room for evolution. Bluntly

---

25. Arie Leegwater, "Editorial," *Perspectives on Science and Christian Faith*, 62/3 (September 2010), 145–46.

26. Sixty-four percent of white Evangelical Protestants remain opposed to evolution; Karl W. Giberson, "2013 Was a Terrible Year for Evolution," *The Daily Beast*, January 2, 2014, http://www.thedailybeast.com/articles/2014/01/02/2013-was-a-terrible-year-for-evolution.html. Giberson, a science professor forced to leave his position at an Evangelical college, comments that when Evangelical students took one of his classes, about half rejected evolution at the beginning but by the end of the semester, most accepted it; "Science and Belief," *The Christian Century*, February 5, 2014, 8.

stated by Peter Enns, an Old Testament scholar, "a literal Adam as a special creation without evolutionary forebears is at odds with everything else we know about the past from the natural sciences and cultural remains."[27] Some posit the interpretation that God conveyed the divine image upon the human species indirectly through evolution. Adam and Eve could then be the first hominid group to evolve to the point where humans were sufficiently self-conscious to know they were created and responsible for their actions. Or a slightly different interpretation argues that Adam and Eve were an actual historical pair living among many about 10,000 years ago when they were chosen to represent the rest of humanity before God. Thus, Adam and Eve would be both historical beings with an evolutionary history and unique in that they were singled out.

Conservative Christians are reluctant to forfeit the historicity of particular texts since to do so implies that Adam and Eve were merely fictional or literary figures. In addition, it becomes necessary to explain the origin of original sin, a critical doctrine when tied to the redeeming work of Jesus Christ. If sin did not have a specific origin and reference to an actual pair of human beings, then it seems to fall prey to the murky waters of evolutionary development over a very long period of time. Even as the debate continues, there is disagreement whether such questions "could produce a huge split right through the heart of conservative, orthodox, historic Christianity" or become simply a peripheral disagreement that will "percolate along as an issue and more of the evangelical church will become fine with it."[28]

Nevertheless, Collins and his coauthor of *The Language of Science and Faith*, Karl W. Giberson, personify a new no-nonsense attitude when it comes to science, and they will have nothing to do with finding a place for supernatural explanations, such as Adam and Eve as a unique creation, when a scientific explanation is adequate. They write unapologetically, "We see no reason to insist that God must miraculously intervene to accomplish things like the origin of species, that God could just as well do by working through the laws of nature."[29] The resurrection of Jesus Christ, though, would be an exception because it is like no other historical event. Here, there seems to be a fair amount of equivocation

---

27. Richard N. Ostling, "The Search for the Historical Adam." *Christianity Today*, June 2011, www.christianitytoday.com/ct/2011/june/historicaladam.html.

28. Ibid. Here Outling is quoting Michael Cromartie and Karl W. Giberson.

29. Giberson and Collins, *The Language of Science and Faith* (Downers Grove, IL: InterVarsity), 71–72.

concerning miracles. Checking the BioLogos web page where questions are asked and answered, miracles are still affirmed both in Scripture and daily life. This means one can hold both views simultaneously; an event could be both miraculous and be explained scientifically.

In the instance of Adam and Eve, it would seem, there are just two alternatives: they were either uniquely created or evolved as one among many. The latter, however, is not very miraculous but that doesn't bother Collins and Giberson. And such a position would not be very far from one expressed by Galileo Galilei: "The task of wise interpreters is to strive to find the true meanings of scriptural passages agreeing with those physical conclusions of which we are already certain and sure from clear sensory experience or from necessary demonstration."[30]

The theological rationale behind this turnabout is stated simply and straightforwardly by one of the widely recognized proponents of rapprochement, Arthur Peacocke, who declares, "Indeed, because the world is created by God, knowledge through science of the world must enhance and clarify and, if need be, correct our understanding of God and of God's relation to creation, including humanity."[31] Keeping in mind that the NR began with an openness to allow scientific discoveries to shape and sharpen theological truth claims,[32] Evangelicals are realizing that a credible theology in a modern context must not only distance itself from a regressive defensiveness but find a way to embrace science as an indispensable resource for the progressive understanding of God.

The Roman Catholic Tradition

Within Roman Catholicism the history of interaction between science and theology has been dominated by four distinct influences. First and most obvious is the hierarchical and authoritative structure of the church. The conflict between Galileo and the Roman Catholic hierarchy was essentially a clash between an established priestly authority and the burgeoning authority of an independent discipline. Galileo conceded the church's authority over matters of faith and morals but held steadfast to

---

30. Letter to Benedetto Castelli, December 21, 1613. Quoted from Nancy K. Frankenberry, ed., *The Faith of Scientists* (Princeton, NJ: Princeton University Press, 2008), 12–13.

31. Peacocke, *Evolution: The Disguised Friend*, viii.

32. See Ted Peters's introductory statement that "scientific knowledge should inform and sharpen theological truth claims" in Peters, *Science and Theology*, 1.

the claim that scientific observation and measurement were not hypothetical (speculative) but deserving of their own authority. The outcome of this particular encounter is well known, but a limited lens in what it tells us about the Roman Catholic tradition of finding a place for science.

Second is the Catholic emphasis on the rational foundations for religious belief. Reason is understood to be a bridge between faith and the natural world since we were created to use reason and the world itself was created with a rational structure, which human intelligence is capable of perceiving. For Catholic thought, then, philosophy plays an enormous role in structuring theology rationally and thus rendering it believable. John Paul II reaffirmed "the positive contribution which rational knowledge can and must make to faith's knowledge."[33] Aquinas and his *Summa Theologiae*, which he began in 1268 and was still amending as death came, represented a willingness to embrace truth wherever it might be found. Along with St. Albert the Great, Thomas was among the first to acknowledge the autonomy of philosophy and (Aristotelian) science as required to complete our understanding of God.

Third is the long-standing commitment to the unity of truth. The unity of truth is a fundamental premise asserting that various modes of knowing will eventually lead to truth in all its fullness. Thus, faith and reason, revelation and natural knowledge, while separate and distinct, "not only in their point of departure but also in their object," cannot ultimately contradict each other because they emanate from the same divine source.[34] Because of the possibility of knowing a universally valid truth, Catholic theologians are motivated to engage other disciplines in a sincere and authentic manner.

Fourth is the dependence on a theology of natural law and the role it plays in what it means to be a moral person. The Catholic understanding of natural law is normally associated with the development of a moral ethic, but it intersects with science because "natural" implies an understanding of what is natural. The concept of natural law is easily misused and misunderstood unless it includes three traditional loci: nature, reason, and Scripture. Briefly stated, natural law refers to those theological principles that arise from the natural givens of human life as understood in the context of Scripture and the goodness of God's creation. "Contrary to what is commonly assumed," Jean Porter points out, "natural law

---

33. John Paul II, *Fides et Ratio*, 71.
34. Ibid., 70.

thinkers did not attempt to derive moral principles from a supposedly self-evident and fixed conception of human nature."[35]

In other words, natural law is a selective process privileging certain aspects of nature rather than assuming our capacity for moral judgment (conscience) is trustworthy. The concept of the natural, then, is a theological notion built on key scriptural texts from Genesis and the Pauline letters that enable proponents of moral law "to distinguish between those aspects of our nature that are normative, and those that are not."[36] A case in point is when Catholic theology privileges procreation as the primary purpose of sexuality while de-emphasizing sexuality as an expression of personal love between two persons. As a further point of clarification, Porter reiterates, "None of this implies procreation is the only legitimate purpose of sexual activity or marriage, or that it is the only purpose that can be defended on theological grounds," but it does promote a particular ideal of marriage on the part of the Christian community.[37]

Unfortunately, the controversies surrounding Galileo Galilei and Charles Darwin have unduly colored how we regard the interaction between Catholicism and science. At the expense of a more balanced perspective, these two controversies accentuated the disparity between an entrenched magisterium and the multitude of priests and scientists who have dedicated themselves to exploring the beauty and rationality of the heavens above and living things below. The Catholic Church acknowledges it erred gravely in these matters by not trusting its own pronouncements concerning the unity of truth and the freedom each discipline requires to pursue truth. In its awakening to the modern science of the twentieth century, the Catholic Church has demonstrated an openness that welcomes what science can contribute to our understanding of human nature and the universe. The Catholic commitment to science is amply evidenced by the widely recognized work of the Vatican Observatory and the Pontifical Academy of Sciences; the latter includes forty-three Nobel Prize winners. Addressing the Pontifical Academy of Sciences, and before his resignation, Pope Benedict XVI recast the famous dictum by Einstein in this way: Without faith and science informing each other "the great questions of humanity leave the domain of reason and truth, and

---

35. Jean Porter, *Natural and Divine Law: Reclaiming the Tradition for Christian Ethics* (Grand Rapids: Eerdmans, 1999), 17.

36. Ibid.

37. Ibid., 221–22.

are abandoned to the irrational, to myth, or to indifference, with great damage to humanity itself, to world peace, and to our ultimate destiny."[38]

Bothersome Questions

This survey of the contemporary scene exposes a number of interrelated questions that only make sense because we are looking at the bigger picture. Insofar as the NR has chartered a new course in bringing theology and science to the same public table of conversation, it deserves to be examined and evaluated. Protestants, Catholics, Evangelicals, and the new atheists bring to the discussion a unique contribution, accompanied by inherent difficulties, which will need to be addressed as the religious-scientific dialogue continues. Undoubtedly, to the extent that one is steeped in a conservative or liberal environment, there are hurdles, or a lack of them, that affect where you begin and where you end. But surely the astonishing discoveries of modern science invite, if not compel, a fresh examination of cherished beliefs. The NR, as I explicate in this book, has demonstrated that a historical, orthodox Christian faith does not have to be compromised in order to accommodate science. But even when we take into account the way many Christians have been shown how to think critically and positively about science, and been led to a mature understanding of their Christian faith, the NR by itself is not all that it could or should be. The questions below are meant to highlight where we need to look if we are to move forward.

Questions Specifically for the New Atheists

The frankness of the new atheists is something of a distraction, but not unwelcomed, because religion is forever in need of a good critique. According to their understanding of the contemporary scene, society would be better off if religion would quietly go away. What they offer in a positive appraisal, however, is overshadowed by the misconceptions they perpetuate. One of their basic arguments is that little would be lost and much would be gained if atheism were to prevail, for then we would be free to enjoy the benefits of a more progressive culture. This is scarcely

---

38. Quoted from Carol Glatz, "Faith, science must cooperate to protect people, planet, pope says," Catholic News Service, November 8, 2012, www.catholicnews.com/data/stories/cns/1204697.htm.

an unarguable position and the first reaction is to point out the valuable contribution of religion to society and individuals. John Haught, one of the foremost contributors to the NR, takes a different tack. He refers to new atheists such as Dawkins, Harris, and Hitchens as soft-core atheists, that is, in comparison to Nietzsche, Camus, and Sartre. He argues that the new atheism is delusional in its own way if it believes that a secular humanism stripped of religion is the answer that puts us on the path of human fulfillment. Evacuate religious beliefs, so the argument goes, and educators would be free to teach science without the interference of creationists, and students would learn that evolution rather than special creation is the ultimate explanation of who we are. Haught's rejoinder cuts to the quick. This, of course, is precisely the kind of atheism or secular humanism that nauseated Nietzsche and made Camus and Sartre cringe.[39] These more muscular critics, Haught retorts, at least had the insight to realize that a full acceptance of the death of God would still leave us with ideals but neither the discipline nor the communities to keep us banging on the doors of poverty, injustice, and hatred.

At the center of what the new atheism gets wrong about religion is a complete amnesia about the other kind of religion. For as much as they get right in their critique, it only applies to a religion that makes promises of inner peace at the expense of any self-searching thoughts, that turns us into fanatics instead of peacemakers who practice nonviolence, and that arouses devotion to tribe and state rather than envisioning an abiding peace among all of God's creatures.[40] Without a doubt, there is a fundamentalism that exists and even thrives by doing exactly what religion should not inspire, but in order to unmask that kind of religion we do not need to perpetuate the impression that religion has never been, nor could it be, the source of an uncommon hope and love that resists all that kills and harms another human being, and the Earth we inhabit.

The new atheists make the claim again and again that only truths based on evidence can count as knowledge worth knowing. The argument I will make is not for theology to find common ground with science by denying that science is superior when it comes to a particular kind of

39. John Haught, "Amateur Atheists," *The Christian Century*, February 26, 2008, www.christiancentury.org/article/2008-02/amateur-atheists. See also his book, *God and the New Atheism* (Louisville: Westminster John Knox, 2008).

40. For example see Nicholas Wolterstorff's description of God's shalom in *Until Justice and Peace Embrace* (Grand Rapids: Eerdmans, 1983); or Miroslav Volf, *Exclusion and Embrace* (Nashville: Abingdon, 1996).

knowledge. Rather, the question before us is whether the knowledge that matters is necessarily of a scientific kind. The new atheism cannot get beyond the presumption that since science is the superior methodology, it should therefore be the great integrator, reminiscent of a time when theology was queen of human knowledge.[41] Theology is readily ignored because the culture is convinced that the only relevant truth is what yields technological advancement. This is an old "battle" between two cultures, notably the humanities and the hard sciences, and the new atheism has targeted religion as a cultural artifact of useless nonsense. But again it must be noted that Christian theology has from the beginning been a culture apart, bearing a word, and a Word, that proclaims the foolishness of God to those seeking signs and wisdom, or in today's language, a Western culture of Baconian *science*, Cartesian *rationalism*, and Lockean *empiricism* (1 Cor 1:22).

Questions Specifically for Evangelicals

In *The Language of Science and Faith*, Collins and Giberson write with a sense of weariness: "It sometimes seems we are constantly protecting traditional doctrines, finding plausible reinterpretations and discovering new compromises that we can make to accept what science has discovered about the world without rejecting faith."[42] The weariness is born of continually fighting the same battles. If one compares the mainstream tradition of the NR with the burgeoning Evangelical turnabout, one observation stands out. Evangelical Christians find it necessary to answer many kinds of questions about evolution and other scientific matters that liberals have simply left behind. The evolutionary history of the human species is simply taken for granted. The BioLogos web page is filled with questions such as, *How should we interpret the Genesis flood account? What role could God have in evolution? How can evolution account for the complexity of life?* (See home page, "The Questions.") This is not to say that mainline Christians can answer these questions beyond generalities. Rather, these types of questions do not matter to them in the same way that they do for conservative Christians. And the reason why is essentially twofold: liberals have a critical historical understanding of the Bible

---

41. For a discussion of when theology was queen of the sciences—when the sciences included law, poetry, and philosophy—and how she was dethroned by modern science, see Coleman, *Competing Truths*, Part 1.

42. Giberson and Collins, *The Language of Science and Faith*, 177.

and think with a modern consciousness. When it comes to empirical evidence—evidence that is well established—the first reaction is not to doubt the evidence but to find ways to incorporate it into the larger body of Christian thinking.

As long as conservative Evangelicals are beholden to a biblical world view, they will make it very difficult to regard science as an ally in understanding the true nature of God. Evangelicals are thoroughly modern in how they live their lives. The difficulty arises specifically when your understanding of God is embedded in a biblical world view, and this world view clashes with the universe described by science. The biblical view of the world is one where Moses parts the Red Sea and Jesus walks on water, where God speaks as if he is another human, where chance and coincidences reflect the hand of God, where history is compacted to reveal those who are with God and those who are against him, where the judgment of God is promised and divine justice assured. The rub comes not only because a natural science will exclude all of this, *methodologically* speaking, but also comes in aces because the *ontology* of a modern world view is indifferent to humankind; it begins and exists at a sub-atomic and molecular level where indeterminacy and mutation proceed at such a slow and invisible pace that God's existence becomes an act of faith. Regardless of whether Adam and Eve were a unique creation or evolved, they lived in a world where everything else evolved gradually and over very long periods of time.

The theory of evolution invites us into a view of the world so different from Scripture that it requires every Christian who thinks in biblical terms to reexamine practically everything. At the very least, the individual Christian, who lives by a personal belief in a God who knows all things and works for the good in all things, is invariably at odds with a world that is capricious and filled with unsettling anomalies. The theory of evolution posits a world view that requires us to relinquish many of our comfortable ideas of divine order and rethink the limits of the divine. While a theistic interpretation of evolution is a valid starting point, it does not resolve a host of questions. Neither can it pick and choose, for it needs to find a place for the gradual emergence of new species by way of natural selection, common ancestry, chance at the quantum level, mutations, bad design, deformity, and the tragic aspects of life itself (e.g., birth defects, Lou Gehrig's disease, genocide). A universe that is cold and indifferent, an earthly world that is red in tooth and claw, and life processes that are meandering and driven by survival of the fittest are not transparent windows to an intelligent designer. A biological history that looks nothing like a straight line guided by purpose just doesn't preach easily in any pulpit. As John Polkinghorne once remarked, "The world is not full of items stamped 'made by God.'"[43] And if you take the next step, you confront the conclusion of Daniel C. Dennett that natural selection is the clear winner over intelligent design, and therefore the burden of proof has shifted to demonstrate how special creation is an adequate or even cogent explanation.[44] The decision will be, then, whether to accept evolution as not only an established explanation about nature but also a view of the world concerning all of creation.

Questions Specifically for Liberal Protestants

With unusual perspicacity Walter Brueggemann identifies the significance of Karl Barth's theological revolt. Commenting on Barth's *Epistle to the Romans* in 1919, Brueggemann discerns how Barth set the stage for a radically new season of theological discourse that "refused the well-established assumption of a self-confident liberalism." In doing so, Barth "committed an overt act of epistemological subversion," breaking with the nineteenth-century valuing of "reasoned universals and a Cartesian program of autonomous reason."[45] In light of this, the question contemporary liberal Protestants might ask themselves is whether the effort to model theology after science impedes all calls for a new overt act of epistemological subversion. Certainly theologians, such as Hans Frei, have warned of substituting a narrative of modernity for a narrative of faith where Scripture ceases to function as the lens through which theologians view the world and instead becomes an object of study.[46] Barth's enduring contribution lies in a methodology that secures Christian theology as a critical voice. In working through his own thoughts of how to write an Old Testament theology that is faithful to the texts, Brueggemann does not ignore the body of historical critical evidence but proceeds on the premise that the "reality of God is an exercise in the daring rhetoric

---

43. Polkinghorne, *Belief in God in an Age of Science* (New Haven, CT: Yale University Press, 1998), 1.

44. Dennett, *Darwin's Dangerous Idea*, 47.

45. Walter Brueggemann, *Theology of the Old Testament* (Minneapolis: Fortress, 1997), 16.

46. See Hans Frei, *The Eclipse of Biblical Narrative* (New Haven, CT: Yale University Press, 1974).

arising from the oddity of the subject."[47] The proposition, then, that needs to be examined is whether the contemporary effort to accommodate science has weakened the unique role of theology to speak a word that always maintains a critical distance whereby no ultimate attachments are permitted. Stanley Hauerwas, who is well known for his dissonant views, tries to set the record straight in this way: "Christian discourse is not a set of beliefs aimed at making our lives more coherent; rather, it is a constitutive set of skills that requires the transformation of the self to rightly see the world."[48]

Not too far removed from this critique is a concern that liberal Protestantism has lost its evangelical voice. This is a generalized critique heard in many quarters but has a particular relevancy regarding theology's rapprochement with science. The NR has not so much compromised a faithful witness to the primary tenets of Christianity as remitted its obligation to voice the peculiar perspective of a nonconforming polemic. Liberal theologians need to risk the consequence of countering a dominant scientific culture with their own particular culture of a "faith that will never let us be assimilated into any judgment about reality."[49] John Yoder writes the following to remind us what it means to be an evangelical witness:

> For a practice to qualify as "evangelical" . . . means first of all that it communicates news. It says something particular that would not be known and could not be believed were it not said. Second, it must mean functionally that this "news" is attested as *good*: *as shalom*. It must be public, not esoteric, but the way for it to be public is not an a priori logical move that subtracts the particular. It is a posterior practice that tells the world something it did not know and could not believe before. It tells the world what is the world's own calling and destiny, not by announcing either a utopian or a realistic goal to be imposed on the whole society, but by pioneering a paradigmatic

---

47. Brueggemann, *Theology of the Old Testament*, 18.

48. Stanley Hauerwas, *Dispatches from the Front* (Durham, NC: Duke University Press, 1994), 7.

49. Jacques Ellul has written extensively on the implications of modern technology for Christian faith. His *Living Faith: Belief and Doubt in a Perilous World* is just one example of someone who understands our modern situation while distinguishing those marks of an authentic Christian faith (quote is from 183).

demonstration of both the power and the practices that define the shape of restored humanity.[50]

Questions Specifically for Roman Catholics

Because an authoritarian structure circumscribes a Catholic way of doing theology, a genuine rethinking of Christian tenets in light of scientific discoveries can be difficult and exasperating. As conservators of Catholic teaching, those theologians engaged with science feel obligated to align science with dogmatic theology. Theologians, such as Karl Rahner and Edward Schillebeeckx, have been enormously creative but at the same time there is an ivory tower air about Catholic theology that does not sit well with experimental science. Science is essentially a bottom-up way of thinking, while Catholic theology begins with a teaching that relies on revelation and Scripture and reasons downward. And to the extent the NR has found common ground with science by being nonfoundational—recognizing the historical nature of all human knowledge—Catholic theology is foundational in the sense that it strives for a unified and organic *system* of truth.

Cardinal John Henry Newman (1801–1890) created an intriguing paradigm. When Darwin's theory of evolution was raising hackles across Europe, Newman stated that he was not frightened by Darwin, declaring evolution to be self-evident. And the most interesting dimension of Newman's admittedly iconoclastic way of thinking was his postmodern understanding of the historical character of Christian faith. In his review of three recent books devoted to Cardinal Newman, Ralph C. Wood writes, "Embracing evolutionary change and historical development, Newman argued that the vitality of dogma lies in its constant deepening and enlargement. Christian doctrine remains true to itself precisely by way of its organic growth."[51] While this is a paradigm worth remembering, it does not alleviate the burden of reconciling scientific evidence that does not square with Catholic teaching.

If one begins with the proposition, as it is asserted by John Paul II, that there are two orders of knowledge, faith and reason, revelation and natural, then the two need to be harmonized in order to reach a unity

50. Quoted from Rodney Clapp, "How Firm a Foundation," 92.
51. For Ralph C. Woods's review, see "Blessed and Dangerous," *The Christian Century*, July 25, 2012, 29.

of truth.[52] One can argue how successful Roman Catholic theology has been in forging a unified truth, but it seems clear that philosophy cannot continue to serve as a mediator as it has in the past. The Catholic tradition of utilizing philosophy to bridge two domains of truth does not transfer especially well when the disciplines are theology and science. The primary reason is the metaphysical nature of theology and the inherently antimetaphysical character of science. Most scientists are not interested in philosophical questions because of their responsibility to stick close to the empirical evidence. Theology is committed to asking ultimate questions while science is not, and this alone is sufficient to pull the two disciplines in different directions. Granted, the pull is not necessarily in opposing directions, but when your governing interests are so divergent the motivation to be dialogical partners is diminished.

It is more than perception that when the immovable truths of revelation meet the confirmed truths of empiricism something has to give, and in the final analysis dogmatic truth trumps all other kinds of truth despite the idealism that in the end there is only one all-encompassing truth. We should not fault Catholicism for insisting that knowledge which is peculiar to faith surpasses knowledge particular to reason when it pertains to knowing the true God. "This truth," John Paul II writes, "which God reveals in Jesus Christ, is not opposed to the truths which philosophy perceives. On the contrary, the two modes of knowledge lead to truth in all its fullness."[53] When we substitute "truths of science" for "truths of philosophy," the issue of reconciliation is intensified. Strictly speaking, truths of science are neutral or objective and it is the believer's faith that perceives the Creator. Nevertheless, Catholic thought certainly is aware of the tension that exists between empirical knowledge and revealed knowledge and is quite willing to use the domain of faith and revelation to criticize the secular domain of scientific knowledge and its effect. Both John Paul II and Benedict XVI spoke out forcibly against the lure of rationalism, reductionism, moral relativism, materialism, a diminished understanding of personhood, individualism, and a culture of death, and that is a positive gain arising from a critical distance. It does not, however, alleviate the difficulty of achieving a unity of truth.

Despite the great strides being made to acknowledge the importance and validity of scientific knowledge, any dialogue reaches an impasse

---

52. John Paul II, *Fides et Ratio*, 18, 70.
53. Ibid., 47.

when a theory of evolution, for example, is incompatible with revealed truth. Thus, to quote Pope John Paul II, who reiterates what he identifies as the essential point made by Pius XII, "if the human body takes its origin from preexistent living matter, [nevertheless] the spiritual soul is immediately created by God."[54] While safeguarding its teachings about original sin and original grace, a substantial difficulty is left to fester. Evolutionary theory, and a multitude of other scientific disciplines, would question how every aspect of human existence evolves except for the spiritual nature of being human. The image portrayed is that of a material vessel suddenly endowed with God's spirit over against an understanding of a species that gradually develops intellectually, emotionally, socially, morally, and spiritually, and does so as an integrated whole. Thus we find (some but not all) Roman Catholic theologians accepting but also contesting some aspect of the consensus understanding of evolution.

An attempt to resolve this kind of impasse is provided by John Paul's II statement in 1996, "The moment of transition to the spiritual cannot be the object of this kind of [scientific] observation, which nevertheless can discover at the experimental level a series of very valuable signs indicating what is specific to the human being."[55] While helpful, the suggestion being made compounds the problem. John Paul II is highlighting a methodological discontinuity between theology and science, where the former posits a creation theology in order to explain the origins of the spiritual nature of being human, and an evolutionary theory to explain the material dimension of being human. Unfortunately, this is just the kind of dualism that impedes dialogue and leaves the impression of two distinct and autonomous disciplines operating with two distinct and autonomous methodologies.[56]

Natural law has served as both a bridge and an impediment toward encouraging a robust exchange of ideas between theologians and scientists. Natural law depends on the supposition that we can know what are the *natural* givens of human life. Apart from the theologizing done within Christian community, it seems a little naive to believe a universal

---

54. Quoted in Stephen M. Barr, "The Design of Evolution," *First Things* (October 2005), 9.

55. John Paul II, "Message to the Pontifical Academy of the Sciences," October 23, 1996, www.ewtn.com/library/papaldoc/jp961022.htm.

56. In his article for *First Things*, "The Design of Evolution," October 2005, 9–12, Barr argues that the reason for the false opposition between Catholic doctrine and scientific theory is the invalid inferences drawn from neo-Darwinism. Yet, the opposition is not entirely false and Barr is trying to make the best of a difficult situation.

and accessible moral rationality is going to come into focus. Keeping in mind that you are extracting those givens selectively in accordance with Scripture and Catholic teaching, you find yourself asking this question. When Maxine Sheets-Johnstone begins her volume *The Roots of Morality* by writing "this book elucidates an understanding of morality grounded in the nature of human nature," do we trust that what she finds based solely on a scientific investigation of what it means to be human will coincide with Catholic teaching?[57] Even within the Catholic community some theologians argue that homosexuality is sinful because it is a violation of the natural order, while others are asking whether science fortifies the conviction that homosexuality is itself part of the human condition, that is, a natural part.

Working from a position of natural law has its limitations, ever more so as traditional moral lines lose clarity within the complexities surrounding euthanasia, cloning, new reproductive techniques, human enhancement, stem cell research, genetic engineering for the purpose of human enhancement, and synthetic biology. The latter highlights the difficulty in assessing what is truly natural when synthetic biology further blurs the line between natural and artificial, since humans are doing exactly what evolution does, only self-consciously; that is, continually refining its creation by means of naturally occurring mutations.[58]

The debate about the ethics of stem cell research is particularly revealing of the predicament natural law presents when there is a Jewish, feminist, Protestant, and Catholic perspective on what is *natural*.[59] The question about what constitutes life, or when human life begins, would seem to be the kind of issue science could decide. Obviously not. The clash between science and theology is not always about the science or even the interpretation of this or that science. Rather, and particularly so for Roman Catholicism, it is the dialogue about how we value or privilege the moral conclusions we draw from the science.

---

57. Sheets-Johnstone, *The Roots of Morality*, 1.

58. See Nicholas Wade, "Genetic Engineers Who Don't Just Tinker," *New York Times*, July 8, 2007.

59. For an informed discussion from a variety of theological perspectives, see Suzanne Holland, Karen Lebacqz, and Laurie Zoloth, eds., *The Human Embryonic Stem Cell Debate* (Cambridge, MA: MIT Press, 2001).

Questions for All

During the centuries when science was establishing itself as an autonomous method of knowing, theologians and scientists were finding ways to accommodate each other. That situation took a decisive turn when the theory of evolution secured empiricism as a methodology capable of encompassing both the physical universe and the biological world.[60] Darwin's publication of *The Origin of Species* in 1859 became a watershed date because a clear choice was now possible between two methodologies, each claiming a superior kind of truth. Consequently, theology and science separated into two distinct and autonomous domains, and scientists wanted to distance themselves from the intrusion of religious assumptions. The science that created the atomic bomb ushered in another era where scientific knowledge became the gold standard for knowledge that is certain and relevant. We now look to science to provide more than technological know-how. Science in the form of technology became the engine for our economy, the source of knowledge with the potential for immense evil and good.[61] Consequently, theology was forced to take a backseat because of its association with speculation, subjectivism, and fideism or a self-authenticating methodology. Theological knowledge could no longer compete with scientific knowledge because it was neither unified, objective, nor universal, and as a result could be deemed to no longer be relevant.

The NR with science represents a definable effort to restore theology's relevancy—a source of knowledge that matters—by aligning itself with science. Process theology, for instance, was a development aimed at reinterpreting traditional forms of theism in order to comply with the latest discoveries regarding the physical universe. The NR continues to dedicate itself to finding common ground between theology and science. Liberal Protestants, joined by a generation of Roman Catholics scholars, and now a growing number of progressive Evangelicals, understand that unless their truth-claims meet the common standard of rationality and accountability they will be ignored and even mocked by the new atheists.

---

60. For a discussion of how difficult it was for Darwin and his defenders to justify a methodology that was statistical in nature and characterized as one long argument in comparison to Newton's equations and precise observational consequences, see Hull, *Darwin and His Critics*, 32–322.

61. See Coleman, *Eden's Garden*, chapter 1.

The central question this survey raises is how to balance Christian faithfulness with credibility. Does theology need to be scientific in order to be credible (taken seriously) and true? Because we live in a scientific era, and will continue to do so for the foreseeable future, one can hardly say, "It doesn't matter." Granting that being faithful to one's history and tradition means something different for Protestants, Roman Catholics, and Evangelicals, Christian theology will still need to find a way to acknowledge science as a legitimate source of knowledge while retaining a critical distance in order to speak a word uniquely Christian. But how do Christians defend and proclaim a word uniquely their own in a way that is persuasive in the twenty-first century? Certainly this is not a new challenge for theologians who, unlike scientists, are obligated to speak a new word to every new generation. Christians know that the path of Protestant pietism, Catholic scholasticism, or Evangelical fundamentalism cannot succeed. A theology that is well informed by the ongoing discoveries of science is a first step, but only that. The next step will be more demanding and while the doors of dialogue have been opened, science and theology are confronted by the exacting task of working out a symbiotic relationship that is satisfying and fruitful for both disciplines.

2

Irreconcilable Differences

Rereading History

THE RAPPROCHEMENT BETWEEN THEOLOGY and science did not spring fully formed from the head of Zeus. The notion of rapprochement implies a conflict in need of resolution. To speak of an original rapprochement, as distinct from a new rapprochement, is awkward but nevertheless justifiable. In order to understand the why and how of the *new* rapprochement (NR) a minimal retrospective is required. This is ground well traveled by historians, philosophers, theologians, and scientists. I have no desire to add another account of religion and science and their history together, but neither can I accept the standard interpretations of that history. A rereading of that history focused on irreconcilable differences is by itself a contrarian notion. Just how irreconcilable those differences continue to be is less important than bringing to light a long history of differences that resist accommodation, and this fact of life being rooted in the very integrity of each discipline (chapters 5 and 6).

Much has been written about the inadequacy of typecasting religion and science as either natural allies or sworn adversaries. The excellent treatment by John Hedley Brooke, *Science and Religion: Some Historical Perspectives* (1991), and the older study by Alexandre Koyré, *From Closed World to the Infinite Universe* (1957), served to wrest this history from the simplicities of caricature and turn it toward fundamental issues. We have moved so far from John William Draper's *History of the Conflict between Religion and Science* (1874) and Andrew Dickson White's two-volume *History of the Warfare of Science with Theology in Christendom* (1896) that David Lindberg judges their effort to now be part of our Western cultural heritage.[1] While Draper and White reflect the nineteenth century's obsession with liberating science from the obscuration of religious dogma, Brooks and Koyré reflect a twentieth-century sensitivity to historical contexts and a variety of encounters between Christianity and science. The scholarship of our time is particularly interested in uncovering the subtleties and continuities of the interaction between theology and science. But in spite of better scholarship and new sensitivities, one can also point to a contemporary inclination to paper over long-standing differences, especially when we take into account the momentum of the last sixty years to find common ground between science and religion in order to foster an environment of mutual cooperation.

The "crisis" precipitating the need for rapprochement is invariably associated with the extraordinary scientific advances initiated by Galileo, Newton, and Darwin. It finds expression in the question, How did Christian theology react to a universe turned upside down by new methods of knowing? This is a story told many times with various interpretations. Richard Rubenstein locates a much older turning point in Western intellectual history to one historical moment in 1210 when the faculty of theology at the University of Paris successfully asserted its dominance over the faculty of philosophy by denying it the privilege of "reading" (lecturing or discussing) Aristotle's books of natural philosophy and commentaries "on pain of excommunication."[2]

Why Aristotle and why at that moment? Known as "the godless philosopher" because he explained the world solely on the basis of naturalistic principles,[3] Aristotle laid the foundation for a scientific methodology. Rubenstein summarizes those Aristotelian principles this way: "The ideas that the world our senses show us is real, not just a shadow of reality; that humans using their reason are capable of discovering general truths about this world; that understanding phenomena means

1. See Lindberg's essay, "Galileo, the Church, and the Cosmos," 58. For a broader perspective see David Lindberg and Ronald Numbers, eds., *God and Nature: Historical Essays on the Encounter between Christianity and Science* (Berkeley, CA: University of California Press, 1986).

2. Rubenstein, *Aristotle's Children*, 6, 162–66.

3. In this book "naturalism" refers to a way or method of knowing, formally known as epistemology. Materialism, on the other hand, is a philosophy about the way the world is, formally known as ontology. Naturalism or naturalistic explanations refer to a method of knowing that excludes supernatural explanations. The result may be an understanding of the universe as consisting of only matter (materialism), but a scientist may still choose to practice a naturalistic methodology while rejecting materialism because he or she believes materialism is unnecessarily reductive.

comprehending the relationship of cause and effect; and that natural processes are developmental, revealing to skillful inquirers orderly patterns of growth and change."[4] In 1210 the critical decision was whether impressionable students should be exposed to Aristotle. As Rubenstein points out, the struggle between faith and reason did not begin with Copernicus' challenge to an Earth-centered cosmology, or with Galileo's claim for universal laws governing all celestial bodies, but rather with the controversy over a natural philosophy emanating from Aristotle and a radically different approach to how we come to know the nature of the universe. What transpired in 1210 is by no means the end of the story. Rather, it is just the beginning of an unfinished story of how theology, science, and philosophy are joined at the hip trying to define their roles in the quest for truth.

The renaissance of Aristotle during the Medieval period had the effect of setting traditionalists (those espousing orthodoxy) against rationalists (those espousing an open inquiry), and setting Dominicans against Franciscans, who defended different ways to reconcile Christian faith with natural philosophy. Thomas Aquinas's *Summa Theologica* (begun in 1268 but unfinished at his death in 1273) demonstrated the possibility of unifying natural and revealed truths, but not even a Thomas Aquinas could quell the feeling that there was truth apart from revelation. The scandalous doctrine of Double Truth—scandalous because if God is the author of all that is true, there can be but one Truth—implied the possibility of an opposition between what is theologically true and what is empirically correct. Assuming that there is more than one kind of or one approach to truth, what happens if neither kind trumps the other? The church acted to protect believers against notions considered dangerous, and this included the notion of Double Truth, by issuing bans, prohibiting certain books, and ferreting out heretics. The Inquisition, notwithstanding, could do little to stop the secular pursuit of knowledge, and the time would come when a scientific way of knowing, armed with all of its brilliant verifiable discoveries, would challenge a solely theological way of coming to know.

While the future of Western intellectual development cannot be given a definite date, we understand that many decisions and many turning points are collapsed into one historical moment. The "revolution" that began with Copernicus and Kepler and culminated with Newton

---

4. Rubenstein, *Aristotle's Children*, 10.

and Darwin is likely to conceal the radical nature of what transpired. Koyré describes the scientific revolution as a "crisis of European consciousness," because the very framework of how humans understood themselves and the world was unalterably changed.[5] Prior to the scientific revolution when theology still ruled as "queen of the sciences," theologians were confident that no one could offer a competing world view with such grandeur and comprehensiveness as theology.[6] The mere peering through a telescope or, for that matter, any instrument that enables us to transcend the limitations of our senses, did not change the nature of the universe. Theologians found ways to accommodate a new picture of the cosmos. To speak of a "crisis of consciousness"—as significant as that may be—slights the import of an alternative methodology that could compete with theology.

Scientist and philosopher Michael Heller has his own list of defining characteristics of the scientific revolution: unification of the "earthly physics" and the "physics of heavens" (universal laws), dehierarchization of the universe, geometrization and infinitization of space, mathematization of science and its mechanization, and the increasing role of controlled scientific experimentation.[7] Heller is inclined to think that too much emphasis has been placed on a revolution that deprived humans their central position in the universe. He prefers to call our attention to the impact of a methodology that removes the self-reflecting subject for the sake of objectivity.[8] Not only was the stage on which the drama of salvation takes place relocated, but the telling of the drama itself became acutely more difficult. This gradual elimination of the self-reflecting knower who questions his knowing meant the gradual diminishment of narrative truth, so essential in Christian thought and Scripture.[9] Koyré's analysis shows us a universe where humans can no longer locate themselves within an embodied hierarchy of perfection and values. We may have been set free to pursue our own values, making of the world what we will—the very hope and desire of the Enlightenment—but we are left

---

5. Koyré, *From Closed World to the Infinite Universe*, vii.

6. For a fuller discussion of theology's reign as queen of the sciences, see Coleman, *Competing Truths*, 4–17.

7. Heller, *Creative Tension*, 41.

8. Ibid., 41–42.

9. See Coleman, *Competing Truths*, 212–38. Providing considerable depth to this eclipse of narration is Taylor's discussion of secular time, higher times, and "homogeneous, empty time" in *A Secular Age*, 54–59, 712–20.

with only a method of knowing that depends on a subject who loves the freedom to know all things more than any good that might guide us. In one of the hyperboles David Bentley Hart employs so well, he describes modernity as an exhilarating and intoxicating promise of a type of personal autonomy inconceivable in earlier ages, leading to "a model of freedom whose ultimate horizon is, quite literally, nothing."[10]

To speak of a scientific revolution is an invitation to pass over the revolutionary aspect of each step along the way: an immeasurable cosmos now measured and rendered infinite, uniform motion occurring across a grid of absolute time and space reconceived as relative and indeterminate, indivisible particles now manipulated and split open, the transmutation of individually created species displaced by a theory of random change and imperceptible mutations. To the degree that classical theology was wed to the Greek idea that perfection exists in the attainment and maintenance of a static state, Aristotle and the science he represented was shaken and discredited. Galileo not only presented a different view of the cosmos. The science he defended eventually removed the presumption of a world hierarchically ordered; an order in which a hierarchy of values was ontologically preserved. The values that mattered—harmony, ideal types, natural place, purpose, and man's place in the scheme of things—had less and less explanatory value. Koyré writes of the "lost man" who is relocated in a world where essences, purpose, divine intervention, and providence rapidly lost their credibility. Christian theologians were able to accommodate traditional teachings with an expanded view of space and time and even found ways to include notions of chance, extinction, development, and probability, but the biblical-Hellenistic-Thomistic world view was steadily being replaced by something very different and incompatible.

The contributors to *When Science and Christianity Meet* (2003) are primarily interested in case studies of particular encounters between science and Christian faith, and its editors David Lindberg and Ronald Numbers assert that "occasionally those conflicts that genuinely existed assumed the form of aggressive hostility, but the norm was interaction of a far more complicated sort, falling somewhere along the spectrum that separates the harmonious from the bellicose, with peaceful coexistence at its midpoint."[11] A fair enough assessment, and I concur that "more often

---

10. Hart, *Atheist Delusions*, 22, 26.

11. Lindberg and Numbers, eds., *When Science and Christianity Meet*, 5. The case study approach to the history of religion and science is also evident in John Brooke's

a workable peace was crafted," and yet I must distance myself from such a rosy picture. Those occasional conflicts of aggressive hostility are by no means a minor footnote, and we are justified in viewing them as disclosing the underbelly of a state of affairs too easily dismissed. The heated and public debates between T. H. Huxley and Bishop Samuel Wilberforce over our origins (monkey or not) or Clarence Darrow and William Jennings Bryan's courtroom battle over teaching evolution in public schools are well known, but the core issues are present in the more subtle differences of Thomas Burnet and the great Danish savant Nicolaus Steno. Both examined the same geological evidence and accepted the authority of Scripture but came to very different conclusion concerning the principles at work. Stephen Jay Gould presses his argument that much the same story is told in the dispute between Georges Cuvier, defender of a theory of geological catastrophism, and Charles Lyell, the champion of the uniformity of law. The real debate, Gould contends, was not dogma versus fieldwork, but "a conflict of metaphor between time's cycle and time's arrow." Yet, we cannot dismiss dogma so easily because Burnet and Cuvier were also defending a biblical world view where change and time were punctual, rather than slow and uniform unfolding, with "no vector of progress in any direction."[12]

In spite of their basic agreement concerning the mechanics of evolution, Charles Darwin and Alfred Russel Wallace differed about the fundamental question of whether or not evolution can account for what makes humans unique. Wallace, for instance, could not suffer a godless universe. Their quarrel however was no isolated event, for it encapsulated an enduring dispute involving chance and providence, teleological and nonteleological explanations, the accidental and the miraculous, special creation and extinction, special revelation and general revelation, impersonal and personal God, and the blood and tooth of evolution over against a loving, all-powerful God. At about the same time as empiricists of the day were lining up for or against Darwin and his theory of evolution, two theologians of considerable stature were making their views known. In his review of *The Life and Letters of Darwin*, appearing in the

---

Science and Religion and a subsequent book coauthored with Geoffrey Cantor, *Reconstructing Nature* (New York: Oxford University Press, 2000), as well as *Science and Religion: New Historical Perspectives*, ed. Thomas Dixon, Geoffrey Cantor, and Stephen Pumfrey (Cambridge: Cambridge University Press, 2010).

12. Gould, *Time's Arrow, Time's Cycle* (Cambridge, MA: Harvard University Press, 1988), 115, 123.

October 1888 issue of *The Presbyterian Review*, Benjamin B. Warfield, a defender of conservative Calvinism and the inerrancy of Scripture, did not think there was an inevitable clash between "the Darwinian form of the hypothesis of evolution and Christianity." A like-minded Princeton Presbyterian, Charles Hodge, was not so accommodating and judged Darwin's view of natural selection to be at odds with supernatural and final causes. While Warfield and Hodge were certainly concerned to protect the authority of Scripture, and notably so when it became a question of verbal inspiration, they did not regard an explanation by natural law to be incompatible with divine supervision. In 1916, Warfield recalled that during his undergraduate days he had been "'a Darwinian of the purest water.'"[13] The decisive point for those who defended Darwin and those who found him either ill informed or a purveyor of atheism hinged on whether or not to include God, whether to continue thinking of God as a causal agent, and whether to insist on a methodology that wanted nothing to do with the supernatural.

A crisis occurs when something sufficiently unsettling provokes a reaction; in other words, a turning point that cannot be ignored. We need to be reminded by an elder statesman in the history of science at Harvard University, Gerald Holton, that concepts such as matter, universal laws, causality, verification, conservation, feedback loops, probability, relativity, the space-time continuum, and quantum complementarity are both the tools we use for thinking and also the way truth and reality are defined.[14] At work is a revolution in understanding that gives birth to a scientific culture where religious values, even though they endure in many forms, become marginalized and contested. Given these circumstances—beginning with an Aristotelian science and culminating with Darwin—perennial and substantial points of contention between an emerging scientific prowess and a reactive religious establishment evolved into a contemporary agreement to go their separate ways and to defend their respective domains.

---

13. Livingstone, "Re-placing Darwinism and Christianity," 195–96.
14. Holton, *Einstein, History, and Other Passions*, 43.

A History of Irreconcilable Differences

Queen of All Knowledge

Throughout the extended history of Christian theology and science, and to the extent they were sibling rivals,[15] each has claimed for itself a superior position. Until science "came of age" and was sufficiently autonomous to function on its own, theology claimed the high ground as queen of the sciences. Natural science was merely one of several handmaiden disciplines, along with philosophy, poetry, law, geometry, and music. For St. Augustine, who articulated the handmaiden image—a rationale that would govern attitudes toward the natural sciences well beyond the end of the Middle Ages—the natural sciences were not to be trusted but to be used. In this regard David Lindberg writes: "Augustine had no use for the natural sciences as ends in themselves, but he accepted them and even esteemed them (if their high profile in his *Literal Commentary on Genesis* is any measure) as valuable, if sometimes problematic, handmaidens."[16] Centuries later Thomas Aquinas was of the same mind that even though all knowledge comes from God, reason alone was limited and only indirectly relevant to salvation. Augustine and Aquinas however did not share identical views, since Aquinas regarded natural knowledge of the world to be worthy in itself and was convinced that the humblest fact could lead to an understanding of a higher truth. It is often said that St. Thomas "brought reason back into theology, and hence into Western thought."[17] But Aquinas's enthusiastic embrace of Aristotle and the logic of his thought were far from being warmly received. Charles Freeman's assertion regarding the reaction to Augustine is "that for centuries any form of independent scientific thinking was suppressed."[18] Even if one leapfrogs over the Middle Ages and the Reformation, Oxford University in the middle of the nineteenth century was principally a theological seminary, and when Rev. William Buckland wanted to establish geology

---

15. "Sibling rivals" is my terminology to describe the relationship of theology and science as belonging to the same family of truth-seekers. See Coleman, *Competing Truths*, especially 42–58.

16. Lindberg and Numbers, eds., *When Science and Christianity Meet*, 30.

17. Freeman, *The Closing of the Western Mind*, 5.

18. Ibid., 5 and passim. David Bentley Hart begs to differ, and quite vociferously, to Freeman's argument that "Christianity is somehow to be blamed for a sudden retrogression in Western civilization that set back the cause of human progress by, say, a thousand years" (Hart, *Atheist Delusions*, 57).

as a legitimate subject for study he had to show how geology would be useful for the training of Anglican clergy, and this in turn hinged on its relevancy to interpreting the Bible, notably the flood.[19]

Francis Bacon (1561–1626) constitutes another significant turning point in the history of science and Christianity. What is often said of Luther is also true for Bacon—neither set out to be a divisive figure. Luther desired reform; Bacon encouraged independent thinking. A deeply religious person, Bacon was respectful of Christian doctrine, but as Galileo argued, Scripture and revelation are limited in their scope. One could, and *should*, examine the world of nature deductively, assuming nothing from the start but beginning with observation and building a case based on an accumulation of evidence. In France a similar "skeptical crisis" was spearheaded by Descartes (1596–1650), who began at an even more fundamental level—the interior thoughts of the knowing subject. Descartes would accept as certain only clear and distinct ideas that had been disentangled and separated from ancient authorities. By this measure even truths of revelation and Scripture would be judged by the same criteria. Such is the beginning of an independent discipline of science increasingly uneasy with the status of handmaiden to theology. The separation between science and theology became more pronounced as the nineteenth century ended. Darwin, unlike Newton, would not tolerate even an occasional reliance on supernatural explanations. They simply have no place in the practice of science, declared a United States federal judge in 1982: "No statement could count as science if it depended on 'supernatural intervention.'" Five years later the US Supreme Court upheld the judge's decision.[20]

We might expect the roles to have been reversed when science matured into the king of all knowledge most certain and relevant. But this did not happen. Science did not expect theology to play an ancillary role. Instead, to be quite frank, scientists asked theologians to stay out of their domain. They remained skeptical of the notion of a theologian-scientist. Theologians, on the other hand, were seldom content to leave science well enough alone. It seems that theologians always want to have the last word. Scientists grow weary and frustrated with every new attempt to interject some form of "vitalism" or divine energy, some suggestion of top-down causation, some purposeful design that is not present or required.

19. Greene, "Genesis and Geology," 144ff.
20. Numbers, "Science without God," 265.

Irreconcilable Differences 39

Speaking from a position of authority as the editor of *The Catechism of the Catholic Church*, Cardinal Schönborn, for instance, says all the right things, such as his dislike of god-of-the-gaps explanations or his concession that we should "not be excessively hasty in wanting to demonstrate 'intelligent design' everywhere as a matter of apologetics."[21] Nevertheless the Cardinal articulates a familiar refrain heard across the theological spectrum that the modern scientific method is intrinsically limited and unable to ascertain the true nature of the universe, as well as declaring that there "is scarcely any doubt that Darwin wished to assist materialism in securing a scientific victory."[22] In his opinion piece for *The New York Times*, Schönborn reacted indignantly to the suggestion that "the Catholic Church has no problem with the notion of 'evolution' as used by mainstream biologists—that is, synonymous with neo-Darwinism."[23] The Catholic Church does have a problem with the extent the modern scientific method is thought able to explain what it is intrinsically unable to explain. Apart from the subtleties of his arguments, the cardinal feels obligated to defend an orthodoxy that overrides science at crucial points. Rumbling in the background is the queen-like status of theology. Usually without the pretense of being the superior discipline, theology sees itself as the grand integrator appealing to a higher truth.[24]

No one likes to be someone's handmaiden and the terminology has dropped out of usage. But remnants of the notion linger and scientists are quick to pick up on it. Theology and science have a difficult time reconciling because most scientists do not really believe good theology translates into good science, or that good science necessarily translates into good theology. Many theologians believe just the opposite, and the NR is committed to the proposition that a fully intelligible universe is only possible by including a theological perspective. And with this proposition comes the lingering suggestion that revelation and faith are theology's aces in the hole.

21. Schönborn, "Reasonable Science," 22, 26.

22. Ibid., 23.

23. Christoph Schönborn, "Finding Design in Nature," *The New York Times*, July 7, 2005.

24. Like the cardinal, Nancey Murphy (theologian) and George Ellis (professor of applied mathematics) argue "that *some* metaphysical or theological account of nature of ultimate reality is needed to 'top-off' the hierarch of the sciences" (*On the Moral Nature*, 21). The cardinal is providing an apologetic, while Murphy and Ellis are looking to elevate theology to a kind of science.

A Plurality of Authorities

For as long as theology reigned as queen of the sciences, she did so with an interlocking network of authorities consisting of Scripture, tradition, and the magisterium. The canon of accepted texts defined the written word. Tradition, whether in the Catholic or Protestant sense, is the living, evolving embodiment of the written word. The magisterium is the authorized interpreter of both Scripture and tradition. In order to close the system and make it both foolproof and impenetrable, the written word is rendered inerrant and the Pope is infallible when speaking on matters of faith and morals. Thus, the church possesses the final word on the meaning of Scripture, and on all matters spiritual. In response, only two moves were possible: one could challenge the authority of the Catholic Church or one could establish other constituent authorities. Either choice would have the effect of diminishing the authority of church-Scripture-tradition.

The Protestant Reformation challenged both the authority of the magisterium and its sole right to interpret Scripture and to be the only legitimate interpreter of the tradition it had authored. The challenge then turned into a wide-ranging, rancorous internal dispute within the Reformation. Questions abounded: Is the authority of Scripture dependent on a literal reading, a reading justified by tradition, a reading where it seems obvious the text is reflecting a cultural norm, such as the days of purification after menstruation and childbirth (Lev 12) or Paul's counsel concerning an unbelieving spouse (1 Cor 7:12ff.)? But the larger problem Luther posed was what right does the priest, representing the church, have to establish his own standard for truth? In the final analysis the audacity of Galileo and Luther rested with their courage to assert their own authority, which resulted in the obligation to defend their understanding of authority. While Luther and Galileo were part of a larger process of self-authorization, they represented very different paths. Charles Taylor provides a very good description of this process and appropriately quotes Alain Renaut: "'The man of humanism is the one who no longer receives his norms and laws either from the nature of things (Aristotle) nor from God, but who establishes them himself on the basis of his reason and will.'"[25]

Luther remained within the context of Scripture and Catholic tradition but added the certainty of personal faith. Galileo, on the other hand, essentially established a parallel authority, and that is of course what

---

25. Taylor, *A Secular Age*, 588.

unnerved the Roman Catholic hierarchy. Bacon took yet another path by caring less about a natural philosophy intended to discover a divine providence in all things and more about an empirical science that improves the condition of humankind. More inadvertently than intentionally, Luther, Galileo, and Bacon prepared the ground of modern unbelief by opening up new spaces for new authorities stemming from an inwardness of self-sufficiency and the autonomous powers of ordering by reason. Charles Taylor summarizes in this way: "We recognize Bacon's double thesis in this passage: the old science is epistemically useless (ending merely in the speculative, the verbal, in unresolvable disputes), and it has turned its back on its proper, moral end of enabling beneficent works."[26]

Luther and Galileo lived in a milieu where authority was conferred by a hierarchy of clerics and guaranteed by the unchallengeable tenets of revelation and inspiration. Such an authority was self-authenticating in the sense that no further justification was necessary or even possible outside the pronouncements of the Pope, the magisterium, and the local priest. This was a kind of authority faithful subjects were called on to obey, a full explanation was not their due. When Locke said, "I have not made it my business, either to quit, or follow any authority in the ensuing discourse," he had no intention of accepting this or that as being true because it was previously claimed to be so. The matter of truth must be a matter of weighing the evidence garnered inductively from careful observations. This was a methodological shift of historic proportions.

Whether speaking of modern science or modern consciousness, the change in "how we come to know" (epistemology) was turned upside down. Any representation of reality must be *constructed* by rational agents who meld together concept and observation, inner thoughts with an outer reality. Only individuals who have freed themselves from all forms of external authority are able to practice *disengaged reasoning*. An *aggressive* methodology—a breaking apart and reconstructing—is preferred to the passive contemplation of the way things are. *Objective knowledge*—the same truth for everyone—is a particular kind of truth, namely, a truth defined procedurally according to a set of established standards. Nor is it just any kind of rationality. "For Plato," writes Taylor, "to be rational we have to be right about the order of things. For Descartes rationality means thinking according to certain standards."[27] The

---

26. Taylor, *Sources of the Self*, 230.
27. Ibid., 156.

ontology of innateness—a reality of eternal forms, essences, ideal types, immutable natural kinds, created species—recedes in the light of reason, which is becoming ever more methodological. The former ontologies must be let go, in part because they cannot be reformed, and with the Reformation we have entered an era of growing desire "to make over the whole society to higher standards."[28]

As heirs to the Enlightenment, we are left to ponder the ramifications of living in an indifferent universe instead of a purposefully created cosmos. But one can see the writing on the wall: ontology is pushed aside in favor of methodology. Inevitably, theology and science find themselves occupying the same intellectual ground and therefore trying to forge a workable peace. But speaking methodologically they are miles apart: revealed vs. constructed, engaged vs. disengaged, passive vs. aggressive, personal vs. objective.

The severest contemporary criticism stems from the self-authenticating or uncritical nature of religious truth. Whether justified or not, Christian truths carry the expectation that they should be accepted faithfully and uncritically. To the extent that such truths are encumbered by a self-authenticating methodology, by dogma, and by judgmental threats, a negative impression regarding religious truth persists. Freeman's discussion of St. Augustine concludes with an assessment by John Rist that "'the tragic side of Augustinianism is that his work was received uncritically for so long . . . his views would be canonized as authoritative proof-texts rather than as starting points for more impartial investigations.'"[29] That, you may say, was many centuries ago, but contemporary critics such as Daniel Dennett (*Breaking the Spell*) discuss Christian theology as if it does not have a self-critical bone in its body. While apparently ignorant of the long tradition of self-criticism beginning in its modern form with Schleiermacher and biblical criticism, Dennett displays a public perception that questions whether theology can speak authoritatively outside of its own domain. Or, to state it otherwise, Christian theology is hard-pressed to show that it can compete in a public square where empiricism dominates and many other authorities seem more relevant. Taking all of this into account, the NR understands itself as addressing our postmodern situation by showing theology to be a science or science-like, but that is a supposition in need of its own critical examination.

---

28. Taylor, *A Secular Age*, 63.
29. Freeman, *The Closing of the Western Mind*, 299.

Naturalism or Supernaturalism

Ronald Numbers reminds us that "long before the birth of modern science and the appearance of 'scientists' in the nineteenth century, the study of nature in the West was carried out primarily by Christian scholars known as natural philosophers, who typically expressed a preference for natural explanations."[30] The preference for natural explanations over supernatural explanations was especially strong in the medical field, where supernatural explanations of disease gradually disappeared. The exceptions proved to be epidemics and insanity, which remained etiological mysteries, and venereal diseases as the wages of sin.[31] Perhaps because size matters, epidemics (smallpox) and natural catastrophes (earthquakes) have a long history of being viewed as God's ultimate scourge to punish sinners and bring them to their knees. Nonetheless, the Puritan Cotton Mather, one of Boston's leading ministerial lights, promoted inoculation when an epidemic threatened to strike New England in 1721. Believing Christians, then, were not opposed to holding two views at the same time. The earthquakes of 1727 and 1755 that shook the northern colonies of America, producing widespread damage to property, provoked the usual call for a public fast, along with a concession that "that the ignition of gases in the earth's interior might have touched off the tremors.[32]"

For every natural event God is the ultimate cause, but works out his purposes through secondary causes. James Gustafson has a wonderful explication along these lines of Jonathan Edwards's twofold interpretation of the disaster that struck his congregation when "'the whole gallery—full of people, with all the seats and timber, suddenly and without any warning—sunk and fell down.'"[33] Edwards's description does nothing to disregard a causal explanation of frost heaving to further weaken a meetinghouse already old and decayed. But this does not count as a full explanation. The event itself might be seen as a sign of God's displeasure, and since it came to pass that, mysteriously and wonderfully, every life was preserved, it does not seems unreasonable to Edwards "'to ascribe it to anything else but the care of Providence, in disposing the motions of every piece of timber, and the precise place of safety where everyone should sit.'" Gustafson suggests that Edwards moves from one framework

30. Numbers, "Science without God," 266.
31. Ibid., 269.
32. Ibid., 270–71.
33. Gustafson, *An Examined Faith*, 1.

of explanation to another: from an observer's account that is objective, informed, and scientific to one that values the religious significance of what has occurred. Edwards the pastor and theologian sought a religious meaning to what happens naturally in an "unthinking world." We are left, however, with several questions, according to Gustafson. "Does the physical account in any way determine—limit or license—the religious and theological account?" And are "these two frameworks of evaluation incommensurate with each other, like two radically different 'language games' used to narrate the same event?"[34]

As it turns out, modern science is not amenable to the idea that a supernatural or theological interpretation is necessary or even helpful. While Robert Boyle and Isaac Newton understood the discovery of natural law as a religious act, and saw those laws as divinely established, Darwin did not see the necessity of deferring to God. Darwin compared himself to Newton and wondered if his methodology is the same. He believed it was the same empiricism, though some of his critics are not so sure, and was well aware of the pressure to admit the supernatural. But Darwin, unlike Newton, had no confidence in supernatural explanations because they are a methodological dead end. He resisted, refused, and insisted on telling a totally consistent naturalistic story or none at all.[35]

Since the onset of a causally determined universe, theologians have found it increasingly difficult to speak of God in the traditional sense. Essentially, just two options are possible. Either God intervenes objectively in special events by breaking or suspending the laws of nature or God acts uniformly in all events. In the former case, objectivity is preserved because the divine event is an anomaly and thus can be singled out. In the latter instance, God does not breach or suspend laws of nature, but as a consequence any divine action is indistinguishable and any sense of special divine providence fades away. Since contemporary theology is inclined to accept the premise of a universe causally bound, it shoulders the burden of defending a superintending God with ever-more sophisticated language and concepts as science relentlessly tightens the causal connections between "events." Theology finds itself in this quandary: the more God is a "sustaining presence" rather than an identifiable "causal event," the more God disappears into the microscopic processes of the subatomic world. In the end, neither alternative is particularly efficacious. The NR

---

34. Ibid., 3.
35. See Hull, *Darwin and His Critics*, 29–32.

fully appreciates the bind theology finds itself in and works diligently to utilize insights of post-Newtonian science and postmodern philosophy to recast "the God who acts" in a noninterventionist way.

No Further Explanation Required

The problem with a God of the unexplained "gaps" and "jumps" is that those gaps eventually get explained (problem-solved) and those evolutionary jumps look less and less like divine intervention. "It is often said," writes historian David L. Hull, "that evolutionary theory brought an end to the practice of including God as a causal factor in scientific explanations." Hull then states what is actually the case. "A more accurate characterization is that it demonstrated forcefully that this day had already passed."[36] For Darwin there could be but one natural law and it must apply to all living things without exception. Little has changed and Hull's verdict stands: As a methodological rule science refuses to include any reference to divine causation. The door is thus closed to a long history of providing theological interpretations for scientific questions. This does not make every scientist an atheist. Rather, the exclusionary rule is a decision with reference to divine causation. In other words, God is not an explanatory principle science can utilize.

For a world view where the whole of nature is invested with meaning and God is responsible for what happens, the earthquake that devastated Lisbon in 1755 was philosophically liberating. Philosophers such as Leibniz, Voltaire, and Kant were quite willing to declare that natural events can and should be explained without reference to God's judgment. The basis of their argument depended on the distinction between what *ought* to be and what *is*. Evil is to be restricted to human affairs caught up in the morality of intentions. Thus, neither nature nor natural events are ever good or evil, they just are. As Susan Neiman points out, philosophers were quite willing to abandon the idea that natural suffering should be understood as a manifestation of sin or evil in order for us to grow up and accept more responsibility for what we do (Nietzsche's hope).[37]

Lisbon is liberating, then, in the sense that the more God is relieved of the onus of cause and effect, the more we assume for ourselves the

---

36. Ibid., 63.

37. Neiman, *Evil in Modern Thought*, 257–58; and her discussion of Nietzsche, 212–19.

responsibility of making our own meaning. Lisbon, however, is not quite so liberating for theology. A philosophical elimination of any distinction between what *is* and what *ought to be* cannot sit well with Christian theology because pivotal Christian tenets uphold the belief that the world is created good, that it is created purposefully, and that it is "fallen" and therefore part of God's redeeming. Philosophers and scientists may be willing to render matter (all that is) opaque and mute, but theologians see a universe that manifests beauty and design in need of further explanation. Thus, theologians continue to return to the question, Why is there something rather than nothing? Why is there design, incredible beauty, a pattern of organization, the emergence of life, an Earth overflowing in abundance; a creation that no less invites our praise?[38] The Christian narrative of sin and redemption simply does not make any sense if you void the goodness of creation, the hope of what ought to be, and the God who in Christ is working out "his" purposes.

Not a Nice World

The notion that a higher power or powers animates and superintends the world is surely ancient. As ancient or primitive as this notion is, it flies in the face of an equally ancient experience of survival in a world that is trying to kill you. The argument for design, then, is a sophisticated leap upward. In both its Christian and Judaic manifestations the benevolence of God is yet another leap forward. Charles Taylor lights up the vision that moves so directly from design to the existence of a good Creator God: "the magnificent design of the whole framework in which our world was set, the stars, the planets, etc.; and then on the admirable micro-design of creatures, including ourselves, with our organs fitted for their functions, as well as on the general way in which life was sustained by the process of nature."[39] Not only is the creation inherently good, not only by design and purpose, but also good in the sense that God wants this goodness to bear fruit in humanity itself. Here is a Creator whose "hand" is to be seen in the heavens above and affirmed in the well-being of his creatures. By melding cosmology with history the Genesis story portrays a single-minded purpose. The chaos is called into order just as Abraham is called

---

38. David Bentley Hart is an Eastern Orthodox theologian who describes with flourishes reminiscent of John Calvin, Jonathan Edwards, and Karl Barth a cosmos infused with divine beauty and intention. See his *The Beauty of the Infinite*.

39. Taylor, *A Secular Age*, 177.

to leave Ur. In such a providential order, each thing and each individual finds its own good while seeking the goodness of the Creator.[40]

In one of his more candid moments Stephen Gould remarked that Christians can sing heartily "All Things Bright and Beautiful," but are rendered speechless by nature nasty, brutish, and destructive.[41] To say the least, theologians have found themselves continually developing theological rationales to defend the Christian belief in a benevolent God in the midst of a heartless world. Theodicy, as Neiman clarifies, comes to the fore in an age where a hierarchy of perfect forms is being replaced by a cold and indifferent universe where chance and chaos are fundamental.[42] After several centuries of championing the order and design of the universe, Christian theology found itself unprepared to cope with disorder, chaos, and evil; and in the twentieth century with the unprecedented elevation of all three.

The very fact that some theologians welcomed Darwin's theory of evolution while others did not is symptomatic of what happens when one tries to reconcile an account of providence and benevolence with an account where natural selection "cares" about one thing: survival of the fittest. Darwin himself did not use the phrase "survival of the fittest" in *The Descent of Man* but it was never far from his thinking. Perhaps even more troubling is the question of why God would create a world replete with so much waste, bloodletting, and cruelty. The truly nonaccommodating factor is not evolution itself but its meandering. In a *New York Review of Books* essay entitled "Saving Us from Darwin," Frederick Crews is even more pointed: "Why, we must wonder, would the Designer of the universe have frittered away thirteen billion years, turning out quadrillions of useless stars, before getting around to the one thing he really cared about, seeing to it that a minuscule minority of earthling vertebrates are washed clean of sin and guaranteed an eternal place in his company?"[43] The broader implication of Crews's perspective is that suffering has no redemptive meaning. Theodicy all over again.

A theological doctrine of "fallenness" might account for why nature meanders. It does falter, though, when trying to explain what is wrong

---

40. See Ibid., 176ff. for a nuanced discussion of mutual benevolence in the eighteenth century.

41. Gould, *Rocks of Ages*, 179.

42. Neiman, *Evil*, 105–9, 119, 257, 318.

43. Crews, "Saving Us from Darwin."

with nature that it needs to be redeemed.[44] The fallenness of nature presents a set of theological problems not germane to human beings who choose between the good and the bad, the right and the wrong. How does one account for fallenness in a universe of exquisite balance between the forces of life and death, where the laws of conservation and entropy have the final say? The fallenness of all things is by no means an appendage to the biblical narrative. It seeps into everything. Should young lambs be food for the wolf? Should the infant live but a few days? Shouldn't the elderly find peace in their old age, and the planters of vineyards find enjoyment in their work (Isa 65:20–25)? Only if all things are measured against a divine intention, and only if all things created share the same yearning to be set free for a glory yet to come (Rom 8:18–25), can it be said that God's good creating is incomplete and ongoing.

Since Christian faith will not concede the goodness of creation even in the teeth of random mutations and indeterminate chaos, it is compelled to rethink the nature of God. David Bentley Hart is prompted to ask: "So, then, what sort of God should a *purely* 'natural' theology invite us to see?"[45] The NR accepts the challenge of confronting the stark reality Stephen Gould thinks Christians can't face, namely, that suffering, bloodletting, and meandering that have their place in a creation that is evolving. Hart, though, takes a somewhat different approach: "The Christian vision of the world, however, is not some *rational* deduction from empirical experience, but is a moral and spiritual aptitude—or, rather, a moral and spiritual labor."[46]

Susan Neiman is justified to affirm the position that metaphysics spring from the rift between *is* and *ought*, and correct again to draw our attention to the new reality. "The first metaphysical question," the Jewish philosopher Emmanuel Levinas proposes, "is no longer Leibniz's question 'why is there something rather than nothing?' but 'why is there evil rather than good?'"[47] Christian theology must do exactly what seems impossible, that is, reconcile the Christian teachings of providence, creation's goodness, and nature's benevolence with a not-so-nice world that is trying to kill us while we are steadily killing it. And on this Earth reigns

---

44. Holmes Rolston asks this very question, "Does Nature Need to be Redeemed," *Zygon* 29 (June 1994) 205–29; and likewise William Drees, *Is Nature Ever Evil?* (London: Routledge, 2003).

45. Hart, *Doors of the Sea*, 52.

46. Ibid., 58 (emphasis mine).

47. Neiman, *Evil*, 322.

a creature, created in the image of its Creator, who is par excellence the purveyor of such suffering that it is evil.

Two World Views

In the minds of many there is a religious world view and a scientific world view. On the other hand, by natural inclination we want to see the world as a coherent whole. Sir Isaac Newton qualifies as a shining example of the latter. Reflecting a new understanding of Newton, Dobbs and Jacob explain the scope of Newton's goal this way: "Now it is no longer necessary to explain away his fierce interest in alchemy or his dogged attempts at the correct interpretation of biblical prophecies, as many earlier biographers and scientists tried to do. If Newton's purpose was to construct a unified system of God and nature, as indeed it was, then it becomes possible to see all of his various fields of study as potential contributors to his overarching goal."[48] Darwin, on the other hand, lived an existence marked by an unresolved tension between Christian belief in a personal and caring God and the impersonal and heartless way nature proceeds. It seems to me that our legacy is from Darwin rather than Newton because belief today still requires of us the difficult task of reconciling two basic orientations, two frames of meaning.

It is naïve to think we can straddle the same two worlds Newton did; one Aristotelian-teleological and the other mechanistic-deistic. In either case a distinction can be made between a *view of the world* and a *world view*.[49] A view of the world is merely a picture of the world while the latter is a picture supported and unified by philosophical-theological presuppositions. The hegemony of Christian theology (as queen) made it feasible for theology to forge a coherent world view. An Aristotelian natural philosophy was Christianized with the consequence that Christian beliefs were intertwined with a natural philosophy. Whether it be outlined in Augustine's *City of God*, Thomas Aquinas's *Summa Theologica*, or by the Great Chain of Being, a divine plan has been written into the very fabric of the universe. By its wariness of ultimate questions and their

---

48. Dobbs and Jacob, *Newton and the Culture of Newtonianism*, 12. Seeing Newton in a new light began with the discovery by John Maynard Keynes of a collection of alchemical papers that had been declared "not fit to print" by the executor of Newton's will. Besides Dobbs and Jacob, see Philip Fanning, *Isaac Newton and the Transmutation of Alchemy* (Berkeley, CA: North Atlantic, 2009).

49. See Coleman, *Competing Truths*, 77–87.

ultimate answers, and by its jumble of separate disciplines, science may be inherently incapable, or simply reluctant, to proclaim a world view. It did however solidify a new picture of the world, which none could eventually resist. And where scientists do adopt unifying metaphysical suppositions, as in the case of materialism, a world view emerges, often sliding into political ideology.[50] To extrapolate, a reordering of the cosmos does not itself make a world view because a world view is not only about what we see outside of ourselves but how we understand ourselves from within.

In order to defend their beliefs as reasonable, Christian theologians found ways to accommodate a scientific *picture* of the world, albeit while still providing answers to ultimate questions. Accommodation, however, can only be stretched so far until it fractures. Beginning with Descartes and Bacon something began to break irreversibly. A mechanistic world picture lays the groundwork for materialism and deism.[51] An intricate machine running on its own without the necessity of divine intervention was the first step toward a universe shorn of all intrinsic meaning, inert, at rest, and fully explainable by universal principles. Evolution suggests imperfection, hints at not getting it right, and thus undercut all instincts of providential care. An understanding of the world this messy, this random, and this heartless could hardly be a plan designed to draw us into God's purposes. The biblical world of Abraham and Jesus had been fashioned into an ideal order designed by God, punctuated with mighty acts of God, and established to move within a defined time scale; and as such it found itself contending with the indifferent and absent God of the Cartesians, or with an impersonal and disinterested First Cause of the Aristotelians, or the deistic God of mindless evolutionary processes.

The most famous mechanical philosopher of his age, Robert Boyle (1627–1691), is an interesting case study. Along with Descartes and the atomist Pierre Gassendi, Boyle embraced a mechanistic understanding

---

50. Karl Popper makes a justifiable distinction between scientific revolutions and ideological revolutions. And while I have been somewhat cavalier in the use of the terminology of revolution, Popper and I are making the same distinction. For Popper, the Copernican revolution is a scientific revolution because it overturned a dominant scientific theory, and also an ideological revolution in that it changed man's view of his place in the universe. See Popper, "The Rationality of Scientific Revolutions," in Rom Harré, *Problems of Scientific Revolutions* (Oxford: Oxford University Press, 1957), 88.

51. See Dobbs and Jacob, *Newton*, 59, 86, 99. Cf. Taylor where he argues an "immanent frame isn't simply 'neutral' but nudges us in the direction of deism, atheism, and materialism (*A Secular Age*, 555ff.).

the world, but none stood more willing to defend the Christian religion against the threat of materialism espoused by the likes of his contemporary, the philosopher Thomas Hobbes. Boyle endowed an annual series of lectures intended to prove the truth of Christianity against the infidels. Boyle's central argument was that even though the world was a vast, impersonal machine, its purpose or design rested solely with the free will of God. The divine sovereignty and power of God was all the more manifested in mechanical explanations than in vulgar notions of nature, which relied on arguments about ideal forms and qualities. In this he opposed those still clinging to an Aristotelian teleology of immanent purpose. For Boyle, teleological explanations short-circuited the search for mechanistic ones and impeded the possibility of genuine progress. A mechanistic universe, then, did nothing to deflate the argument from design. The argument merely shifted from a God of First Cause to a God revealed and known through knowledge of secondary causes, which was the primary aim of science. There should be no doubt that Boyle had committed himself to an experimentally based knowledge. At his house in Stalbridge he had set up his own laboratory and was transfixed by experiments using a vacuum pump he had created. Curiously enough, Boyle could express sincere belief in the "manifest impositions we call miracles" while showing a reticence concerning an intervening God. In his most important essay, "A Free Enquiry Into the Vulgarly Received Notion of Nature," Boyle wrote, "To conclude . . . God does sometimes in a peculiar, though hidden way, interpose in the ordinary phenomena and events of crises; but yet this is done so seldom, at least in a way that we can certainly discern, that we are not hastily to have recourse to an extraordinary providence."[52] We see in Boyle the beginning of a struggle that reached for accommodation but ended with a sense of ambivalence.[53] In Boyle's world view, pressure and volume are inversely proportional at a constant temperature (Boyle's law), God *willing*.

In his exploration of the scientific revolution, Steven Shapin calls attention to the development of a new natural philosophy, to be known as natural theology, championed by the religiously motivated English

[52]. In this depiction of Boyle I am following closely the introduction by Edward B. Davis and Michael Hunter, eds., *Robert Boyle: A Free Enquiry into the Vulgarly Received Notion of Nature* (Cambridge: Cambridge University Press, 1996), 101 (quote from p. 101). Also very insightful is Steven Shapin's discussion of Boyle, *The Scientific Revolution*, passim.

[53]. Taylor uses the terminology of "cross-pressured" to describe a situation of tension between two basic orientations. See *A Secular Age*, e.g., 548ff.

mechanical philosophers of the seventeenth century (Robert Boyle, John Ray, Robert Hooke). Shapin reads this history of reforming natural theology as one where religion and science acted to reinforce each other. This may be accurate for this century, but only if you exempt Descartes and Hobbes, whose atheistic inclinations posit a more consistent nature without divine interventions. Trouble was brewing, nevertheless, in the very distinction between a Book of Nature and a Book of Scripture. Shapin recognizes that "science and theology might be identified as distinct enterprises . . . but it was this very separation that allowed a reformed natural philosophy to contribute *independently* to religious concerns."[54] But from the beginning the existence of two independent sources of truth was a catalyst for theology and science to claim the higher ground or simply go their independent ways.

Once the natural sciences began to propose alternative explanations for natural occurrences without recourse to a Creator, a Christian world view was rendered suspect. This view of the world held together by Christian tenets such as creation and providence, by philosophical tenets such as teleology and essences, and by an epistemology of intuition and inspiration, was teetering on collapse. A Christian metanarrative was feasible only because both the cosmos above and the world of human affairs below found their purpose in divine will. The argument from design made perfect sense, as did the notion of a Great Chain of Being, because a hierarchy of created things was how we found our place in a disorderly and unjust state of daily affairs.[55] Just the same, theology could no more ignore evolution as a principal paradigm of the universe than it could snub Newton's three fundamental laws of classical physics. Christian theology did find ways to adopt an evolutionist point of view.

Once again natural theology proved to be incalculably elastic and amazingly resilient, even so by extending the argument from design to the level of the oddity and minuscule. The power, wisdom, and goodness of God was readily adapted to the oddly fish-like reptiles known as *Ichthyosaurus*, which was exactly what the Rev. William Buckland (1784–1856) demonstrated in his *Curiosities of Natural History*. He wrote, "'These deviations [from ordinary reptilian form] are so far from being fortuitous, or evidencing imperfection, that they present examples

---

54. Shapin, *The Scientific Revolution*, 138.

55. Taylor unpacks this world view by describing it as "an order of hierarchical complements" (*A Secular Age,* 438ff.).

of perfect appointment and judicious choice."[56] Writing about the relationship between Genesis and geology in nineteenth-century Britain, Mott Greene nicely summed up how Buckland and his fellow nineteenth-century geologists were able to maneuver from defending "geology as evidence of providential intervention to geology as evidence of providential design."[57] Whether by mechanical models of clockwork precision or living organisms exquisitely designed for their purpose, God was still the Creator of a universe in need of a divine explanation.[58]

Alongside accommodation and a growing obsession with knowing the world as it is, mystery began to fade in proportion to the adequacy of natural explanations. The mystery of bread and wine becoming the actual body and blood of Christ could no longer stand simply as mystery per se but required the support of a sophisticated cause and effect explanation (the doctrine of transubstantiation). What happens during the mass was still mysterious but the porous boundary between spirit and matter was no longer easily assumed. And this was symptomatic of a larger transition from an open, spirit-filled world of porous boundaries to a closed, impersonal world of atoms. The very context of thinking theologically had been altered. A self-sufficient and self-ordered universe was one where God could still be envisioned, but only with heavy lifting on the part of defenders of the faith.

Christians increasingly bore the responsibility of reason. A line of thinking emerged that went something like this: Since God expects humans to use their powers of reason to understand the laws that govern the universe, it would defeat his purpose to intervene miraculously. If God were to adjust laws to specific instances, would that not make God capricious and untrustworthy? Once the notion of an order sufficiently good that it does not require divine interference took hold, miracles and saving events became an embarrassment to the scientifically minded. Faith was no longer sufficient. Heard for the first time were a litany of

---

56. Quoted in Gould, *Time's Arrow, Time's Cycle*, 99-100.

57. Greene, "Genesis and Geology Revisited," 159.

58. In their joint Gifford Lectures, John Brooke and Geoffrey Cantor delve deeply into the adaptability of natural theology, and the argument for design, to move almost seamlessly from the celestial order to human anatomy. See their *Reconstructing Nature: The Engagement of Science and Religion*. However, as David Fergusson points out, a shift was taking place. After Darwin the prospect of a knockdown argument receded and theology settled for an apologetic goal of showing that the Christian faith can coexist in a positive relation with the best insights from other fields of knowledge. See David Fergusson, "Types of Natural Theology," in F. LeRon Shults, ed., *The Evolution of Rationality* (Grand Rapids: Eerdmans, 2006), 380-93.

sins regarding bad reason, bad education, sloth, customs that inhibited the naturally curious mind, and the irrationality of astrology and black magic.[59]

Along with the diminished faith in an all-powerful, interceding God was an eclipse of grace. Any doctrine of transformation involving the saving action of God found itself competing with a growing sense that we are responsible for our own actions. Preaching turned from sin as our original condition from which we need to be saved toward sins of wrong behavior that we can overcome with education and willpower. Rousseau struck a responsive chord when he emphasized the basic goodness of human nature, goodness we can pretty much realize without the help of God. Self-empowerment was the perfect complement to a scientific methodology that continued to demonstrate the power of an instrumental reason to manipulate the universe for human purposes.[60]

Given that the goal of science is to seek natural explanations for natural phenomena while the goal of theology is to seek ultimate explanations for natural phenomena, are the two disciplines totally irrelevant to one another? Bear in mind that science and theology would have little to dispute if they looked at the universe in the same way. Ultimately a clash of world views and mind-sets is what happened. Even though space does not permit a fuller discussion, the questions posed by New Testament scholar N. T. Wright are sufficiently suggestive to indicate a Christian world view that stands over against a scientific world view: Who are we? Where are we? What's wrong? What is the solution? What time is it?[61] The beliefs, hopes, and faith of orthodox Christianity give rise to a definitive world view, and while this world view may be superimposed over an empirical way of looking at the world, it is sophomoric to think religious and empirical values have meshed. We need not presume that Christians are morally superior or that scientists cannot personally hold Christian values. The issue before us is whether or not there are values that adhere to empiricism that influence how one construes a coherent and adequate understanding of the universe, just as there are values particular to

---

59. Cf. Taylor, *A Secular Age*, 71–74, for his discussion of the revolt that carries over to include the church's good magic. Also, see the important contribution of Hans Blumenberg, *The Legitimacy of the Modern Age* (Cambridge, MA: MIT Press, 1983); and note his treatment of curiosity, so important for the scientific spirit, ch. 10 and passim.

60. According to Taylor, "we feel a new freedom in a world shorn of the sacred," and thus "a great energy is released to re-order affairs in secular time" (*A Secular Age*, 80).

61. N. T. Wright, *The Resurrection of the Son of God*, 581.

theology that affect how Christians frame a meaningful universe. What the NR has failed to do consistently, and with any depth, is to explore and expose those points of tension and opposition arising from the world view implicitly or explicitly held, and what ultimately counts as true.

A Clash of Methodologies

Even from hindsight we are likely to miss that something radically new was afoot, but the principal actors in the burgeoning new science were very much aware that nothing would be the same. Neither Galileo nor Bacon set out to introduce a rival methodology but they appreciated well enough the significance of two sources of truth. Nothing so defined the "new science" as the claim that an empirical method is new. In physics, Galileo offered his *Discourses and Demonstrations Concerning Two Sciences* (one traditional and one new); as Kepler did in his *New Astronomy*; as Robert Boyle did in chemistry and experimental philosophy with a series of tracts called *New Experiments*; as Pascal wrote about in his *New Experiments about the Void*; as Boyle discussed his experiments using an air pump in *New Experiments Physico-Mechanical: Touching the Spring of the Air*; and as Bacon did in the *Novum Organum* ("New Instrument").[62] Some were more courageous than others in declaring a definitive break with tradition and orthodoxy, but always and everywhere was the awareness that truths supported by observational evidence and argument by induction were different from truths arising from logic, deduction, and revelation. What ultimately connected philosopher and experimenter was the attention being given to methodology or epistemology and how it related to securing and validating knowledge—a discussion that would continue for centuries and range from the proper use of reason to the employment of instruments and the artificial manipulation of matter, the validity of thought experiments and mathematics, the role of probability, and the importance of direct experience and observation. Along with a greater emphasis on methodology came a reassessment of how to value different kinds of knowledge and how they should be used.

What exactly was new about empiricism? First and foremost was the introduction of evidence and making evidence primary. Many things count for evidence that have little or no place in a theological system

---

62. Steven Shapin explores in depth the emerging ways of knowing that garnered the title "new." See his *The Scientific Revolution*, ch. 2.

of dogmatics: results of experiments, accurate measurements, the application of mathematics as a way to solve problems, and meticulous observation often with the use of instruments. Second, scientists jettisoned a closed system of self-authenticating authorities in favor of an open process of verification, by inviting others to validate or invalidate their results. Third, science brought into play the revolutionary idea of probability. Ian Hacking and Jeffrey Stout have fleshed out just what probability means for the formation of a modern consciousness.[63] Before the emergence of notions of statistical and evidential probability in the second half of the seventeenth century, anything proposed as hypothetical or probable was dismissed as inferior to the certainty of revelation or deductive reasoning. For St. Thomas and the Roman Catholic Church a demonstrated proof was drawn from a correct application of deduction, and a deductive proof that was certain had to begin with the certainty of a self-evident truth, and the Catholic Church was the sole guardian of those truths. "The only way to attack Aquinas," as Lawrence and Nancy Goldstone point out, "was within the accepted bounds of scholasticism, that is, to quibble over points of logic, and in this Aquinas was without peer."[64]

The threat of Double Truth was only as real as the credibility of each methodology. The Catholic Church sensed the possibility that Galileo was opening a door to an alternative source of truth utilizing an entirely different methodology. While Galileo showed little interest in setting truths of nature over against truths of revelation, he did pursue a course of limiting the authority of revelation.[65] Galileo was quite willing to grant the

63. Ian Hacking, *The Emergence of Probability* (Cambridge: Cambridge University Press, 1975) and Stout, *The Flight from Authority*. See also Paul Jerome Croce, *Science and Religion in the Era of William James: Eclipse of Certainty, 1820-1880* (Chapel Hill, NC: University of North Carolina Press, 1995).

64. Lawrence and Nancy Goldstone, *The Friar and the Cipher* (New York: Doubleday, 2005), 129.

65. Galileo did not directly confront the authority of revelation but did so indirectly by restricting its scope. Further sleuthing by Richard Blackwell brings to light a tract written while the trial was being conducted by Melchior Inchofer, S.J., with the explicit intention of expanding the long-standing category of "matters of faith and morals," and thereby laying the groundwork to accuse Galileo of denying the literal sense of Scripture. Inchofer set out to demonstrate that the Bible explicitly states that "the earth is at rest at the center of the world," while Galileo asserted just the opposite, and in this case science was correct and Scripture was wrong. This would be heretical but only if one accepted Inchofer's argument that texts referring to the movement, or nonmovement, of the Earth are teachings about faith and morals. See Blackwell, *Behind the Scenes*, ch. 2 (the book includes the first English translation of Inchofer's tract).

church the authority to interpret Scripture regarding matters of faith and morals. His fight to the end was to convince the magisterium to accept as true, and not merely as hypothetical, his discoveries and demonstrations regarding the Earth's rotation and position.[66] Even though a good case had been made for the rotation of the Earth about its axis prior to Galileo, it could never be accepted if it contradicted the established interpretation of Scripture, such as Psalm 92:1 ("For God hath established the world, which shall not be moved"). Galileo did the sensible thing. Rather than making us choose between rival truth claims, he discounted a literal or wooden interpretation and put forth the hermeneutic that texts such as Psalm 92 were not in error about the Earth's rotation since they have nothing authoritative to say about the structure of the cosmos, that is, about matters of observation and measurement.

David Bentley Hart characterizes Galileo's trial as "[A] single instance of institutional purblindness and internal dissension, which was entirely anomalous with the larger history of the Catholic Church's relation to the natural sciences . . . but demonstrates only how idiotic a conflict between men of titanic egotism can become."[67] Though Hart is certainly correct that Galileo "squandered good will with remarkable abandon," the trial brought to the surface issues that still have not been settled. There are four. The first is the scope of "faith and morals," and since this rule can be defined narrowly or expansively it is not an effective tool to discern what is extraneous and what is fundamental to the Christian faith. Second is the difficulty of knowing when to interpret a particular Scripture text literally, and what the biblical authors intended. These two issues were clearly recognized. Questions involving a scientific methodology (the third issue) and the value assigned to different kinds of knowledge (the fourth issue) are still ongoing. Galileo did not have a good handle on what constitutes a scientific methodology but he knew that it differed from what theologians did, he understood it was not

---

66. The Catholic Church would designate something "hypothetical" to indicate that it was provisional, and indirectly, that it was a second-tier truth and not an authentic description of nature. Owen Gingerich is especially alert to the part played by Andreas Osiander in adding an *ad lectorem* to Copernicus' *De revolutionibus* intended to imply the treatise is nothing more than a mathematical device for calculating heavenly bodies and therefore of no permanent value. A theologian-pastor in Nuremberg, Osiander was doing little more than acting on the widespread impression that hypotheses of this kind could not "hope to attain true reasons." See Gingerich, *The Book Nobody Read* (New York: Walker & Company, 2004), 138–39.

67. Hart, *Atheist Delusions*, 62.

hypothetical but certain in its own way, and he valued natural knowledge more than most of his peers. He valued it so much that he was willing to risk imprisonment and even worse. Galileo himself did not believe he had to choose between two kinds of truths because he thought he had found a way to interpret Scripture that skirted the problem. And even if we agree with Galileo's intuition that the Scriptures ought not to be read as a scientific description of reality, and we grant Scripture the authority over matters of faith and morals, there remains the issue of epistemological authority. Traditional ways of securing and validating knowledge centered on textual authority and appeals to biblical revelation cannot be reconciled easily with ways of securing and validating knowledge dependent on careful observation leading to universal laws. Thus, David Lindberg, in contrast to Hart, writes that we must not allow our enthusiasm for the local and human aspects of the struggle to obscure the central methodological issue in the Galileo affair.[68] Lindberg also refers to a lack of resolution and the potential for conflict concerning epistemological authority and whether matters of truth are "to be determined by exercise of the human capacities of sense and reason, by appeal to biblical revelation, or by some combination of the two."[69] Given this historical context, we begin to appreciate the impetus for science and theology to go their separate ways in order to diminish the specter of dissonance. Further down the road is the added complication that society will value one kind of knowledge over the other, and this too has the effect of driving religion and science into their own spheres of respectability and legitimacy.

The burgeoning interest in exploring and measuring the world by telescope and microscope stirred questions about how to access truths of nature. Clearly Francis Bacon was intent on articulating the features of a separate and distinct methodology. For Bacon the divide was clear and determinable. By the middle of the nineteenth century Aristotle was considered by scientists to be the author of infinite error because of his dependency on word-type truths. Bacon does not squander many opportunities to deride any procedure tainted with deduction and intuition. Aristotle could not be trusted because in the final analysis he trusts deduction to be the highest form of truth. We cannot deny that Aristotle is

---

68. Lindberg, "Galileo, the Church," 58. See also Alasdair MacIntyre who writes about what he calls an "epistemological crisis" and how it applies in full measure to a conflict over rival answers to key questions that can no longer be settled using the warrants and justifications on hand, in his *Whose Justice?*, 361ff.

69. Ibid.

a keen observer. Rather, in the pithy words of David Hull: "For Aristotle, scientific knowledge had to be universal, immutable and absolutely certain. The existence of essences assured that truth would be universal and immutable. Intuition guaranteed that it would be certain."[70] Bacon thought just the opposite to be true. Intuition guarantees nothing, essences constitute an unwarranted idealism, and immutable propositions are most likely speculation. On the other hand, gathering data based on careful observation and experimentation makes it possible to formulate a hypothesis that can be tested in a way that word truths cannot.

Empiricists sneered at the idea that essences could be intuited, therefore making observation superfluous. Theologians are no better than philosophers because they merely substitute inspiration and revelation for intuition in order to begin with infallible premises. But as Hull so correctly clarifies, the real difference is not about induction or deduction because both are lines of reasoning ending in certainty: either the certainty of conclusions that follow necessarily from the premise, or the certainty of conclusions built up by gathering data. Neither method of reasoning is a method of *discovery* but what invariably must happen after discovery. This is not to lose sight of what Newton's *Principia* and Darwin's *Origin* have in common: both engaged in careful observation and reasoned their way to universal principles (e.g., the inverse square law and natural selection). While centuries in its making, science demonstrates success at building a body of knowledge by a distinct methodology. And as a consequence all other methods of knowing must prove themselves to be as good at marshaling evidence and utilizing procedures that can be duplicated by anyone who follows the same methodology. Whether this success means theology is beholden to empiricism is another issue.

During the interval between Newton and Darwin the inevitable clash of methodologies reached a tipping point. A decision was forced, loyalties were declared. The days of the gentlemen-scientist were fading. Alongside professional religious clerics a new profession of scientists was being established with its own professional institutions, degree programs, and sources of income. The denouement came when most intellectuals considered the empirical method capable of certain knowledge. Increasingly so, science and theology competed for the same intellectual and social spaces; that is, if one was going to be intellectually honest one needed

---

70. Hull, *Darwin and His Critics*, 20.

to declare oneself. Either the geological record supported a belief in a universal flood or it didn't.

Around the time of Darwin's death in 1882 accommodation was still very much in play. In his book *On the Genesis of Species* (1871), George Jackson Mivart, a convert to Catholicism and Professor of Comparative Anatomy at St. Mary's Hospital Medical School in London, agreed with Darwin that species evolved but disagreed regarding Darwin's mechanisms. In this Mivart was not alone since many intellectuals accepted the general notion of evolution but objected to particular points, such as natural selection. Mivart believed evolutionary theory could be reconciled with Catholic dogma, but in order to achieve this he needed to suggest an alternative mechanism (some unknown "internal innate force" that guides the evolution of species) and restrict evolution to the material world (excluding the mind and soul). About this time a petition was being circulated among eminent students of science to counter an uneasy feeling that theology and science were about to collide. The idea that there could be two kinds of truths—one empirical and one theological, each arising from distinctive methodologies—seemed to be a conclusion to be avoided at all cost. But Mivart was fighting the inevitable. The very places where he could accommodate Darwin's theory of evolution were the very places Darwin and his supporters would not accommodate theology. Darwin was willing to leave well enough alone when it came to the ultimate origin of life, but he did not bow to supernatural escape clauses that referred to some unknown force, or a dualism that claimed evolution applies to the body but not the mind. The inclusive nature of adaptation and accommodation reached a place where a line had to be drawn and sides taken.[71]

Phrases such as "new frame of reference" or "paradigm shift" do not quite get to the heart of the matter because the modern era is different from the premodern era in that it reverses the ontological-epistemological fit. Insofar as the cosmos consists of ideal forms, immutable species, indestructible atoms, and ontology dominates, there is nothing humans can do to change what is. Meaning is derived from aligning the mind and heart with what already exists, and we are called to contemplate the beauty and perfection of a world created, and to find our rightful place in

---

71. David Hull notes that 1874 marked a final break between Mivart and the Darwinians, and just as Mivart was being excluded from the scientific community by Darwin and his associates he was being excommunicated from the Catholic Church because of his article on happiness in hell (*Darwin and His Critics*, 415).

the scheme of things divinely ordered. Such is the ontological-methodological fit that held sway until an alternative way of knowing became a legitimate alternative. A scientific methodology was that alternative way, and when it came it reversed the ontological-epistemological fit so that methodology now predominates.[72]

Insofar as the universe consists of mechanical or biological parts, parts that are interchangeable, the knower is encouraged to manipulate and construct what never was but is always becoming. The new methodology invites us to create a new order by thought and experiment, and since Mother Nature will not easily give up her secrets, probing, breaking apart, splitting, and colliding are called for. Passivity has no place in a world of doers and makers. The reason humans look to the starry heavens above and read their horoscope is the belief that meaning is somehow embedded in the order of the universe. Here the proper method of knowing is a passive form of meditation and reception, a seeing behind natural properties to the true reality, a getting in touch with the hidden nature of things. Alter your perspective and presume that meaning is discovered and constructed, and the appropriate methodology is an assertive form of experimenting, observing, engaging in thought experiments, and reaching consensus. No longer is knowledge the consequence of apprehending the immutable essence of things, where each thing is a God-given type nestled in a hierarchy of meaning, but the testing of a hypothesis utilizing objective standards.[73]

Beginning with the distinction between revealed truths and empirical truths, the possibility of competition between the two arises. In addition, a reversal takes place. Revealed truth is rooted in the rationalist tradition where truths of reason are considered to be necessary and eternal because they are discerned by reason (intuitive certainty) and by faith (inspirational certainty). They are called rational truths because they are "true in all circumstances and can never—never in all eternity—be anything else."[74] Natural or empirical truths represent the other fundamental Western tradition where truth gains certainty by the way things are observed or experienced. Whereas revealed truths were once

72. See Coleman, *Competing Truths*, 112–23.

73. For an expanded discussion of a new epistemology of doing and constructing that shuns a passive methodology of contemplation and exposition of texts, see Amos Funkenstein, *Theology and the Scientific Imagination from the Middle Ages to the Seventeenth Century* (Princeton, NJ: Princeton University Press, 1988).

74. Nygren, *Meaning and Method*, 78–102.

considered eternal and all other truths were contingent (or hypothetical), now empirical truths, once regarded as contingent, are understood as universal and timeless. And to the extent that biblical criticism had a deteriorating effect on both revelation and inspiration—and the resulting defensive reaction to assert infallibility and verbal inspiration—a liberal theology is compelled to reconceptualize revelation and inspiration, and at the same time cover itself with the mantle of the "scientific," especially in a methodological sense.

Over the course of a maturing modern science, theology was displaced as queen by a method of knowing with greater potential to provide the knowledge needed to change the world. Consequently, theology was isolated and marginalized, even to the point of being ostracized from the marketplace of relevant ideas and critical information. What was theology to do? The broad fracturing of theology into liberal and fundamental constituents is well known, but this division was more than an in-house theological squabble because in their modern forms fundamentalism and liberalism are two opposite reactions to the emergence of modern science.

There are good reasons, then, to reserve the language of rapprochement to the period succeeding Darwin's death. There is no unqualified way to describe the trafficking between theology and science prior to Darwin's death except to say the conversation was sometimes mutually supportive and sometimes divisive. The decisive change in climate as the twentieth century ended was none other than the growing feeling that separation might be the best possible solution to mediate an impossible situation of irreconcilable differences. That some scientists and some theologians did not, and do not, understand their differences to be irreconcilable becomes the basis for finding grounds for a new rapprochement.

Conclusion

Of course there are other valid readings of the entanglement of religion and science. The collection of case histories in *When Science and Christianity Meet* exemplifies an approach that is wary of generalization and focused on "locating particular encounters in their specific circumstances."[75] But generalizations as an extension of particular cases are useful if they are valid generalizations. To speak of irreconcilable differences is a

---

75. Livingstone, "Re-placing Darwinism and Christianity," 202.

generalization that I am willing to defend, if for no other reason than to redress an imbalance in the standard historical reading of theology and science. Likewise, while I agree with Taylor's observation that the "pure face-off between 'religion' and 'science' is a chimera, or rather, an ideological construct," and that in reality "there is a struggle between thinkers with complex, many leveled agendas, which is why the real story seems so confused and untidy in the light of ideal confrontation," it too can leave the impression that Christian theology and science share the same intellectual space without substantial and enduring tension.[76] More so than almost any other philosopher Taylor understands that Christian orthodoxy is losing ground in more than one way. The charter of modern belief, he argues, is the discovery of intrahuman resources to make the world a better place. The transition to an era when human beings want to set the agenda is established by a sentiment that God's help is neither wanted nor needed.[77] Muscular, self-confident "man" will do what needs to be done, and science will be the means by which it gets done.

The spirit of rapprochement is such that it papers over history as if there are no defining points. Even if there was no scientific revolution or single tipping point, Darwin's publication of *The Origin of Species* in 1859 represented a point of no return. Darwin died a conflicted individual regarding his religious beliefs. David Livingstone notes Darwin's divided mind about whether to "truckle" to public opinion and use the world "creation" in the second edition of the *Origin of Species*.[78] Likewise, Frank Brown remarks that "at low tide, so to speak, [Darwin] was essentially an undogmatic atheist; at high tide he was a tentative theist; the rest of the time he was basically agnostic—in sympathy with theism but unable or unwilling to commit himself on such imponderable questions."[79] Both authors are especially sensitive to the essential ambivalence running through Darwin's adult life, but that should not hide the fact that Darwin was thoroughly consistent and immovable about his methodology. Here he took a stand against the many who urged him to make an exception for human beings, and could he not include a divine purpose regarding the processes of natural selection? He could not!

A world picture is more easily amendable than a world view, and Christian belief holds tenaciously to the latter because so much is at

---

76. Taylor, *A Secular Age*, 332.
77. Ibid., 257.
78. Livingstone, "Re-placing Darwinism and Christianity," 187.
79. See Brown, *The Evolution of Darwin's Religious Views*, 27.

stake. David Hull's comment is apposite: "Galileo and Newton replaced one physical theory with another, but they left the teleological world-picture intact."[80] In other words, Christians could still locate themselves in a heliocentric cosmos, and intelligent design could be recaptured in a mechanistic system of parts. But the growing clash of authorities is another matter. Who are you going to trust when it comes to observable facts about the universe? Theology eventually concedes this province of observable facts in order to claim some alternative higher ground, and while that ground might be matters of faith and morals, it leaves unsettled which discipline can claim the highest prize of all, a superior methodology.

I have highlighted the remarkable agility among theologians to remain faithful to core Christian tenets while incorporating and accommodating the rising tide of science. The doctrine of divine providence, for example, proved to be surprisingly elastic; capable of accommodating a new world order even as it is continued to be reconceptualized over a number of centuries. Instead of emphasizing a world created by special acts of God—one for each species— theologians pointed to God's *general* providence in creating the world by means of natural laws and secondary causes (*creation continua*). Theologians had little difficulty incorporating natural law explanations as long as they were natural laws worthy of their understanding of God. Under the maxim that only a perfect God could create a perfect world, theologians found themselves defending a perfect world of universal laws. Christian theology was first attracted to the Aristotelian notion that each thing possesses its own natural perfection, its own intrinsic good. A natural perfection becomes a created perfection; whereas if the cosmic order was seen as the embodiment of Platonic-type ideas, the cosmic order was transformed to embody the mind of its Creator, and everything bent to the will of God. Given the pervasive notions of teleology and essentialism—the very foundation of the conceptual framework for Western thought— it was impossible for theologians to dismiss them, and it became their task to incorporate them into a theology of divine providence. In both hymns and liturgy, in both heart and mind, God was working out his purposes in both cosmos and history, albeit more subtly. Likewise, each species was complete in its essence and in the purpose it fulfilled. Fitting human beings into this paradigm of

---

80. Hull, *Darwin and His Critics*, 54.

perfection however required a little more finesse since our fallen nature is blatant in a way nature is not.

Thus, a liberal theological tradition grew up alongside modern science believing their differences to be reconcilable. Conversation with science was a positive influence, and a necessary fact of life in the public square. Nevertheless, the sounds of dissonance became louder over time. In his discussion of the geological or deep time, Gould chronicles the progression from Thomas Burnet, who wrote his *Sacred Theory of the Earth* in the 1680s, to James Hutton, who wrote his *Theory of the Earth* a century later, to Charles Lyell, who wrote his seminal book, *Principles of Geology*, just fifty years later in the 1830s. From hindsight we can say, as Gould does, that Burnet epitomized "the entrenched opposition of church and society to the new ways of observational science." But placed in his own particular historical circumstance, Burnet was defending a world view that made sense "only if a wise agent of order governed the cosmos and established laws that make the products of history unfold in such simple and rigorous patterns."[81] Because Hutton was willing to place field observation before preconception—allowing nature to speak to us—he jettisoned the biblical strictures of a compressed time scale and embraced a deep time of change and gradualism.[82] Anticipating Darwin, Lyell carefully constructed his argument from a mind-boggling compendium of observed information about the rates and modes of geological processes. Gould hails him as "one of history's greatest triumphs of observation and objectivity over preconception and irrationalism."[83] The irrationalism Gould refers to is the reliance on supernatural explanations when none are needed.

Unquestionably, the role of observation cannot be overlooked because it was foundational. In his study of Isaac Newton the alchemist, Philip Fanning draws our attention to what constitutes the "advent of modern science." Considering Newton's theory of universal gravitation,

---

81. Gould, *Time's Arrow, Time's Cycle*, 4–5, 59. Compare Loren Eisley's equally engaging discussion of deep time in *The Firmament of Time* (New York: Atheneum, 1984), and the more scholarly book of Stephen Toulmin and June Goodfield, *The Discovery of Time* (Chicago: University of Chicago Press, 1965), and Paolo Rossi, *The Dark Abyss of Time: The History of the Earth and the History of Nations from Hooke to Vico* (Chicago: University of Chicago Press, 1984). All the authors, but especially Rossi, show how the tyranny of biblical time and history towered over more rational and empirical approaches.

82. Gould, *Time's Arrow, Time's Cycle*, 5–6.

83. Ibid., 6.

Fanning writes that if "something is subject to gravity, it was matter; it could be seen, touched, heard, smelled or tasted," and that made it distinct from a mere idea. "By giving the senses a common denominator, Newton solidified the conviction that perception was an approach to knowledge in its own right, superior to all others."[84] No longer could superstition and experience be merged, and no longer could ideas be accepted without proper experiential collaboration.[85] In the history of ideas, then, people began to see the world differently by drawing a sharp distinction between objective and subjective experience. A new world began to emerge—objective, machinelike, and publicly verifiable. This was an understanding of the cosmos where alchemy had no place simply because it blurred the boundaries between matter and spirit, the natural and the supernatural.

A rereading of history is not complete without considering the cause-and-effect connections between the rise of modern science and secularism. The so-called scientific revolution should not be conflated or identified with the forces of secularism. As powerful as modern science becomes, it is subsidiary to the pressures of secularism. Charles Taylor's many-layered arguments in *A Secular Age* unearth a complex picture where a scientific rationality is *one of many* reformations at work to reorder society and the intellectual landscape. Taylor finds the usual subtraction accounts of secularism to be inadequate because something was added as well as taken away in order to bring us into a secular era. If we speak only of a falling away of religious beliefs or the weakening of religious influence, we have not dug deep enough to reach the very conditions of belief. "The shift to secularity in this sense," he writes, "consists, among other things, of a move from a society where belief in God is unchallenged and indeed, unproblematic, to one in which it is understood to be one option among others, and frequently not the easiest to embrace."[86]

To this unarguable conclusion I draw two more conclusions. First, while science and theology are subject to various secularizing forces, such as the instrumental uses of reason, modern science is the *primary*

---

84. Philip A. Fanning, *Isaac Newton and the Transmutation of Alchemy*, 220. Fanning's argument is not a simplistic one where Newton disowned alchemy in order to establish a new science. Rather, by arguing that Newton's alchemical activities were at the very heart of the scientific revolution, he claims Newton turned alchemy into science.

85. Steven Shapin makes an important argument by clarifying that a new understanding of experience was taking place; experience extended by artificial experiment, scientific instruments, and subjected to technological intervention (*The Scientific Revolution*, 80–89).

86. Taylor, *A Secular Age*, 3.

force behind the shift from a theistic construal of the cosmos to a non-theistic universe from which all intrinsic purpose has been expelled. This I have argued is not so much the consequence of a scientific revolution but the outcome of incremental steps. Just the same, in the hands of both philosophers and experimenters the new science leaves no space for God to "operate," and theology is put on the defensive. And yet, as Peter Berger points out, modernity is not characterized by the absence of God. Nietzsche's proclamation of the death of God is not what we see globally. Berger highlights two particularly powerful religious explosions: resurgent Islam and Evangelical Protestantism in South America. But given the fact that both explosions are taking place in cultures without a strong scientific culture, can we conclude that where science is the dominant condition for knowing, religion becomes problematic and questioned? Thus, while it is true that theology and science have found ways to coexist, it is important to unpack the manner of this coexistence and what price theology has paid.[87]

The least we can say, to follow the lead of Taylor and Berger, is that belief in a Creator in a secular age has become "not the easiest to embrace," and modern science is the primary reason that makes it so. Those alternative construals of meaning Taylor elucidates include the emergence of a self-sufficient humanism, that is, a humanism that excludes dimensions of transcendence. Again, it is not fair to lay at the feet of science the dissipation of a world view anchored in the divine will and the new conditions underlying a rampant epistemology of materialism. Yet, one would have to turn a blind eye not to see the impact of modern science. Irreconcilable differences or not, the framework of meaning has been changed irrevocably by science, and theology is forced to make the best of a new situation. With this in mind, one can appreciate why Cardinal Schönborn finds it necessary to write about "overcoming the materialistic vision of evolution" and the necessity of recapturing a "holistic understanding of reality."[88] No theologian, not even the fundamentalist, can begin to make an argument at exactly the same place as did Augustine or Newton, because we will never be as naïve as we were in the time of Augustine or

---

87. Peter Berger, "Secularization Falsified," *First Things*, February 2008, 23–27.

88. Schönborn, "Reasonable Science," 25, and "The Designs of Science," 37. The cardinal does however claim the higher ground—"Indeed, my argument was superior to a 'scientific' argument since it was based on more certain and enduring truth and principles" ("The Designs," 37).

Newton.[89] Newton, after all, spent a significant amount of time mixing religious truths with scientific truths as if they could be blended in the way ingredients are mixed according to the recipe.[90] That kind of mixing is no longer tolerated by modern science, and as a consequence theology is compelled to follow a course of respecting boundaries in a way that it never had to before.

This leads to my second conclusion regarding how we should understand the impact of science when separated from secularism. Science has its own trajectory quite apart from secularism, and at times in opposition to secularism. To the degree that secularism opens up spaces for a plurality of viewpoints leading to a leveling of all viewpoints, science works toward a winnowing of viewpoints (hypotheses) until there is but one accepted paradigm (theory). As much as the philosophy and sociology of history want to paint science with the same colors as secularism, what scientists are about is problem solving with a definitive end in mind, and for the most part they work toward a consensus resolution (see chapter 5).

My argument, therefore, is different from the polemic that science is intrinsically atheistic or materialistic. Nor would I phrase the question as physicist Stephen M. Barr does, since it is prejudicial and misleading. "The question before us, then, is whether the actual discoveries of science have undercut the central claims of religion, specifically the great monotheistic religions of the Bible, Judaism and Christianity, or whether those discoveries have actually, in certain respects, damaged the credibility of materialism."[91] Depending on your presuppositions and perspective, certain discoveries of modern science, such as the big bang, have served to weaken materialism while strengthening Christian belief. But by claiming science as an ally against materialism, Barr is avoiding the question of whether modern science complicates and undermines pivotal tenets of Christianity. Barr places considerable weight on the changes wrought by the scientific revolution beginning at the end of the nineteenth century and spilling over into the twentieth century, and seems to think *modern*

---

89. One thinks of Paul Ricoeur, who anticipates Charles Taylor's assessment, because he drew our attention to the necessity of moving beyond the naiveté of "immediacy of belief" and the first naiveté of trying to live life according to the great religious symbols of the past, and thus his belief that modern thinkers should aim at a second naiveté in and through criticism.

90. For example see Gail Christianson, *In the Presence of the Creator: Newton and His Times* (New York: Free Press, 1984).

91. Barr, *Modern Physics and Ancient Faith*, 3.

science is more compatible with the central teachings of Christianity and Judaism. That we find ourselves speaking of rapprochement is an indication that Barr's reading of history is deficient because something has happened that begs for reconciliation. Unless you are starry-eyed with optimism, the emergence of a scientific world view exerts substantial pressure to rethink traditional ways of conceptualizing God. We understand intuitively that we no longer live in a cosmos that can be naïvely construed as bounded and filled, created and ordered (as the Great Chain of Being), fixed and contained, imbued with spirits and powers, rich and beneficent (plentitude), guided and superintended, and reflective of ideas and higher purposes (providence). Instead, we find ourselves living in a universe immense and unbounded, atomized and mechanized, violent and indifferent, random and capricious, reflective of nothing except the human mind that sees it, leaving scant place and little reason for a narrative account of fall and redemption. Contemporary theologians do not see their task to be one of holding onto a cultural artifact. Theologians of the NR find the new cosmic stage invigorating and stimulating, and the "great discoveries of modern physics" (Barr) as a new and hopeful venue for interdisciplinary dialogue. Everything that has been said underscores both the importance and the difficulty confronting those who are committed to reconciling two disciplines, which, by the end of the nineteenth century, one had conceded to the other a principal domain of influence and competency.

3

The New Rapprochement with Science

Amicable Separation

MODERN SCIENCE IS IRREVOCABLY identified with an empirical methodology that excludes supernatural explanations or divine interventions. Yet, to cite Ronald Numbers, "the study of nature in the West was carried out primarily by Christian scholars known as natural philosophers" and "for centuries men of science had typically gone out of their way to assure the religious of their peaceful intentions."[1] Darwin's *Origin of Species* served to complete a naturalistic understanding of the world—the heavens above, the Earth below, and life itself.[2] But by the last third of the nineteenth century any implied and theretofore respected agreement to keep the peace between naturalists and supernaturalists was being ignored. Ronald Numbers and I concur that a shift in sentiment took place during that time.[3] For example, we find T. H. Huxley (1825-1895) and the Irish physicist John Tyndall (1820-1893) engaged in a new antagonism

---

1. Numbers, "Science without God," 281.

2. While the focus had been on the evolution of life, a full account of a naturalistic science would include William Herschel's proposal, as early as 1802, of an evolving universe. Based on thirty years of observing nebulae through telescopes he had made, Herschel argued that nebulae and large star clusters were being born, growing older, and dying out. See Holmes, *The Age of Wonder*, ch. 4, especially 203–5. The evolution of planet Earth in geological terms was the account given by Sir Charles Lyell in his *Principles of Geology* (1830–33) while Alexander von Humboldt took five volumes and nearly two decades to write an all-embracing view of the world simply called *Kosmos* (1845–62).

3. Numbers, "Science without God," 281.

toward religion. As keen as Huxley was to defend Darwin's methodology, he devoted himself to expanding the influence of science to the educational system. Tyndall not only wanted to root out supernaturalism from science, but also wanted to have traditional religion replaced by a rational "religion of science."[4] Religion of science foreshadows a philosophical positivism where meaning is reduced to what is verifiable. The historian Frank M. Turner points out that these polemicists sought "'to expand the influence of scientific ideas for the purpose of secularizing society rather than for the goal of advancing science internally. Secularization was their goal; science, their weapon.'"[5] We can see where this is heading. A direct line of attack extends from Huxley to E. O. Wilson, who argues that civilization is better off when science, not religion, is given the responsibility to establish those human values worth pursuing.[6]

During the nineteenth century not everyone understood the situation to be an irreconcilable crisis, but everyone recognized the perennial nature of contention inherent in a tug of divergent cultural forces. A divorce did actually happen by the close of the nineteenth century. Perhaps *divorce* is too strong a word if we understand what happened to be an amicable separation of two mature disciplines. The world's oldest scientific academy, The Royal Society of London for Improving Natural Knowledge, was established in 1660. By 1847 the society decided that in the future fellows would be elected solely on the merit of their scientific work, thus ending one tradition of rewarding patronage and establishing a new one of identifying professional scientists. In America, a similar shift was taking place. According to Roberts and Turner, Charles Darwin provided the nudge, and the doxological character of science and its intimate associations with defending Christian theism gave ground to methodological naturalism. By 1870, an arbitrary but reasonable marker, American intellectuals were enthusiastically and aggressively justifying, even privileging, scientific inquiry.[7] The separate domains "agreement" becomes established not only in the formation of separate professional organizations but also with the formation of distinct faculties within

---

4. David A. Hollinger is very instructive in the development of a science-centered culture or an "ethic of science" from about 1870 to 1930, especially at the hands of Huxley and William James. See his *After Cloven Tongues of Fire*, chapters 4 and 6.

5. Quoted from Numbers, "Science without God," 281.

6. Namely, E. O. Wilson, *Sociobiology: The New Synthesis* (Cambridge, MA: Harvard University Press, 1975), as well as his *On Human Nature* (Cambridge, MA: Harvard University Press, 1978).

7. Roberts and Turner, *The Sacred and the Secular University*, 33, and 129 n.27.

universities and colleges. Professionalism not only fostered specialization, it required scholars and researchers to commit to one discipline under increasing pressure to maintain proper boundaries and credentials. In their study of the rise of the secular university, Roberts and Turner conclude: "If disciplinary specialization was one chief manifestation of epistemological secularization, the humanities reinforced the other, naturalism."[8] Whether a divorce or an amicable separation, certain individuals were not content to let the status quo stand. In his 1932 *Nature, Man and God*, William Temple called for mutual respect, a common reverence for truth in all its forms, where even though there may still be differences and tension, "there will be no quarrel."

Overall, theology was doing its best to reestablish its credibility while conceding to science its own domain. On one front, fundamentalists chose to challenge science, wanting nothing to do with accommodation. From where they stood the cumulative effect of a succession of compromises was nothing less than a compromised orthodoxy. A universe closed to divine intervention was simply intolerable because the God who creates natural laws can supersede them at any time. Even though Scripture is not a science book, when its writers speak, Christians are obligated to accept their words as "the way it actually is."

The broader and somewhat more conciliatory Evangelicalism adopted a different approach.[9] Beginning with the presumption that both theology and science are interested in "objective facts"—whether they are objective facts in respect to God or facts about the universe—they share a commensurate epistemology. Nancey Murphy makes the interesting observation that a conservative Evangelical theology does not want to dismiss science; rather, it sees itself as a parallel epistemology. She cites the influence of Thomas Reid, the founder of the common-sense realism school of philosophy.[10] Influenced by Reid, Charles Hodge emphasized the parallels between scientific facts and scriptural facts, calling on

---

8. Ibid., 121.

9. I am making a common distinction between Fundamentalism and Conservatism or Fundamentalists and Evangelical conservatives. There are many good historical studies that trace the history of both streams of Protestant Christianity, such as Donald G. Bloesch, *The Evangelical Renaissance* (Grand Rapids: Eerdmans, 1973) and Gary Dorrien, *The Remaking of Evangelical Theology* (Louisville: Westminster John Knox, 1998). The key distinction in this context is willingness of conservative Evangelicals to converse with other traditions of truth when Fundamentalists are not.

10. Murphy, *Beyond Liberalism and Fundamentalism*, 15–16, 32.

theologians "to ascertain, collect, and combine all the facts which God has revealed concerning himself and our relation to Him."[11]

Contemporary advocates of intelligent design represent both a continuation of natural theology and the intention to reclaim science in the name of God. The principal premise driving natural theology has always been the presence of design, and the intelligent design movement (ID) has pressed the argument that the more we know about the universe, the more we are certain of an intelligent design. Rather than attacking methodological naturalism as atheistic, scientists sympathetic to intelligent design keep pressing the argument that a nontheistic methodology is inadequate and cannot explain the unexplainable, such as the emergence of life.

In this regard, conservatives see themselves as adding a corrective to the reigning theory of evolution. The public schools, they contend, are not teaching the whole truth, and so a theistic perspective needs to be added to complement science. Thus, we find ID advocates and established scientists accusing each other of "bad" science.

The liberal theology of mainline Protestantism, on the other hand, does not share the premise that science and theology are interested in the same kinds of facts, regarding attempts to harmonize Scripture with science as simplistic. Creationists and intelligent designers are not only exhibiting bad science but also bad theology. Liberals are more likely to honor the integrity of scientific methodology by exploring ways theology and science complement each other.

Nancey Murphy also exposes the underbelly of two types of theology arising from different understandings of language. Murphy turns to the contemporary philosophical distinction between "outside-in" and "inside-out" theories of language.[12] In the former model "words get their meaning from the things in the world to which they *refer*, or sentences get their meaning from the facts or states of affairs they *represent*."[13] Priority is given to the ontological givenness of what lies outside the mind, and language functions to bring to light what is already given. In this outside-in approach to reality and language, conservatives find support for a theology that begins with objective facts and honors a tight fit between language and reality. The inspired author, then, is someone who

---

11. Quoted in Murphy, *Beyond Liberalism and Fundamentalism*, 42–43.
12. Ibid., 36–51.
13. Ibid., 38.

is superintended by the Holy Spirit in order to use not merely adequate language but the only language necessary to express what God intends.

By way of contrast, an inside-out approach to language and reality begins with what happens in the mind. This is the Cartesian turn to the subject, which progressed through modern philosophy and modern theology from Descartes to Richard Rorty, from Schleiermacher to Bultmann, from existentialism to postmodernism. Here, language functions to bring to expression, experience, emotions, attitudes, and intentions. Truth is more expansive since words themselves, without referring to anything external, can generate their own meaning, as they do in fiction and poetry. Objective facts, therefore, do not exist, because there is no such thing as a fact waiting to be discovered since language (the act of bringing to expression) is what renders every experience meaningful. It does not matter if the experience is religious or observational in nature since both depend on "language in use" to bring an experience or observation to expression in order for it be communicated.

The distinction between outside-in and inside-out methodologies is helpful in understanding why conservatives and liberals have difficulty finding common ground. An ongoing discussion of the relationship of language to reality is essential to both our understanding of science (chapter 4) and theology (chapter 5), and how theology and science relate to each other. We can begin to see the validity of making a distinction between words that become meaningful as they correspond or represent an external reality and words that become meaningful because they bring to light a new understanding by the way the words are put together; between language that adheres to reality and language that creates its own reality; between a reality that is discovered and a reality that needs to be interpreted; and between language that is culture-free and language that is necessarily conditioned by the subjective nature of all experience.

Roman Catholicism seems to have made its peace with science, and notably with Galileo and Darwin. The problem with making peace with the past is that often the past does not always want to make peace with us. There is, for instance, the official position of the Roman Catholic Church. In 1996, Pope John Paul II acknowledged the theory of evolution to be "more than a hypothesis." Nevertheless, a theory of evolution does not override revelation, and in particular, science cannot fully explain a species that is endowed with a soul that is immediately created by God. In order to further clarify the church's attitude and position toward evolution and empirical science, John Paul released *Fides et Ratio* in 1998, followed in 2004 by *Communion and Stewardship: Human Persons Created in the Image of God*. To say the least, a considerable degree of careful analysis and theological sophistication is required to reconcile truths of science with truths of revelation. But unlike the history of conservative and liberal theology with its generalized disposition toward science, Roman Catholic theology "picks its fights" with science only when it contradicts "divine and catholic truth."

The displacement of a natural theology by a natural philosophy, and the rising tide of a dominant empirical science, foretells the appearance of a new atheism. Even a theistic natural philosophy could not withstand the onslaught of a secular science, but in one sense an atheistic secularism was already imbedded in a mind-set that pushed God further into the background, effectively eliminating belief in inspiration and divine intervention. Modern science was opening new avenues of discourse but closing others, and most certainly compelling most Christians to either dig in their heels or revel in the prospect of finding God anew in places never expected.

Antecedents

Rapprochement is always possible when a desire to reconcile is present. During the period from Bacon until the end of the nineteenth century, rapprochement ebbed and flowed in the sense that science and theology made space to accommodate each other. Historians do not normally use the terminology of rapprochement to describe what was happening during this period, and the reason I suspect lies in the fact that neither science nor theology were sufficiently self-defined as distinct disciplines but existed together under the blanket of natural theology or natural philosophy (or even natural science). When I speak of rapprochement, then, I have in mind a very specific interaction arising from a particular historical circumstance. In order to understand the antecedents to what I am calling the NR, we turn to Alfred North Whitehead and Teilhard de Chardin.

De Chardin and Whitehead, but notably the latter, are best understood against the backdrop of the "new physics." Anticipating and preparing the way for a new rapprochement (NR) was the revolution in modern physics, especially as it was interpreted by Niels Bohr (1885–1944) and Werner Heisenberg (1901–1976). Bohr argued as early as 1935 that recent discoveries in quantum mechanics required a radical revision of the classical understanding of causality. Historian John Brooke mentions a number of characteristics of the revolution in physics as encouraging a dialogue with theology: (1) the recognition that physicists deal with an elusive reality, and that no one model can give an exhaustive account of subatomic phenomena, (2) the indeterminacy of reality creates a space for speaking of divine activity and human freedom, (3) the concept of complementarity and complementary models of description suggests parallels within theology when speaking of the mystery of God, (4) the holistic implications of the new physics reverberate with holistic explanations theologians often employ, (5) the "fall" of determinism allows for a little humility to enter into the conversation, and (6) the impossibility of removing the observer entirely from the act of observing suggests that "even in science, the object of research is no longer nature itself, but man's investigation of nature" (Heisenberg).[14]

Whitehead and Chardin were singularly self-aware of a need to break down the barriers of separate domains. Neither fit the mold of adaptation or reconciliation, for both did their thinking from the ground up with unmatched originality. After a distinguished career as a mathematician and logistician at the Universities of Cambridge and London, Whitehead, at the age of sixty-three, changed direction by accepting the position of Professor of Philosophy at Harvard University in 1924. He went on to formulate a process metaphysics that provided the foundation for what became known as process theology. His most important publications in this area were *Process and Reality: An Essay in Cosmology* (Gifford Lectures 1927/28) and *Science and the Modern World* (1925). Throughout his career as a mathematician and philosopher, Whitehead was an independent thinker. He was born into a family firmly rooted in the Church of England. His father and uncles were vicars. Religious minded but not interested in institutional religion, Whitehead wrote as a philosopher-theologian. He died in 1947 in Cambridge, Massachusetts and was buried without a funeral. All of his papers were destroyed by his family, honoring his request to do so at his death.

In order to appreciate Whitehead one needs to understand that he was living during a time when the foundation of an Aristotelian-Newtonian world view was crumbling as modern physics was rewriting the Book of Nature. The stability and visualizability of Newtonian physics

---

14. Brooke, *Science and Religion*, 330–31.

was made for a calculable, rational, and God-given universe. Consequently, Christian theologians were able to make appropriate adaptations without compromising basic tenets of the faith. But if reality at its deepest levels is part of a process having temporal extension rather than existing as permanent substance, then the God of traditional theism is suspect. For Whitehead, God must partake of the very reality that God creates. If Creator and reality are of one piece, and Whitehead will not have it otherwise, God cannot stand apart as omnipotent and self-contained. If we take seriously what particle physicists say about the core nature of reality, Whitehead argued, every particle of reality, instead of constituting an approximate point in itself, extends from the previous fragment to the next in an invisible thread running back to infinity. In other words, no "event" is complete in itself but is always part of a continuous process. So too, God must exist as interdependent with the universe, a universe constituted by change, process, and development.

Pierre Teilhard de Chardin stood in that unique Roman Catholic tradition of Jesuit priest-scientist. Born in France in 1881, he received a doctorate in geology from the Sorbonne. He spent much of his life in paleontological research in China while engaged in paleontological expeditions to India, Africa, and Southeast Asia. Everything he wrote, except for a few scientific papers, appeared after his death in 1955. More than fifteen volumes of his writings have since been published, among which *The Phenomenon of Man* (1955) and *The Divine Milieu* (1960) are the best known. When he began writing *Le Phénomènen Humain* during the 1920s and 1930s, his religious superiors were fearful of his radical religious ideas. As a result, Teilhard and his writings were literally exiled to China. Teilhard found himself wrestling with a similar but distinctive paradigm shift that was organic rather than inorganic. Here too was an understanding of reality where "every element of the cosmos is woven from all others." Nothing characterizes the living world more than change, and the most appropriate way to describe this change is to say everything is evolving into something new. Like no one before him and few who followed, Teilhard adopted an unrestrained embrace of evolution. The redeemer Christ is delivered from a fossilized past and projected into a future where Christ is the Omega Point. The universe, Teilhard writes, "is physically impregnated to the very core of its matter by the influence of his [Christ's] super-human nature."[15] Like Whitehead, Teilhard wanted

---

15. See Teilhard de Chardin, "My Universe," 252.

to break down rigid distinctions between matter and spirit since both are different aspects of a radial energy that draws the universe towards ever-greater complexity and centricity.

Although very distinctive in their approaches—Whitehead assumed the role of philosopher-metaphysician and Teilhard the role of christo-centric mystic—the central conviction for both was the obligation to face up to an evolutionary perspective. Neither was familiar with the work of the other but both acknowledged their indebtedness to Henri Bergson, the French pioneer in evolutionary thinking. Change in all its manifestations permeates the essence of being, so that being is always a becoming. Whitehead and Teilhard leave us with the unmistakable feeling that the old wineskins of classic theology cannot sustain the new wine of relativity, quantum mechanics, and evolutionary biology. Whitehead and Teilhard did not look to solve specific issues of contention between science and Christian doctrine. Instead, they set forth to construct a framework or perspective sufficiently comprehensive to incorporate new paradigms of time and divine action. The school of thought known as process theology was the result of an extended interpretation of Whitehead's process metaphysics. Over decades, Whitehead inspired a more coherent train of thought, particularly as it was developed at the University of Chicago, and in the writings of Charles Hartshorne, W. Norman Pittenger, Bernard E. Meland, Schubert Ogden, and John B. Cobb Jr.[16]

It is difficult to judge the reach of Whitehead and Teilhard's influence because we are more likely to remember the criticism they received than their ground-breaking contributions, which we are likely to take for granted. Neither the scientific nor theological communities embraced Whitehead or Teilhard, judging them as drifting, or even betraying, their respective core disciplines.[17] Orthodox theologians were uncomfortable with the mix of philosophy, religion, and science. For many, process

---

16. Somewhere in the mix of names, Joseph Sittler should be remembered as questioning whether theologies of the word, such as neo-orthodoxy, were capable of addressing a global environmental crisis of our own making. For a reassessment of Sittler, see H. Paul Santmire, "A Reformation Theology of Nature Transfigured," *Theology Today* 61 (January 2005) 509–27. We should also not forget Santmire's own contribution in the recovery of a theology that "encompasses the world of nature"—*The Travail of Nature* (Minneapolis: Fortress, 1985).

17. Phillip M. Thompson does an admirable job of placing Teilhard into a larger Catholic context; namely by examining the writings of Jacques Maritain, Bernard Lonergan, and Thomas Merton. See his *Between Science and Religion: The Engagement of Catholic Intellectuals with Science and Technology in the Twentieth Century* (Lanham, MD: Lexington Books, 2009).

theology had the feel of pantheism (seeing God everywhere) while making light of a personal God of history who performs saving acts. Already taking place was a shift away from working out a natural theology à la Whitehead or Teilhard and toward a more modest theology of nature. In addition, Teilhard was measured against the orthodoxy of Roman Catholicism and found to be too mystical. Teilhard characterizes his purpose as making a place for God in a universe always evolving, and Whitehead is intent on developing a theistic philosophy where becoming is not inferior to being. Together they prepared the way for a new rapprochement, setting in motion one of the pivotal issues of the twentieth century: How will Christians reconcile God, whose essence is unchanging and omnipotent, with a universe that knows nothing of either?

Paul Tillich remains a quintessential example of someone who defines the task of modern theology as that of deonticizing Christian theology.[18] While not as well known, Leslie Dewart sets out to accomplish a similar de-Hellenization of traditional Roman Catholic theology. He formulates the pivotal question for Christian theology this way: "Can the Christian faith be said truly to develop and unequivocally to evolve, on the assumption that this faith is *true* and that its object is *real?*"[19] Since humans, as Dewart argues, continuously evolve by a progressive process of self-awareness, so truth is a process of progressive differentiation. Truth, therefore, cannot be conformity to something that was. Given this premise about the evolution of all things, "the experience of truth implies the possibility of error."[20] The Roman Catholic hierarchy did not warm to Dewart's revisionist theology, but that does not eliminate the profound issue for Christian theology of how to reconcile a received truth of revelation found in Scripture and tradition when they are indubitably the product of an evolving human consciousness.

The New Rapprochement

The NR is *new* by virtue of its historical situation, as well as its salient features. Whitehead and Teilhard have been absorbed or found wanting.

18. See Tillich's article entitled, "Science and Theology: A Discussion with Einstein" in Paul Tillich, *Theology of Culture*, ed. Robert C. Kimball (New York: Oxford University Press, 1964); and Roy D. Morrison II, *Science, Theology and the Transcendent Horizon* (Atlanta: Scholars Press, 1994), 187 and 338.

19. Dewart, *The Foundations of Belief,* 12.

20. Ibid., 328.

The move toward rapprochement is different this time around. A new generation of historians, philosophers, and scientist-theologians are in place to try a new approach. A spirit of openness and affirmation has for the most part displaced a reactionary defensiveness. Absent is the grand sweep of a synthesis comparable to Whitehead and Teilhard, or any obligation to write a natural theology. Practitioners of the NR are not enamored with the argument from design nor with arguments that smack of a proof for God.[21] Scientific discoveries are allowed, even invited, to shape and sharpen theological truth claims. Conscious of the orthodoxy they are defending, the language of the NR thinkers is not one of compromise but of respect. One of its primary spokesmen, Arthur Peacocke, reminds us that because the universe is created by God, our understanding of that universe through science "must *enhance* and *clarify* and, if need be, *correct* our understanding of God and of God's relation to creation, including humanity."[22]

Enhance, clarify, and correct nicely summarizes the impetus and purpose of the NR. What sets the NR apart from other approaches to bridging the theology-science divide is a broad and deep appreciation of the philosophical and theological shifts within Christianity coupled with equally important changes in science. Also present is a sense of urgency to halt any further marginalization and isolation of theological claims. A new opportunity has opened up, and the time to begin a new and creative interaction between theology and science is now—"an interaction which honors and respects the integrity of each partner, an interaction in which convictions are self-critical and honest engagement is prized, an interaction which focuses specifically on the most rigorous theories of mainstream natural sciences and the most central positions of mainline theology."[23] Motivated by finding common ground and initiating a new dialogue with science, the NR is no less than a new discipline.

---

21. John Haught offers the most sustained skepticism regarding intelligent design as being "too restrictive, theologically speaking, to capture the deeper and ultimately more compelling meaningfulness that a robust theological vision may discern in an evolving universe." See Haught, *God After Darwin*, 46 and 5–6, 55–56.

22. Peacocke, *Evolution: Disguised Friend of Faith?*, viii. Italics mine.

23. The quote is from Robert John Russell's short summary of "Bridging Science and Religion," http://ctns.org/russell_article.html. For a general overview of the NR, see Ted Peters, ed., *Science and Theology: The New Consonance*. A wealth of information can be found in both Peter Harrison, ed., *The Cambridge Companion to Science and Religion* (Cambridge: Cambridge University Press, 2010), and Christopher Southgate, ed., *God, Humanity and the Cosmos: A Companion to the Science-Religion Debate* (London: T & T Clark, 2005).

While it is difficult to say what the following individuals have in common, they do demonstrate a passion for thinking critically and holistically about matters scientific and theological: Thomas Forsyth Torrance, Wolfhart Pannenberg, John B. Cobb Jr., Ian Barbour, Arthur Peacocke, John Polkinghorne, Keith Ward, Ernan McMullen, Holmes Rolston III, Philip Hefner, John Haught, Nancey Murphy, Willem B. Drees, George L. Murphy, Jürgen Moltmann, Ted Peters, Alvin Plantinga, Hans Küng, Niels Henrik Gregersen, Wentzel van Huyssteen, John D. Barrow, Francisco J. Ayala, Francis S. Collins, Keith B. Miller, Alister E. McGrath, John H. Brooke, William Stoeger, Ronald Numbers, Robert John Russell, and Michael Heller.[24] They all consider, as I do, theology and science to be vitally and historically interconnected. Additionally, they would agree with Stephen M. Barr, a theoretical particle physicist, that what many mistakenly take to be the conflict between religion and science is actually one between religion and materialism.[25] In other words, science is not intrinsically atheistic, nor is there an inherent antagonism between religion and science. The point is often made that many great scientists have been religiously motivated and many clergy have been deeply interested in science. Since the 1960s, an explosion of books and research centers have emerged with the purpose of reversing the status quo of separate ghettos of knowledge.

At times the NR is associated with another set of names, such as Theodosius Dobzhansky (*The Biology of Ultimate Concern*, 1967), E. Schrödinger (*What Is Life?*, 1969), Fritjof Capra (*The Tao of Physics*, 1975), David Bohm (*Wholeness and the Implicate Order*, 1981), Paul Davies (*God and the New Physics*, 1983), and J. D. Barrow and F. J. Tipler (*The Anthropic Cosmological Principle*, 1986). But this trajectory is not identical with the NR that I have in mind. Motivating this group of thinkers is a renewed enthusiasm for pursuing religious types of questions as they grow out of "the new physics" and evolutionary theory. Capra, for example, is inspired to write books about the possible religious implications of the new physics and parallels with the mystical traditions of Hinduism, Buddhism, Taoism, and Zen. The same mind-set is found in the recent book by the Dali Lama—*The Universe in a Single Atom: The Convergence of Science and Spirituality* (2006)—where the Dali Lama considers the neuroscientific basis of Buddhist meditation practices and

---

24. This list of names is by no means exhaustive but does try to identify those who have a sustained commitment to the dialogue between science and theology.

25. Barr, *Modern Physics and Ancient Faith*, 28.

the similarities between Eastern concepts like emptiness and those of modern field theory. Paul Davies and Frank Tipler have written a number of popular books that are difficult to define except to say they are neither fish nor fowl.[26] Tipler proposes that Christianity can be approached as a science, and its claims can be empirically proven, including bodily resurrection. Davies is more reserved but his *The Mind of God* is subtitled *The Scientific Basis for a Rational God*. Both Tipler and Davies are physicists who pursue ultimate questions but only in the most generalized form.

This is a diffuse trajectory because it makes religion the counterpoint to science, resulting in many ideas going in many directions rather than taking a more disciplined approach represented by articles in *Zygon: The Journal of Religion & Science* or *Theology and Science*. The NR of which I speak, however, is not of this ilk. By comparison, Polkinghorne is a physicist and a theologian who pursues deep questions within an orthodox framework rather than trying to prove something. Certainly there are religious implications incited by the new physics worthy of exploration, but to be quite frank, Capra, Tipler, and Davies are not knowledgeable theologians and therefore are incapable of or disinterested in a sustained theological discussion. And this is a critique I will extend to most scientists who do not know the difference between Augustine and Aquinas, or Barth and Pannenberg, or a theology of nature and a natural theology.

A much more important seedbed for the NR is the making of American liberal theology, to borrow a phrase from Gary Dorrien's book by that name, and in particular the Chicago school of thought during the 1930s and '40s. Dorrien defines liberal theology as the idea of a Christian perspective based on reason and experience, not external authority. As he traces the historical roots of liberal theology, especially as it takes shape in America, we encounter a diverse group of thinkers who are excited by crossover possibilities in the wake of modern science. Here is the beginning of a liberal tradition committed to a methodology adequate to establish an empirical foundation for doing Christian theology. Process theology emanates from the dominating influence of Whitehead, but it was Charles Hartshorne and Henry Wieman who theologized Whitehead's philosophy at the University of Chicago Divinity School. A

---

26. For example, Paul Davies, *Fifth Miracle: The Search for the Origin and Meaning of Life* (New York: Touchstone, 1999), *God and the New Physics* (New York: Touchstone, 1983), *The Mind of God* (New York: Simon & Schuster, 1992); and Frank J. Tipler, *The Physics of Christianity* (New York: Doubleday, 2007), *The Physics of Immortality* (New York: Anchor, 1994).

succession of creative thinkers, including George Burman Foster, Shirley Jackson Case, Edward Scribner Ames, and Gerald Birney Smith, forge a school of realism.[27]

Still more relevant to the NR is the development of two new disciplines: the history and philosophy of science (and one might add the sociology of knowledge). This legacy belongs to Werner Heisenberg, Karl Popper, Paul Feyerabend, Michael Polanyi, Norwood Russell Hanson, Larry Laudan, Mary Hesse, Imre Lakatos, Ian Hacking, Gerald Holton, Stephen Toulmin, and Thomas Kuhn. In hindsight, we see how much broader and deeper our understanding of science is when enlarged by an introspective and historical perspective. Specifically, philosophers provide a wider interpretive framework for science, while historians provide a needed interrogation for what constitutes scientific knowledge.

Running along a parallel track is the emergence of philosophers of religion such as Frederick Ferré, Ian Ramsey, and William Austin, who opened new ways to think and talk about religion. In addition, J. L. Austin and the later Wittgenstein shifted the focus from meaning as *reference* to meaning as *use*, and so put another nail in the coffin of positivism.[28] What these disciplines interject into the conversation between theology and science are new ways to frame the questions, new ways to look at the language of religion, and new ways to understand empiricism.

Sometime in the twentieth century the hard, arrogant objectivity of modern science became a softer, humbler objectivity. We see the empiricism of Newton and John Stuart Mill give way to the critical examinations of Popper, Feyerabend, and Kuhn, severely undercutting the strong claims for observation, experimentation, and inductionism. In addition, the subject-centered rationalism of Descartes and the associated claims of intuitive knowledge are thoroughly discredited. Despite Einstein's lifelong reservation, the observer and the observed are understood as inextricably bound together. Some would say the entire project of empiricism is no longer viable in the sense that language is incapable of representing things-in-themselves.[29] Nor can science portray itself as making steady

---

27. See Gary Dorrien, *The Making of American Liberal Theology: Idealism, Realism, and Modernity 1900–1950* (Louisville: John Knox, 2006), 235–56. This is volume two of a three-volume history of liberal theology from 1805–2005.

28. For a fuller discussion of this shift, see Nancey Murphy, *Anglo-American Postmodernity* (Boulder, CO: Westview, 1997), 23–26.

29. I have in mind the broad critique of Richard Rorty and Charles Taylor. See for example Clifford Geertz's essay, "The Strange Estrangement: Charles Taylor and the Natural Sciences," where Geertz quotes Taylor's own confession that he is "a hedgehog,

progress toward a truth waiting to be discovered. The presumption, if we are to follow the NR, is that developments in the latter half of the twentieth century, especially as they have taken place outside of science proper in the disciplines of history, philosophy, and sociology, have resulted in a "softer" science, have reshaped the conceptual landscape, and have thereby opened a new space for theology and science to mutually enrich each other.

Without any doubt the three kingpins of the NR are Ian Barbour, the consummate teacher; John Polkinghorne, the impeccable scientist-theologian; and Arthur Peacocke, the discerning freethinker. Over a period of forty years they have given us a body of work epitomizing the NR.

Born in Peking, China in 1923, the second of three sons to an American Episcopal mother and a Scottish Presbyterian father, Barbour grew up among teachers. At Yenching University, his father, a close friend of the Jesuit paleontologist Pierre Teilhard de Chardin, taught geology, and his mother taught religious education. In 1949 Barbour completed a PhD in high-energy physics at the University of Chicago, but another vocational calling could not be ignored and Barbour enrolled at Yale Divinity School, completing his degree in 1956. In 1955 he joined the faculty at Carleton College in Minnesota where he taught physics and religion for thirty years, until he retired, professor emeritus. Barbour's ground-breaking contribution to the science-religion debate was duly recognized when he was invited to present the Gifford Lecture in 1989. In 1999 Barbour was also honored when named by the Templeton Foundation as the winner of the prize for Progress in Religion for his lifelong dedication to fostering dialogue between religion and science. The publication of his *Issues in Science and Religion* in 1966 became one of the markers of a new rapprochement, and for a generation this text defined the issues and set forth the alternatives. Barbour summarized his life this way: "The years in my twenties were devoted mainly to physics, in my thirties mainly to studying and teaching religion, my forties to relating science and religion, and my fifties (starting in 1973) to technology and

---

a monomaniac endlessly polemicizing against a single idea—'the ambition to model the study of man on the natural science'" (Geertz, *Available Light*, 143). In the same vein compare Wendell Berry's assault on what he regards as E. O. Wilson's scientific hubris and radical reductionism, *Life Is a Miracle: An Essay against Modern Superstition* (Washington, DC: Counterpoint, 2000), ch. 3. Also pertinent is Gerald P. McKenny's discussion of the Baconian project and "the technological utopian quest of medicine" in *To Relieve the Human Condition*.

ethics."[30] Barbour died at age ninety in Northfield, Minnesota, lauded for giving birth to the contemporary dialogue between science and religion.

Born into a devout family, early on John Polkinghorne displayed his academic gifts that led to a scholarship and degree from Cambridge University (Trinity College). He began his career doing research in theoretical particle physics but found a calling as a Lecturer at the University of Edinburgh and as Professor of Mathematical Physics at the University of Cambridge. For twenty-five years, Professor Polkinghorne was content as a theoretical physicist, playing a significant role in the discovery of the quark, and then, like Barbour, pursued a theological education, being ordained an Anglican priest in 1982. Over the subsequent twenty-plus years, Polkinghorne served as an Anglican curate and vicar of a country parish in Kent. But his standing in the academic world made him a unique candidate to become College Dean at Trinity Hall, and then President of Queen's College, Cambridge. During this time, and into retirement, he wrote more than thirty-five well-received books exploring in readable language the mysteries of science (principally physics) and illuminating where science and theology intersect. On the world stage, Polkinghorne has been a tireless advocate for interactive exchange between the scientific and theological communities. His distinguished career includes roles as (past) President and (now) Fellow of Queen's College; Fellow of the Royal Society; and the first President of the International Society for Science and Religion.[31] Like Barbour, he was invited to give the Gifford Lectures in Scotland, and also like Barbour was honored with the Templeton Prize for Progress in Religion (receiving the award in 2002).

Barbour found a home and a vocation teaching undergraduates in a small midwestern college in America. Polkinghorne's first love was physics and Cambridge was where he became a prominent professor and dean. Arthur Peacocke was an Oxford man, spending almost his entire adult life living on St. John Street. By his own admission he lived a double vocation divided into roughly equal periods of researcher and lecturer in physical biochemistry and "worker-priest," bridging the academic worlds of science and religion.[32] Born in 1924 in Watford near London and

30. Barbour, "A Personal Odyssey," 27.

31. Polkinghorne's life is told no better than by himself: *From Physicist to Priest: An Autobiography*. One chapter outlines in chronological order his theological writings and his motivation for writing each book.

32. Peacocke gives a brief autobiographical account in *From DNA to Dean*. The book also serves as a concise account of his theological beliefs in the context of a

raised in a traditional Church of England household, he finished a PhD in physical biochemistry from Oxford University in 1948, then spent over twenty-five years doing research and teaching at the Universities of Birmingham and Oxford. A self-described "mild agnostic" in his earlier years, Peacocke found himself pulled toward more a robust explanation of the natural world and like Polkinghorne pursued a theological degree and was ordained in the Church of England (in 1971). At the age of forty-eight this Oxford scientist became a Cambridge Dean at Clare College, where he taught both biochemistry and theology for eleven years. Returning then to Oxford, he served as honorary chaplain and canon. Following in the footsteps of Polkinghorne and Barbour, he delivered the Gifford Lectures in 1993/94. He too received the Templeton Prize, in 2001. A member of many learned societies, author of numerous respected books and scientific articles, founder of the Society for Ordained Scientists, Director of the Ian Ramsey Center, and President of the Science and Religion Forum from 1995 until his death in 2006, Peacocke devoted himself to broader issues, but especially to the intersection of theology and evolutionary biology.

Barbour's *Religion in an Age of Science* (1990), Polkinghorne's *The Faith of a Physicist: Reflections of a Bottom-Up Thinker* (1994), and Peacocke's *Theology for a Scientific Age* (1993) were all originally given as Gifford Lectures and are "attempts to articulate Christian belief in ways that seem natural and congenial to the scientific mind" (Polkinghorne). On a broader scale, the NR signals a movement beyond the positivism, reductionism, materialism, fideism, and atheism that inevitably turn theology and science against each other. In his preface to the festschrift dedicated to Barbour, *Fifty Years in Science and Religion*, Robert Russell summarizes the significance of what makes his contribution crucial and unique: "A willingness to hold . . . beliefs self-critically and hypothetically in hopes that such dialogue will lead to deeper understanding and even mutual transformation."[33]

In a book entitled *Scientists as Theologians*, Polkinghorne undertakes a comparison of himself with Barbour and Peacocke. The critical criterion according to Polkinghorne is "the degree to which scientific concepts should be allowed to mold and influence the conceptual apparatus of theological thought, and the degree to which theology must retain

scientific world view.

33. Russell, ed., *Fifty Years in Science and Religion*, xiii.

(as science does unquestioned) its own portfolio of irreducibly necessary ideas."[34] At stake then is the value one places on autonomy, orthodoxy, and the unity of knowledge. Remembering Barbour's original fourfold taxonomy of possible ways of relating science and religion—conflict, independence, dialogue, integration—Barbour tilts toward integration with his preference for a metaphysical framework akin to Whitehead's proposal.[35] Polkinghorne, who takes more seriously the "detailed substance of traditional Christian theology," is an advocate of dialogue but vigilantly guards theology's autonomy.[36] Peacock is something of a maverick, eschewing metaphysics and process theology while advocating a revision of traditional Christian doctrines in order to accommodate recent scientific discoveries. Peacocke is more adventurous and less dedicated to preserving orthodox Christianity than Polkinghorne, while Barbour occupies a middle ground. It is clear, though, that all three move between the poles of convergence and consonance. Here it is possible to distinguish between strong and weak forms of consonance. The strong form works toward convergence, a true integration of consistency and coherence. The weak form is content, at least for the moment, with constructive engagement. The distinction is not absolute, but I think of Barbour as tilting toward the strong end of the spectrum, Peacocke toward the weak end, with Polkinghorne in the middle.

A discussion of the NR is incomplete without mention of two prominent institutions. Established in 1987 by the late international investor and philanthropist Sir John Templeton, the Templeton Foundation supports numerous and varied projects, studies, award programs, conferences, and its own worldwide publications. The stated purpose of the Foundation is to "stimulate a high standard of excellence in scholarly understanding which can serve to encourage further worldwide exploration of the moral and spiritual dimension of the universe and of the

---

34. Polkinghorne, *Scientists as Theologians: A Comparison of the Writings of Ian Barbour, Arthur Peacocke and John Polkinghorne* (London: SPCK, 1996), 82.

35. There have been many alternative proposals to Barbour's fourfold taxonomy. A good review of them plus a creative new proposal is found in Mikael Stenmark's *How to Relate Science and Religion: A Multidimensional Model* (Grand Rapids: Eerdmans, 2004).

36. Polkinghorne says as much as he begins his Gifford Lectures. In comparing his own to other fashionable books, such as Barbour's *Religion in an Age of Science* and Peacocke's *Theology for a Scientific Age*, Polkinghorne states that he "differs from my predecessors in wanting to make much more detailed contact with the core of Christian belief" (*Science and Christian Belief*, 1).

human potential within its ultimate purpose.[37]" Each year the foundation awards the Templeton Prize for Progress in Religion to a living person who has devoted his or her talents to "those aspects of human experience that even in an age of astonishing scientific advance, remain beyond the reach of scientific explanation."[38]

By its own admission the foundation is biased toward life's biggest questions and new insights at the boundary of religion and science. If for no other reason than the large sums of money the foundation expends annually, the breadth of its reach is commanding. Remove it from the picture and the NR is a much smaller player among the principal actors of secular scientists. Critics complain that in trying to reconcile science and religion the lines between the two become blurred. The unspoken presumption is that religion has been marginalized and can gain some much-needed credibility if backed by scientific studies. When grants are let, for example, to explore if prayer can make a difference and to spur competition for "Gods in Minds: The Science of Religious Cognition," the hopeful effect is to cover religion with the mantle of medical and scientific respectability. Such seems to have been the case in the $2.4 million study, funded in large part by the Templeton Foundation, to test whether prayer can pass the test of science.[39] As in turns out, cardiac patients who were prayed for did not have a better chance of recovery than those who were not. Patients who knew they were being prayed for actually did worse, possibly because of performance anxiety. Regardless of how the "experiment" turned out, the Templeton Foundation is a barometer showing there is no shortage of academic types willing to participate in the "business" of reconciling science and religion.[40] To its credit, though, the Templeton Foundation is willing to ask and fund collaborative explorations of the big questions, something science is reluctant to do on its own. Thus, a $1.3 million grant in 2013 to three Johns Hopkins University theoretical physicists to develop new ideas for the origin of the universe and alternative ways to test those ideas.

37. See www.templeton.org.

38. Ibid.

39. See Benedict Carey, "Long-awaited Medical Study Questions the Power of Prayer," *The New York Times*, March 31, 2006, www.nytimes.com/2006/03/32/health/31pray.html.

40. A decidedly negative assessment from a UK perspective is given by Sunny Bains, "Questioning the Integrity of the John Templeton Foundation," *Journal of Evolutionary Psychology* 9 (March 2011), accessible online at www.epjournal.net.

Founded in 1982, the Center for Theology and the Natural Sciences (CTNS), an affiliate of the Graduate Theological Union in Berkeley, California, is committed to the critical and creative exploration of the relation between theology and the natural sciences, including physics, cosmology, evolutionary and molecular biology, genetics, neurosciences, the environmental sciences, and mathematics. In partnership with Taylor and Frances, a division of Routledge publishing, CTNS publishes the journal *Theology and Science*, dedicated to promoting creative and mutual interaction between the natural sciences and theology. The center's purpose is well-rounded and anchored in three programs: the center's teaching program at the Graduate Theological Union and, by extension, local churches, universities, and seminaries; its support of various research programs including the STARS program;[41] and its public service by way of public forums, workshops, CTNS news, its journal, and its website (www.ctns.org). Its board of directors is a virtual who's who in the academic environs of the NR. While accepting grants from the Templeton Foundation, the center embodies a more critical and creative approach. It does not give off the aura of trying to prove something or garner the support of science.

Typical of the new interest in bringing together theology and science is the newly named Zygon Center for Religion and Science located at the Lutheran School of Theology at Chicago (LSTC). As a program arm of the school, the center is "dedicated to relating religious traditions and the best scientific knowledge in order to gain insight into the origins, nature, and destiny of humans and their environment."[42] Under the leadership of its new director, Philip Hefner, longtime editor of the journal *Zygon*, the center is a place where scientists, theologians, and other scholars can explore our world and our place in that world. In addition, theological

---

41. The STARS program of the Center for Theology and the Natural Sciences awards grants funded by the Templeton Foundation. In 2009 the center awarded grants totaling $1.3 million. Recipients of two $200,000 grants include those studying a scientific approach to moral action and virtue, and doing research "on the ways science, in light of philosophical and theological reflection, points towards the nature, character and meaning of ultimate reality" (online at www.ctnsstars.org/). Besides the sophistication of research projects involving teams of scientists and humanities scholars, the research bears the Templeton trademark of science being harnessed to probe interdisciplinary questions. The conspicuous absence of similar efforts being made by secular universities indicates a skeptical attitude regarding the worthiness and relevancy of this kind of interdisciplinary research.

42. See http://zygoncenter.org.

seminaries and colleges, and to a lesser extent universities,[43] are now sponsoring interdisciplinary courses and centers devoted to bridging the separation of religion and the sciences. For the most part these efforts are intended to advance the dialogue between religion and science by educating those with a minimal knowledge of science or religion. At the denominational level, and beyond, one finds a diversity of approaches to promote interdisciplinary dialogue at the interface of faith, science, technology, and ethics.[44]

While there is no neat way to summarize the NR, there are consistent themes that are easily identifiable. I present them here without assessment, for that will come in the next chapter.

Common Ground in a Shared Postmodern Situation

The first and overriding premise of the NR is the presumption that theology and science share a common ground, opening the way for a fresh and invigorated interdisciplinary conversation. The impetus comes from two directions: science itself and a more generalized shift in philosophy. From a different perspective the prospect of common ground arises from a new way to look at reality (ontology) and a postmodern assessment of how we come to know (epistemology).

Advocates of the NR point to the way scientists themselves have been rethinking their claims for truth. From an ontological perspective, Einstein rewrites the book of physics and then upends our understanding of the universe. The absolutes of Newton's time and space, as well as the absolutes of matter in motion, give way to statistical methods, field theories, relative motion and time, and a universe finite but without boundaries. My own preferred way of speaking of this change is from the *hard* reality of Newtonian physics to a *soft* reality of Einsteinian

---

43. A typical university center is the Center for the Study of Science and Religion, which operates within The Earth Institute at Columbia University. Founded in 1999, the center is a forum "for the examination of issues that lie at the boundary of these two complementary ways of comprehending the world and our place in it" (Center for the Study of Science and Religion website, http://cssr.ei.columbia.edu/). One does notice a distinctive difference when a center for the study of science and religion is located in a university setting. The subject matter is broader, such as "Muslim Hermeneutics and Modern Arabic Views of Evolution."

44. A convenient link to this network of organizations can be found online: www.ucc.org/science/links.html.

interconnectedness.[45] By postmodern standards no one thinks in terms of hierarchical ladders of meaning where each truth leads to a higher truth. The reason is again the interconnectedness of reality, and thus the interconnectedness of truth. Electrons do not rotate about a nucleus in splendid isolation, any more than time and space are independent of each other, or a gene is a "thing unto itself." Kant's thing-in-itself is not only an illusion, it proves to be pernicious. One of the reasons the Enlightenment overpromised and oversold rationality rests with the presumption that the world is composed of things-in-themselves that can be known objectively and absolutely. Science rode the crest of its initial success, displacing theology as queen of human knowing, because it convinced just about everyone that it possessed the perfect methodology (empiricism) to know the true nature of things-in-themselves (an absolute ontology).

In addition, a softer scientific methodology, for instance, concedes that we cannot know the way things are because we can only construct representations of what is "out there." Near the end of *The Hunting of the Quark* Michael Riordan writes, "We cannot know the quark-in-itself. And anyone familiar with quantum theory has to admit that no representation is ever the one unique description of a subatomic entity. There is always an element of choice—the act of a willing subject—in every such picture."[46] The new softness of ontology and epistemology arising from the revolution in physics becomes the basis for theology to engage science as a discipline that is itself a softer science.

Looking at our postmodern situation more broadly and philosophically, the common ground on which science and theology tread is conditioned by how *all* knowledge is acquired. Scientific knowledge is not privileged insofar as it is like all knowing. It bows to the postmodern declaration that all knowing develops historically, is culturally located, and is collectively produced. Consequently, the epistemological privilege of empiricism is relativized by making space for other methodologies. Succinctly stated, postmodernity marks the end of our Enlightenment quest to know the true nature of things intuitively, unmediated, and unaffected by history or culture. Postmodernism is no less than the relentless criticism of any foundational knowledge that relies on a methodology of knowing that is self-evident and self-authenticating. The subsequent conclusion is that all knowledge is contingent and constructed. Van

---

45. See Coleman, *Competing Truths*, 28, 87, 132, 141 and passim.
46. Riordan, *The Hunting of the Quark* (New York: Touchstone, 1987), 367.

Huyssteen declares that "science and religion have now woken up to find their identities challenged and changed by a new and pervasive postmodern culture."[47]

In a gem of an essay on the legacy of Thomas Kuhn, Clifford Geertz summarizes the upshot of what Kuhn passionately defended, namely that "the history of science is the history of the growth and replacement of self-recruiting, normatively defined, variously directed, and often sharply competitive scientific communities."[48] Even if Kuhn goes too far by reducing science to the work of self-recruiting communities, as Weinberg complains about most historians and philosophers of science,[49] most scientists will concede that scientific knowledge develops historically. The interlocking nature of ontology and epistemology—the method of knowing is affected by the object of your knowing (subject/object), and the object of your knowing (ontology) affects the method you employ to know it (epistemology)— comes to the fore in modern science.[50] Modern science is itself the clearest example of this dovetailing of ontology and epistemology, and rightly so if everything in the universe is connected to everything else. Consequently, a relational (softer) ontology requires a softer methodology in order to understand the true nature of the universe. The quandary of quantum physics is often cited: In order to make a measurement the observer must "intervene" and this intervention precipitates one of many possibilities. "It is only the observer's intervention," Barr notes, "that takes one out of the realm of the hypothetical and into the realm of the actual."[51] So too at the largest scale of things, astronomers are not sure whether finding a larger number of galaxies moving counterclockwise is reality or a strange phenomena revealing something about how our brains perceive spirals.

While the history and philosophy of science were reshaping postmodern science, contemporary liberal theology found it necessary to move toward a nonfoundational theology given the following tenets.

47. Van Huyssteen, *The Shaping of Rationality*, 3.
48. Geertz, *Available Light*, 163.
49. Weinberg, *Facing Up*, 85–87, 132, 266.
50. Polkinghorne speaks of "the epistemic circle" where "how we know is controlled by the nature of the object and the nature of the object is revealed through our knowledge of it" (*Science and Christian Belief*, 32). In referring to Torrance (above), Polkinghorne writes of the idea that reality is known in accord with its nature and that "we cannot determine beforehand what these epistemological modes will be" (*Belief in God in an Age of Science* [New Haven, CT: Yale University Press, 1998], 81).
51. Barr, *Modern Physics and Ancient Faith*, 230.

(We leave for a later discussion of whether these tenets apply equally to science.)

- The rejection of the autonomous knower—the punctiliar self—who is able to apprehend universally valid truths once one extricates oneself from the authority and prejudice of a dominant text or tradition. In its place is a nonfoundational presumption that "neither science nor theology can ever have demonstrably certain foundations" since all knowing happens within a particular tradition or conceptual framework.[52]
- The acceptance of a plurality of languages for a plurality of meanings because no understanding is exhaustive and every meaning is conditioned by its context.
- The need to distance ourselves from metanarratives or grand stories which understand history, sacred or secular, as moving toward some culmination, as well as from all attempts to describe or explain the true nature of the universe by way of universal principles.
- Interpreted experiences are the only kind of experiences we have. Therefore, observational data is theory laden (already framed by a theory, otherwise it would be meaningless) and religious experience (data) is already languaged before it is understood (otherwise it would be meaningless). In short, all understanding is linguistic through and through.

Pulling together these various strands that shaped the last century, a new rapprochement became possible. Stephen M. Barr, professor of physics at the Bartol Research Institute at the University of Delaware, argues that the great discoveries of modern physics have the cumulative effect of making science and the teachings of Christianity and Judaism more compatible. Specifically, the big bang theory as a confirmed reason to believe that the universe actually does have a beginning, that the universe actually does look like it has been designed by a Designer, and that humans are by no means incidental but a natural fit in the great order of things. Similarly, Polkinghorne identifies seven salient "scientifically disclosed" features of the universe that invite a further response: a deeply intelligible universe, a universe with a fruitful history, a relational universe, a universe of veiled reality, a universe of open processes, an information-generating universe, and a universe of eventual futility.[53] Polkinghorne speaks of a remarkable turn of events while Barr speaks

---

52. Van Huyssteen, *Essays in Postfoundationalist Theology*, 264.
53. Polkinghorne, *Science and the Trinity*, ch. 3.

of an astonishing reversal, and both make the same point concerning an "inviting" universe. With the end of a mechanically deterministic world, and with the advent of ontology open to the future, the door was opened to a new level of theological discussion. Barr goes still further. A world view that looked more and more like the materialistic picture of atheism is being reversed by recent discoveries that have "to confound the materialist's expectations and confirm those of the believer in God."[54] Polkinghorne and Barr, then, reflect a consensus sentiment that contemporary science itself has created the conditions for a common ground that did not exist before.

Besides creating a level playing field where diverse methodologies can compete under the umbrella of clarity, intelligibility, and inference to the best argument, the postfoundational theme becomes important for another reason. Van Huyssteen writes forcefully, as he should, of the "epistemological isolationism" of theology.[55] This isolation and lack of credibility is due in large measure to a history of claiming methodological superiority predicated on revelation and inspiration of a God who speaks ("thus says the Lord") and a text that contains "the very words of Jesus." Such epistemic protective strategies with their own special form of internal rationality simply will not make the grade in a postmodern culture. Thus van Huyssteen explains, "In developing my notion of a postfoundationalist rationality, I argue for the abandonment of modernist notions of rationality, typically rooted in foundationalism and in the quest for secure foundations for our various domains of knowledge."[56] Thus, theology helps itself by becoming science-like by foregoing self-authenticating truth-claims and by joining the world of acceptable truth-claims by weighing credible evidence.

Critical Realism as a Bridge

If finding common ground is the most important plank in the NR, critical realism is its backbone. The language of critical realism is introduced into the theology-science dialogue by Barbour in *Issues in Science and Religion* (1966).[57] Barbour in turn acknowledges his debt to philosophers of

54. Barr, *Modern Physics and Ancient Faith*, 29.
55. Van Huyssteen, *The Shaping of Rationality*, 73.
56. Van Huyssteen, *Alone in the World?*, 10.
57. See Barbour, *Issues*, 162–74; *Myths, Models*, 34–38; *Religion in an Age of Science*, 43–45. Four insightful discussions of "Barbour's Contribution to Methodology" can be

science Ernst Nagel, Ernan McMullin, Hilary Putnam, and Ian Hacking. For Barbour, realism is a point of agreement between science and religion over against approaches that disregard realist claims. Initially Barbour wanted to distance himself from two language systems—one for religion and one for science—and the tendency to think of science as an objective description and religion as a subjective description. In *Issues in Science and Religion* Barbour writes that "most simply realism accepts the existence of a mind-independent world with specific characteristics." Barbour also adds a second postmodern condition related to the knowing subject who starts "not from bare, separate sense-data but from patterns of experienced relationships in which interpretation is already present."[58] Polkinghorne speaks of a "tightening grasp of an actual reality" and Peacocke emphasizes a "continuous historical reference in a continuous linguistic community."[59]

Critical realism, then, is neither a naïve objectivity that expects an exact correspondence between data and theory, nor mere functionalism where an operational application, such as the manipulation of particles, is all that matters. By way of contrast, an uncritical realism remains confident of fixing a perfect fit between the "real" world and its representation (with words or mathematical symbols). The upshot of the move toward critical realism is that both science and theology are called on to make truth-claims about the way things actually are.

The linchpin of critical realism is the way reality reacts in a certain and consistent way to human probing and thereby limits what we can say is true about it. Philosopher Frank Farrell, for instance, writes, "The important idea here is that reality is not the child of our abilities for organizing, meaning, and evidence gathering, but is an independent measure of how good those abilities get to be."[60] Critical realism makes the modest claim that it is possible to accrue knowledge that is reliable without claiming to be exhaustive or absolute.[61]

---

found in Russell, ed., *Fifty Years*, Part II. See also Andreas Losch, "On the Origins of Critical Realism," 85–106.

58. Barbour, *Issues in Science and Religion*, 163.

59. Polkinghorne, *One World: The Interaction of Science and Theology* (West Conshohocken, PA: Templeton Foundation, 2007), 22, and Peacocke, *Intimations of Reality*, 27.

60. Farrell, *Subjectivity, Realism and Postmodernism*, 149.

61. For an expanded discussion of critical realism see Niekerk, "A Critical Realist Perspective," and the essay by ed. Gregersen, "Critical Realism and Other Realisms." For an in-depth discussion see Losch, "On the Origins of Critical Realism."

In a broader context of public acceptance, critical realism becomes a necessary step for theology to be regarded as credible. Critical realism is meant to demonstrate that theology is an empirical discipline to the extent that its assertions are related to a critical understanding of experience and the real world. To this end, Polkinghorne will frequently invoke the use of "bottom-up" thinking, which is reflective of a method that starts from the basement of phenomena, experience, and evidence rather than from the top floor of general principles or dogma.[62] Since scientists are likely to think of theologians as wedded to top-down types of methodologies, Polkinghorne wants to show that such an assumption is not necessarily so. Theologians are quite capable of starting with data and reasoning to the best possible conclusion, then allowing those conclusions to be subjected to criticism from within (intradisciplinary) and from without (interdisciplinary).

Critical realism has both its staunch critics and defenders. Barbour originally adopted the term in order to return theology to a position of making realist claims, both in the sense of making truth-claims about reality (the created universe) and epistemic claims such as Polkinghorne's bottom-up thinking. There was never any serious consideration of returning to a foundationalist type of theology where knowledge is self-authenticating. What has persisted is a viewpoint that theology forfeits a much-needed credibility if it cannot accept the role of critical realism. Yet to be discussed is whether theology should have its own distinctive methodology and language, and to what degree it should feel obligated to make explanatory claims about the nature of the universe. Barbour, though, was clear from the beginning that critical realists, whether speaking theologically or scientifically, find common grounds in making truth-claims about the nature of reality.[63]

Science Is a Positive Resource

The NR has left its mark by changing the mind-set to one where science is viewed as a positive resource. Historically speaking, theology found it necessary to put a positive spin on a difficult situation, finding itself in a position of defending its truth-claims against the corrosive nature of an

---

62. Polkinghorne, *Science and Christian Belief: Theological Reflection of a Bottom-Up Thinker*, passim.

63. Barbour, *Religion in an Age of Science*, 92.

intrinsically secular and atheistic culture. The engagement with science has served to do what every positive interaction with the culture at hand should do: stir the reexamination of cherished truth claims, and to distinguish what is fundamental and particular from what is incidental. When truth-seeking communities engage each other, dissonance is exactly what stirs them to rediscover facets of what they hold true while exploring dimensions of truth they barely know. Christian theologians, especially in the Roman Catholic tradition, have a very long history of interacting with philosophy in its various cultural expressions while acknowledging philosophy to be "an indispensable help for a deeper understanding of faith and for communicating the truth of the Gospel to those who do not yet know it."[64]

The language of the NR is revealing. In developing "a theology of evolution," John Haught sees his engagement with Darwin "as an *invitation* for us to enlarge our sense of the divine." "What Darwin does," Haught writes, "is *challenge* religious thought to recapture the tragic aspects of divine creativity." Furthermore, "evolutionary science *compels* theology to reclaim features of religious faith that are all too easily smothered by the deadening disguise of order and design." Striking another common chord is Haught's statement that "theological engagement with evolution can bring us a *fuller and more satisfying understanding* of the many religious references to an 'ultimate reality' than we might otherwise have ever attained."[65] Working within the more focused topic of human uniqueness, van Huyssteen expects an engagement with science should at least "inspire the theologian to carefully trace and rethink the complex evolution of the doctrine of the *imago Dei*."[66] Throughout his Gifford Lectures van Huyssteen uses phrases widespread in the NR: "theologians are now *challenged* to take seriously . . . ," or the important question that still remains is "how can theology possibly be *enriched* by the insights gained from the sciences on the evolution of . . . ," or "how interdisciplinary dialogue provides for us an accumulating argument for radically *rethinking* theological notion of the *imago Dei*."[67] And the language of the NR does not change if the science is physics or cosmology, chemistry or biology. And why shouldn't theology be motivated positively to engage science

---

64. John Paul II, *Fides et Ratio*, 13.
65. Haught, *God After Darwin*, 5-6, emphasis added.
66. Van Huyssteen, *Alone in the World?*, 215.
67. Ibid., 267, 269, 273; emphasis added.

when there is an already extant history of mutual enrichment, inspiration, and challenge?

As former Director of the Georgetown Center for the Study of Science and Religion,[68] John Haught has for many years expressed his enthusiasm for the ways "the Darwinian vision has already affected theological understanding of the notions of creation, eschatology, revelation, divine love (or grace), divine power and redemption."[69] Because the universe is permitted, even encouraged, to evolve as something ontologically distinct from God, and because it is a work in progress, we learn that God is the disturbing wellspring of novelty, that chance and contingency are not antithetical for a God who loves the world by "letting the world be itself," and that God's power and action in relation to the world takes the form of persuasive love rather than coercive force. Haught argues to the effect that "a coercive deity—one that an immature religiosity often wishes for and that our scientific skeptics almost invariable have in mind when they assert that Darwin destroyed theism—would not allow for the otherness, autonomy, and self-coherence necessary for the world to be a world unto itself."[70]

Haught's long-standing engagement with Darwin and evolutionary theory is one of many examples of taking science seriously and accepting the challenge to rethink cardinal teachings of the Christian faith. The NR in itself is an example of "more truth and more light still to break forth" (John Robinson) when truths of one discipline meet truths of another discipline. To say science has been a positive stimulus is an understatement. There is scarcely a principal tenet of Christian doctrine that has escaped, either directly or indirectly, the sphere of influence radiating from modern science. Because of science, theologians watch what they say, reconsider what they deem relevant, and rethink how they go about saying it. To its credit the NR has not gone down the path of confirmation or refutation (science confirms or refutes this or that tenet). Instead, theologians of the NR tackle scientific discoveries with the excitement that here they might run into "mysterious sacred depths of reality previously unfathomed."[71]

---

68. The Jesuit provincials announced the closure of this theological center in June of 2013, thus ending an important Jesuit institute for cross-disciplinary study.

69. Haught, *God After Darwin*, 38–39.

70. Ibid., 41.

71. Ibid., 10.

Science Constrains or Complicates Theology

Another thread weaving its way through the NR is the belief that science constrains or limits theology. Polkinghorne's statement is succinct and to the point: "Science does not determine theological thought but it certainly constrains it."[72] By showing us what the physical world is actually like, science acts as a healthy corrective for theology's persistent propensity to indulge in ungrounded speculation. Theologians have a responsibility to be deeply informed by the natural in order to carry out the premise that a created universe reflects its Creator. For the NR, science is not dictating what theologians should write and teach. Theology's integrity is still intact, but theologians no longer have the luxury of "esoteric and baroquely abstract notions of human uniqueness," at least not if theology wants to be taken seriously by other disciplines.[73]

In resisting Roman Catholic teaching, Galileo did not choose a course of reconciliation by way of harmonization. His response was more in keeping with a plea for theology to limit what it claims to be revealed truth; in this case, the way celestial bodies orbit other celestial bodies. One could say, as many have, that an Augustinian interpretation of original sin as originating from the "fall" of a single disastrous ancestral act of the first two human beings is not tenable because it is not consonant with what is known about the history of the Earth and the evolution of human life. If we take our evolutionary history seriously, human spirituality must be viewed as a feature of emergent capacities, and the "soul" must refer to a dimension of human existence that is addressed by God.[74] That admission alone recasts the "fall" as something that happened as humans evolved into spiritual beings self-aware of their place before God. And let us not forget the considerable theological rethinking that went on, and is still going on, in order to find an acceptable interpretation of God's personal relationship with a universe of physical causation. In many ways, C. S. Lewis's masterful *Miracles* (1947) epitomized a last-ditch effort to hold onto the miraculous as divine initiative while cognizant of all the arguments against such a belief.

---

72. Polkinghorne, *Scientists as Theologians*, 6.

73. Van Huyssteen, *Alone in the World?*, 219.

74. See the editorial by Patrick D. Miller and the issue of *Theology Today* devoted to "Whatever Happened to the Soul?" (January 1994). Also, see Nancey Murphy's sophisticated arguments in *Bodies and Souls, or Spirited Bodies?* (Cambridge: Cambridge University Press, 2006).

I submit another limited perspective. The term "natural evil" is a theological staple referring to natural events that wreak havoc and take millions of human lives. The great earthquake that leveled Lisbon on All Saints' Day, 1755, is often cited as a turning point in that philosophers and theologians were finally induced to break the moral bond between evil and natural events.[75] Natural events are no more the work of God than they are the work of humans. They simply are, neither good nor evil. While it is difficult to imagine the tsunami of 2004 as the will of God, both Christians and Muslims find it difficult to sweep it aside as happening outside of the will of God. In either case—whether the will of God or not—science adds another layer of complexity by understanding nature to be a "delicate balance" and the universe to be "finely tuned." The universe, then, is not only just there; it can be nothing except what it is, for the universe we know is the only universe that makes any sense to us, scientifically speaking.

New Testament scholar N. T. Wright mounts a forceful argument that the New Testament speaks of a *bodily* resurrection. Referring to what both Paul and the Gospels write about Jesus, Wright elucidates what he means by resurrection: "an event involving neither the resuscitation nor the abandonment of a physical body, but its change into a new mode of transformed physicality, what I have called 'transphysicality'; that is an event for which there was no precedent."[76] Science complicates this assessment not by asking historical-type questions (whether the biblical sources present a coherent witness) but by asking whether the transformed body of Jesus the disciples encountered was composed of the very same atoms the historical Jesus was, or how a corporeal body could be recognized if the very atoms of our bodily existence are scattered across the universe beginning with our death. Of course, the incorruptible physicality that is God's new creation of us—incorruptible for the sake of abiding with the triune God for eternity, and therefore "existing" beyond space and time where corruption is the rule—cannot be the same kind of physicality of Jesus while on Earth. We could suppose that God did not need any of Jesus' earthly physicality in order to recreate the incorruptible Jesus, but that would entail a very different conceptual framework than Wright considers.[77] It all gets very complicated.

---

75. See Neiman's sensitive discussion of Lisbon and natural evil in *Evil*, 241–50.

76. Wright, *The Resurrection of the Son of God*, 612.

77. For Polkinghorne's discussion of resurrection complicated by science, see *Science and Christian Belief*, ch. 9.

In the writings of the NR, two other constraining issues rise to the surface again and again. I will only mention them because to discuss them at length is a book in itself. The first is the radicalization of our understanding of time. From the viewpoint of quantum physics, and general and special relativity, the biblical conception of time seems quaint. Our modern understanding of time and eternity is a quantum jump from how they were perceived in the first century. And because the Christian faith is so thoroughly rooted in time, including theologies of history, the end time, eternal life, and the triune God, there is barely anything left not to rethink.[78] Second is the radicalization of cosmology, and here I have in mind the sheer immensity and complexity of the universe. Perhaps it requires science fiction writers and movies, such as the *Star Wars* films, to drive home how provincial Christian theologizing can be. Since we have yet to enter the age of true space flight (star flight), theologians seem to be content with earthbound questions. But as with time, so with space, the reality science continues to explore is not the biblical world of nomads, patriarchs, and disciples traversing a corner of the only planet they can know.

While Polkinghorne will speak of theology as being constrained by science, he never thinks of himself as compromising theological orthodoxy. As a scientist he adheres to the premise that scientific accounts are not merely true within the context of empiricism. They are valid to the extent that they are true. As a theologian he also does not forget one of the quintessential questions of this book: "At issue is the degree to which scientific concepts should be allowed to mold and influence the conceptual apparatus of theological thought."[79] Because the language of limit and constraint carries with it an unnecessary negativity, could we not just say that science adds a level of *complexity* that theologians need to consider, while theology adds a level of *complexity* that scientists should value?

---

78. Pannenberg and Polkinghorne have both sought to reformulate the relation between time and eternity as they relate to God's eternity. See the collected essays of Pannenberg in Niels Gregersen, ed., *The Historicity of Nature: Essays on Science and Theology* (West Conshohocken, PA: Templeton Foundation, 2008). See Polkinghorne, "Natural Science, Temporality, and Divine Action," *Theology Today* 55 (October 1998) 329–43. Michael Heller, the Polish philosopher-scientist-theologian, has also written perceptively about time and space as they impact theologizing about God (*Creative Tension*). Also relevant is Robert John Russell, *Time in Eternity: Pannenberg, Physics and Eschatology in Creative Mutual Interaction* (Notre Dame, IN: University of Notre Dame Press, 2012).

79. Polkinghorne, *Scientists as Theologians*, 82.

Embracing Kenosis Theology

The turn toward kenosis theology is so prominent within the NR that it serves as an example of what can happen when the integrity of nature is taken seriously. Kenosis, from the Greek "*kenosis*," meaning "emptying," is a profoundly Christian idea when it refers to the self-emptying of Christ who takes for himself the form of a servant (Phil 2:6–7). In its classic exposition, kenosis theology is a working out of complexities regarding the dual nature of Christ and the attributes of God.[80] Theologians of the NR have avoided for the most part the subtle arguments that become necessary when parsing the nature of Christ and the attributes of God. Their point of entry has been twofold and somewhat unavoidable. First is the nature of the universe itself. Second is theodicy, where the claims of divine love and divine power meet the realities of meaningless suffering and evil. On both accounts it became necessary to find new language and metaphors to speak of God the Creator and Redeemer as science solidified a world view of internal coherence and self-generation.

The renaissance of kenosis theology might be traced to the influential publication of Jürgen Moltmann, *The Crucified God*. Moltmann, who was writing in the aftermath of World War II and the Holocaust, was confronted with a level of death and depravity which pushed theodicy to a new level of urgency.[81] Regardless of the context, the enduring question of how an all-loving and all-powerful God can tolerate, allow, or include in his will the atrocities, both natural and human, that devastate our world is perennial. At the core of both Testaments is the witness to an eternal God whose creation is good, whose steadfast love endures forever, and who in the fullness of time "comes down" to live a fully human life. The NR goes a long way to sort out both positive and negative possibilities, and in the end argues that a cosmos empirically understood reveals some powerful insights into the nature of God.

Until the era of Darwin, the shortcomings of a metaphysical framework of perfection or a theology of the "eternal now" were tolerable. The consequence of such a framework was to think of creation as fixed episodes in time, as a hierarchical order punctuated by supernatural events

---

80. Jürgen Moltmann gives a glimpse of those subtleties in *Science and Wisdom*, 55–67.

81. For a broader context for why theodicy becomes the unavoidable question, see Neiman, *Evil*, Charles Taylor, *A Secular Age*, 232, 305, and Nancey Murphy et al., eds., *Physics and Cosmology: Scientific Perspectives on the Problem of Evil* (Notre Dame, IN: University of Notre Dame Press, 2007).

from time to time. Perfection and omnipotence were a match made in heaven because a static perfection matched a God who is the supreme reality (*summum ens*) and pure act (*actus purus*). The Roman Catholic theologian John Haught sizes up the problem: Darwin's theory of natural selection challenges Christians to rethink God's omnipotence because a metaphysics of perfection stifles God. A nostalgia for a lost perfection and preoccupation with order and design has shown itself to be incompatible and inadequate if everything is evolving. The Greeks did not really have an accurate understanding of nature and the universe, and if we can free ourselves from their constraints, we can develop a theology of possibilities. In the conclusion of his *God After Darwin*, Haught writes that instead of attributing to God a rigid plan for the universe, evolutionary theology prefers to think of an unfolding vision where the world is energized not so much from what has passed, as from what lies up ahead.[82]

Haught is a voice among a chorus of voices who speak of a world meant to embody the divine gifts of freedom and autonomy. All around us, and at the deepest levels, we see a created autonomy that strives to realize the fullness of God's good intention. We can no longer accept notions of divine power where that power is used to manipulate, overpower, dominate, and control. Of the three nonnegotiable attributes of God— all-present (omnipresence), all-knowing (omniscience), and all-powerful (omnipotence)—it turns out that the latter is, after all, negotiable, or a least open to fresh rethinking. If the universe is truly set apart from God and possesses a real autonomy of its own, then there are things God will choose not to do. And while *ultimately* nothing may be beyond God's will, for the moment, God will allow creation to unfold apart from divine manipulation. This leads Moltmann to write of God's self-limitation as God's first act of grace: "If God is in his very essence infinite, then any such limit or frontier exists only through his self-limitation." Moltmann completes his kenotic theology this way: "For the limitation of his infinity and omnipresence, is itself an act of his own omnipotence. Only God can limit God."[83]

Characteristic of contemporary rapprochement with science is this statement that could be from almost any liberal-minded theologian: "God does not sustain and rule the world like an autocrat or a dictator, who permits no freedom; he is more like the suffering servant who

82. Haught, *God After Darwin*, 188–89.
83. Moltmann, *Science and Wisdom*, 61–62.

bears the world and its guilt and its griefs as Atlas carries the world on his shoulders."[84] While kenotic theology is very helpful in revising our theological understanding of God the all-powerful, it leaves us with a more deistic picture of God. By answering why God does not intervene, and why we should not read a divine purpose into the earthquake that devastated Haiti, we are left to ask if God does anything more than sustain, participate in, suffer with, and imperceptibly bring to fulfillment the ultimate purpose of creation. The core of Haught's argument is that while God's self-absenting is manifested in God's nonmanipulation of events, God "can still be deeply present and effective in the mode of *ultimate goodness.*"[85] Similarly, Moltmann repeatedly speaks of God's patient and silent presence in order to understand the history of nature and human beings.[86] While Haught and Moltmann make theologically sound statements, they underestimate how difficult it is to hold together God's omnipotence and God's self-absenting, God's goodness and the evil that seems to have no bounds.[87]

Distancing Ourselves from the Supernatural

A hallmark of the NR is its distaste for all things that look like overt divine intervention. Polkinghorne states the principle this way: "God's activity in creation is not to be located with intervention in the world, either with or against the grain of physical law. Rather, it is to be found in those laws themselves, of which God is the guarantor."[88] The NR has taken up the challenge of answering this: How does the Creator reveal "himself" when universal laws and mathematics provide a satisfactory understanding of how the universe is? Once you accept cause and effect relationships as the underlying principle of reality, miracles become the exception and, for some, the impossible; and divine intervention looks like meddling in matters that were casually determined from the moment

84. Ibid., 65.
85. Haught, *God After Darwin*, 197, n.13.
86. Moltmann, *Science and Wisdom*, 65–66.
87. George L. Murphy is another Christian theologian who pursues a consistent kenotic approach at the expense of minimizing the inherent conflict between a God who brings to fulfillment cosmic salvation and at the same time creates a *relatively* autonomous physical universe that can and does stand over against God's goodness ("relatively" being the key qualification Murphy makes). See Murphy, *The Cosmos in the Light of the Cross* (Harrisburg, PA: Trinity International, 2003).
88. Polkinghorne, "Creation and the Structure of the Physical World," 54.

of the big bang. Initially, and then persistently, theologians were obliged to explain themselves when discussing miracles, and what religion does not have its share of miracles? Miracles testify to the existence of God, and they testify because God is not powerless to intervene and disclose. The irony of this predicament was exposed by Hume's argument that the more extraordinary the claim, the greater the evidence required to establish it. The more a divine act stands out, the more it cries out for an explanation; and these acts stand out precisely because they defy the normal course of events. They are anomalies par excellence. Science, on the other hand, cannot abide unexplained anomalies. It prefers instead to seek ever-deeper explanations until it has explained away miracles. Once again theologians demonstrated a wonderful resourcefulness by realigning theological notions with the natural. Just as there was an urgent and intense effort to show how rational the Christian faith was, there was a similar effort to speak of God as self-revealing in the natural course of events, albeit, understood at a deeper or secondary level.

The NR operates at a level of sophistication well beyond C. S. Lewis's *Miracles* since it takes into account chaos theory, quantum mechanics, information theory, the presence of chance, and mutation. The thrust has been both to move the argument (actually the argument for design) to the quantum level, and to show the inadequacy of thinking of the universe as a closed causal system. In this regard the NR becomes very creative by suggesting new ways of thinking about divine action. A physicist himself, Robert John Russell has written extensively on this topic.[89] He argues, for instance, for a "noninterventionist objective special divine action" at the quantum level with potential for a special event at the macroscopic level, or what we would call an event of special providence. This is quite a mouthful because his arguments try to meet all the criteria of noninterventionists while affirming traditional orthodoxy (objective, special, divine, action). Russell gives us a very subtle Creator and recognizes that God's action is a hidden action when one of many possibilities becomes actualized (á la Whitehead). In a similar vein of theological finesse, Polkinghorne speaks of an input of new information that "influences the mo-

---

89 Russell, *From Alpha to Omega: The Creative Mutual Interaction of Theology and Science* (Minneapolis: Fortress, 2008). In addition see R. J. Russell et al., eds., *Chaos and Complexity: Scientific Perspectives on Divine Action*. All the essays included in *Chaos and Complexity* are pertinent but especially the introduction by Russell. The level of sophistication is clearly on display, as it is in "Project Saturn—Scientific and Theological Understanding of Randomness," on the research program of the same name sponsored by the Center for Theology and the Natural Sciences in 2013.

tion of a quantum entity by directional preferences but not by the transfer of energy (it is active in a non-energetic way)."[90]

In an exercise of respecting both science and theology, van Huyssteen lays considerable emphasis on the technical term "evolutionary epistemology." With an interdisciplinary conversation with science in mind, van Huyssteen believes theology should move toward "embodied notions of humanness where our embodied sexuality and moral awareness are tied directly to our embodied self-transcendence as believers who are in a relationship with God."[91] So, instead of relying on overly abstract disembodied notions of human uniqueness in the tradition of the *imago Dei*, van Huyssteen prefers to think of the "image of God" as "having emerged from nature by natural evolutionary processes."[92] And while the context has shifted from physics or quantum mechanics to biology and evolution, the reluctance to reference divine intervention in the classical sense is clearly operative. The NR gives us fully embodied human beings within evolutionary processes, and any theological talk will have to acknowledge, if not begin with, this fact.

No matter how subtle God's action is—and it needs to be very subtle at the micro level— it is either an intervention (a distinct divine initiative that changes the course of events by bringing about something new) or it is not. The more God's presence is enfolded into the fabric of reality, the more difficult it is to speak of an "objective event." It is not clear to me how "events" at the quantum level or molecular level translate into an identifiable "event" at the level of observation. And that may be the point: The NR takes away a verifiable God found "poking an occasional divine finger into the processes of the universe" and gives us a subtle God whose presence is discerned by faith in the "guiding and enticing the unfolding of continuous creation."[93]

The difference between atheist and theist is, in the end, the argument from design, and the critical question is not whether the universe exhibits design and purpose but how to account for it. In both *Climbing*

90. Polkinghorne, *Belief in God in an Age of Science*, 66–67.
91. Van Huyssteen, *Alone in the World?*, 219.
92. Ibid., 322.
93. One notices a new emphasis on the Christian teaching of *creatio continua* at the expense of special creation, and this is perfectly understandable in the displacement of a prescientific world view by a modern one. What is not recognized is the cost to theology of relying on ever more subtle and scientific language in order to make the biblical God of creation and history credible. Perhaps, though, this is an inescapable "fact of life" in an era where scientific thinking predominates.

Mount Improbable and *The Blind Watchmaker*, Richard Dawkins flatly states the problem is not "complex design" but how to explain it. The atheist will offer a solely naturalistic argument and be satisfied with it. Daniel Dennett goes a step further and argues that the burden of evidence has shifted to the point that "since I cannot imagine how anything other than natural selection could be the cause of the effects, I will have to assume that the objection [say, intelligent design] is spurious."[94] A typical theistic response is Stephen Barr's distinction between order that comes from order, and order that comes from greater order.[95] You belong to the NR if you are willing to let go of a world view where God intervenes visibly and supernaturally, while not forgoing a world view where the hand of God still sustains and guides, no matter how subtly.

A Holistic Approach

Theologians of the NR are unanimous in claiming the higher ground for a holistic approach to truth. Almost without fail you can bank on reference to a holistic methodology. Expressed in a wide variety of ways, the role theology claims for itself is to provide answers to metaquestions that arise from science and transcend the province of science. Nancey Murphy and George Ellis, for instance, support Arthur Peacocke's argument that theology should be understood as the science at the top of a hierarchy of sciences. "Some metaphysical or theological account of the nature of ultimate reality," they write, "is needed to 'top-off' the hierarchy of the sciences."[96] Theology is uniquely equipped, so their argument goes, to paint a broader canvas. Polkinghorne captures both the motivation and the purpose of the NR by describing it as a mutual effort to reach "a coherent and deeply intellectually satisfying understanding of the total way things are."[97]

Another, and perhaps an even more helpful way to think about holism, since it circumvents the language of *ultimate* questions and *ultimate*

---

94. Dennett, *Darwin's Dangerous Idea*, 47.

95. Barr, *Modern Physics and Ancient Faith*, ch. 11. Making more sophisticated arguments but in the defense of "arguments for theism," Robert J. Spitzer is excellent. See his *New Proofs for the Existence of God* (Grand Rapids: Eerdmans, 2010). On the other hand, Stephen Hawking makes his case that God is not a required hypothesis even for a universe of grand design. In conjunction with Leonard Mlodinow, see *The Grand Design* (New York: Random House, 2010).

96. Murphy and Ellis, *On the Moral Nature of the Universe*, 21.

97. Polkinghorne, *Reason and Reality*, 51.

answers, is Polkinghorne's reference to *thicker explanations* or *thicker narratives*. The motivation is the same: "Therefore, to some degree theology must take account of all forms of truth-seeking investigation into the nature of what is."[98] Thicker means more robust and less reductive in order to match the many levels of complexity required to adequately understand the nature of the universe. If everything is connected to everything, reality needs to be explained holistically and relationally. Almost by definition, a *narrative* account is thicker than an empirical explanation. And not incidentally, theologians are adept and committed to those kinds of accounts that explain by connecting diverse understandings, some more objective and others more subjective.

The NR is no less than a drive toward a richer account of reality and truth. The reason usually given by theologians for why holism is necessary concerns the way modern science comes up against phenomena it cannot explain by further reductive procedures.[99] One only needs to think of de Chardin and Whitehead to appreciate what a thicker narrative looks like when science is augmented by a religious-metaphysical perspective. The present context, though, is different once again. Scientists are more reluctant than ever to jump into the metaphysical quicksand of ultimate questions. Why the change? The conservative right is pushing an agenda that clouds the distinction between science and theology, and science naturally reacts by protecting its turf. It is fitting to say that science needs theology (and philosophy) when it wants to be more metaphysical, but the key phrase is "wants to," and any statement to the effect that physics is moving in a more holistic direction overlooks the observation that science has been trying to divest itself of metaphysical questions since its emergence as an independent discipline. Polkinghorne is not speaking for all scientists but surely for himself when he reflects that to their surprise physicists feel an urge to concern themselves with metaphysical issues.[100]

It is one kind of argument that science is inadequate if metaquestions are excluded for methodological reason, and another kind of argument if science itself is fundamentally limited. If one is looking at general historical movements, theologians may be more willing now to stake out their "higher" ground by being critical of a reductionist science. When

---

98. Polkinghorne, *Science and the Trinity*, 1.

99. Polkinghorne's essay "Creation and the Structure" is still one of the best and most concise arguments for the kind of phenomena empiricism cannot explain.

100. Polkinghorne, *Science and the Trinity*, 11, 75.

van Huyssteen proposes that "theology also offers a more comprehensive, complementary perspective on the deeper philosophical/theological meaning of what it means to be human," he is finding a place for theology at the table of interdisciplinary discussions.[101] Haught takes direct aim at science in his book *Is Nature Enough?*, where he offers five fields of meaning in order to balance a scientific method that "lacks both the rich empiricism and the layered explanation essential to take the fact of subjectivity fully into account."[102] With his long-standing interest in science, Hans Küng observes that "the most recent history of both physics and mathematics has produced admirable results, but it also shows fundamental limits to physical and mathematical knowledge."[103]

The second kind of argument voiced by Haught and Küng goes further than saying science is inherently or fundamentally reductionistic and therefore unable to fully explain human nature and the universe. It invokes, either directly or indirectly, the Barthian principle that theology has the last word when it comes to knowing the *real* truth or the *real* reality. Theology then becomes complementary not only by providing thicker explanations, it becomes a criticism of science itself. Just as you can depend on scientists to react to the inclusion of metaphysical questions, so you can depend on theologians to be dissatisfied with the exclusion of wider fields of meaning. In carving out a role for itself, theology, and the NR in particular, is probing the question about what theology's role should be in the public square when discussing vital issues. And making that question even more difficult for theology is the present attitude that most issues deemed vital and relevant are scientific ones.

---

101. Van Huyssteen, *Alone in the World?*, 305.
102. Haught, *Is Nature Enough?*, 176.
103. Küng, *The Beginning of All Things*, 30.

4

Lingering Questions and Some Tentative Conclusions

As argued in chapter three, the NR depends on a number of specific suppositions. Some of these arise from the desire on the part of theology to engage science, while others are simply postmodern presumptions that cannot be taken for granted. Together they constitute the field of inquiry prompting my lingering questions. I also offer some tentative conclusions because they flow naturally from the critique being offered, and because they anticipate the last chapter.

Lingering Questions

1. Has theology been bent out of shape by its effort to emulate a scientific methodology?
2. Is the common ground premise overstated?
3. Is critical realism the bridge between science and theology we think it is?
4. Is this an asymmetrical conversation?
5. Are science and theology at a methodological impasse?

1. Bent Out of Shape

Without a doubt, modern science has significantly impacted Christian theology. The deeper question is whether theology has been bent out of shape trying to emulate science. After living in the shadow of Queen Theology for so many centuries, science emerged as an autonomous discipline with a distinctive methodology that proved to be superior in describing and explaining the nature of physical reality. Theology, as I argued in chapter one ("The Contemporary Scene"), went in several different directions as a consequence, but in the liberal tradition theology does not so much compete with science as work to incorporate its truth claims. The long-standing tradition of natural philosophers to trace the hand of God in the Book of Nature—whether professional or amateur, whether philosophers or theologians, whether Kepler's painstaking charting of the heavens or Gregor Mendel's meticulous recoding of a genetic mechanism at work in plants—was dying. John Brooke and Geoffrey Cantor note that the "great age of natural theology had long passed by the time Adam Lord Gifford penned his will in 1885."[1] Natural philosophy, natural theology, the Book of Nature, science the handmaiden of theology, discovering the glory of God in the design of nature—their time had come and gone. They were eclipsed by a new "glory"—the excitement, enthusiasm, confidence, and optimism of seeing what the hand of man can do. Even as far back as Mary Shelley's *Frankenstein*, the young Victor Frankenstein is inspired by a lecture of the visionary Professor Waldman.

> "The ancient teachers of this science," said he, "promised impossibilities and performed nothing. The modern masters promise very little; they know that metals cannot be transmuted, and that the elixir of life is a chimera. But these philosophers, whose hands seem only to dabble in dirt, and their eyes to pore over the microscope or crucible, have indeed performed miracles. They penetrate into the recesses of nature, and show how she works in her hiding-places. They ascend into the heavens; they have discovered how the blood circulates, and the nature of the air we breathe. They have acquired new and almost unlimited Powers."[2]

The inevitable happens: theologians begin to speak of a "scientific theology." The word "science" or "scientific" begins to appear in titles signaling a need to readdress some deficiency.[3] Alister McGrath's three-volume *A*

---

1. Brooke and Cantor, *Reconstructing Nature*, 177.
2. Mary Shelley, *Frankenstein* (New York: Penguin Classics, 2003), 32–33. Richard Holmes places Shelley and her novel in its historical context (*The Age of Wonder*, 325–36).
3. While I have in mind the more recent predilection in American theology to think

Scientific Theology is but one of many in a long list of volumes compelled, so it seems, to don the title of "scientific."

Thomas F. Torrance is an interesting example of the road taken. His landmark book of 1969, *Theological Science*, sets the stage for turning the corner from neo-orthodoxy to a new realism.[4] Still within the tradition of Calvin and Barth, Torrance holds that faith is required to know things as they *really* are. For instance, Torrance writes, "Theological knowledge pivots upon what is *given* from beyond it, and which does not depend upon our discovering it."[5] Theology, therefore, is obliged to pursue an "objective ontological reality," where each word reverberates with modern science. Torrance and McGrath follow Barth believing theology trumps science because to know things as they really are means to know their ultimate beginning and end, and this is possible only through faith and from revelation. But Torrance points out that modern theology in its distinctive form begins when John Calvin reverses the medieval order of questions, *quid sit* (what is it?), *an sit* (does it exist?), and *qualis sit* (what is its nature?) by making the question of *qualis sit* primary.[6] The question of a thing's nature answers the question of what it is. Calvin's reversal meant that theology, like science, could be a genuine interrogator of actuality without being governed by preceding abstractions regarding possibility and essence. Torrance concludes: "Thus instead of starting with abstract questions as to essence and possibility, he [Calvin] starts with the question as to actuality, 'What is the nature of this thing that we have here?'"[7] Calvin effectively moves theology away from scholasticism and its endless speculations into the sphere of critical testing. Torrance's *Theological Science* is not explicitly a dialogue with the natural sciences but a way of doing theology that is scientific; that is, scientific in the sense of an inquiry into the *ultimate* nature of God and creation as we find it ontologically (the way things are).

---

of itself as scientific, there is the considerably older German tradition of *Wissenschaft*. For instance, the making of modern disciplines and what that meant for theology—if it could demonstrate an ability to adapt to the new scholarly demands of *Wissenschaft*—is visibly demonstrated in the establishment of the University of Berlin in 1810. See Thomas Albert Howard, *Protestant Theology and the Making of the Modern German University* (Oxford: Oxford University Press, 2009).

4. For a balanced appraisal of Torrance, see Holder, "Thomas Torrance."

5. Torrance, *Theological Science*, 27.

6. Ibid., ix. One can also argue that Calvin is picking up where the Aristotelian renaissance in Roman Catholicism began but then faltered.

7. Ibid., xiii.

Nor should we forget that the first page of Barth's *Church Dogmatics* includes the word "scientific": "Dogmatics is the scientific test to which the Christian Church puts herself regarding the language about God which is peculiar to her."[8] Here Barth's intention is to irrevocably commit Christian theology to a critical examination of all its dogmas, and not to exclude the written word of God. By sharply distinguishing between the word of God as the content of the Bible and the Word of God incarnated in Jesus Christ, Barth gained the freedom to set the gospel over against the word of man. It was just this stance that enabled Barth to let loose his resounding "*Nein*" against Nazism (also against natural theology and the German Evangelical Church's alliance with Hitler). There is nevertheless a price to pay for exempting the Word of God from all forms of rational dissent. Like Aquinas, Barth built a theological fortress impenetrable except for a better citadel. Not only barring the door to natural theology, Barth eliminates other approaches to make Christian thought credible; namely, to defend the rationality of Christianity, establish a core historicity, align Christian theology with empirical experience, restate the essence of the Christian message, and adopt a scientific-like methodology.

From hindsight we can see that Torrance is attempting to save theology from a kind of fideism that further isolates theology and renders it incredible in an age of science. Rodney Holder is correct to identify Torrance's most important contribution to be his assertion that theology is scientific, not methodologically speaking, but by letting the reality we confront to determine our knowledge of it.[9] By attempting a middle course, however, Torrance creates a scientific theology that is neither scientific in the German sense of *Wissenschaft* nor in the modern sense of confirmable evidence. At best, we have a critical realism that informs theology. The rub comes when the reality of God and the physical reality of the universe require their own particular kind of methodology, and when the two are not easily reconcilable.

Theology's domain of credibility continued to shrink. D. Stephen Long concludes that "while theology could still be practiced through faith alone, through revelations inaccessible to reason, or through private personal experience, theology could not reasonably be employed in a decisive political, philosophical, or ethical sense."[10] What we see then in

8. Barth, *The Doctrine of the Word of God; Church Dogmatics* I/1 (Edinburgh: T & T Clark, 1975), 1.

9. Holder, "Thomas Torrance," 292.

10. Long, "Radical Orthodoxy," 131.

Torrance, and more acutely in the Radical Orthodoxy movement, is an attempt to reclaim ontology. Stephen Long is again instructive by clarifying how the theological tradition of Barth-Torrance-Milbank[11] resists the presumed premise that the essence or nature of a thing is fully known by abstracting from things as they exist. Instead, a true ontology is to be tied to the knowing of it, and the knowing of it includes subjectivity, and true subjectivity arises from sensuality and from ethical demands "the other" places on us.[12] In other words, a methodology of objectivity or distilled reason neglects the knowing that happens when we acknowledge our desires, our sensuality, and our moral responsibilities. And in no case can we act in an unmotivated way, for one will always act in a way that reflects what one perceives as one's good.[13]

The long simmering divide between theology and science over issues of objectivity and subjectivity is itself misplaced. Almost all of the attention has been centered on an inherent subjectivity associated with religion, and thus theology by association, and the inherent objectivity of science and the empirical method. Granted there is a substantive measure of stereotyping in play here, ranging from viewing science as value free, whereas theology is compromised by personal values arising from religious beliefs.[14] While some stereotyping is strictly for the benefit of knockdown arguments, what needs to be said in order to bring the discussion back on track is to acknowledge that both theology and science strive for knowledge that has been cauterized by prejudice and personal biases arising from one's culture, personal identity, and historical moment, leaving an enduring body of understanding. Nevertheless,

---

11. John Milbank (*Theology and Social Theory* [Malden, MA: Blackwell, 1990]) became a leading spokesperson for a movement of Cambridge trained theologians well versed in French poststructuralist theory under the name "Radical Orthodoxy."

12. Long, "Radical Orthodoxy," 139–43. Torrance sets the stage for this inclusion of the subjective, and traces the shift to science itself. "Natural science," he writes, "has been forced to take the human subject into theoretical account in the development of its explanations" (*Theological Science*, xi). But Torrance misreads what the inclusion of the subject means for science and theology. For science, it is all about the intrusion of ourselves "distortingly [sic] into the picture"; but for theology, it is all about "man himself assuming the role of Creator" (xiii). We cannot presume the latter is a pivotal concern for science, as Torrance does.

13. This last sentence is a paraphrase from Hinlicky, *Paths Not Taken,* 24. This take on subjectivity, as Hinlicky points out, brings us back into the sphere of Augustine, Luther, and Leibniz.

14. See van Huyssteen for his discussion of typical stereotyping (*Shaping of Rationality,* 22–27).

there is objectivity peculiar to science in that mathematical signs are directly related to a reality outside the mind; and those signs and equations interpret intrinsic properties of that reality. Likewise, there is a subjectivity peculiar to theology in that the mind (consciousness) is directed to inner states of self-knowing, such as matters of motivation, evaluation, moral choices, and self-examination. This process of self-examination is of singular importance to theology because theology is a reflection of the self in relation to God. The neglected issue, then, is whether the objectivity peculiar to science and the subjectivity peculiar to theology becomes a substantial point of contention.

The lure of a scientific objectivity cannot be denied, and perhaps the most blatant manifestation of theology modeling itself after science is its obsession with methodological issues. Beginning somewhere in the 1960s, doing theology rightly meant beginning with an examination of one's methodology. The prolegomenon devoted to methodological justification is often longer than the exposition itself. Theologians are writing essays about "issues" while eschewing systematics as attempting too much and dogmatics as too presumptuous. Surveying the theological scene as an outsider (not as a professional theologian but a philosopher), Jeffrey Stout characterizes theologians who try to find a way to adapt orthodox Christianity to new standards of credibility as being reduced to "seemingly endless methodological foreplay."[15] In the preface of his *Unapologetic Theology*, William Placher, writing as a theological insider, acknowledges that a "good many people—myself included—have urged contemporary theologians to abandon their preoccupation with methodology and get on with the business of really doing theology." But then Placher apologizes for writing yet another "extended preface to contemporary discussions about theological method."[16] In his analysis of the collapse of epistemological foundationalism, Ronald Thiemann also draws a similar conclusion that "modern doctrines of revelation inevitably become epistemological doctrines." And like Placher, Thiemann expends his theological acumen, trying to find a way to advocate for a nonfoundational theology that is holistic, descriptive, and narrative.[17] Perhaps all

---

15. Stout, *The Flight from Authority*, 147.
16. Placher, *Unapologetic Theology*, 7.
17. Thiemann, *Revelation and Theology*, 43. See chapter 4, "Toward a Nonfoundational Theology." Placher, Thiemann, Lindbeck, and the "school" they inspired clearly engage in their own style of methodological foreplay. They do not look to science as an appropriate methodological model but react against it. Nevertheless, they "go with the

of this seemingly endless methodological foreplay is necessary given the rise of empiricism to a dominant position. In hindsight, though, it looks like methodological envy on the part of theologians.

The question that begs to be asked is why this obsession or need to justify a theological methodology in the first place, and why should theology be scientific? Or, to ask an alternative question: Is the pull of empiricism—the gold standard of what it means to know—so strong that it proves irresistible to theology? The question invites a number of responses (below).

I have hinted at one obvious motivation: for the sake of credibility. That in itself is a lame but understandable reason, for the predicament (lack of credibility) theologians face is a serious one. Professor of theology at Hardin-Simmons University at Abilene, Texas, Dan Stiver speaks of a catch-22. "The catch-22 of modern theology is between either sacrificing the mystery of God to meet objectivist standards, or of sacrificing the cogency of belief in God altogether by placing theology in a risk-free fideistic zone of private belief."[18] Stout comes to the same conclusion by pointing out that while paradox, mystery, incoherence, and anomaly are what make Christian theology distinctive, they are the first to be sacrificed when theology engages a modern culture.[19] Stout argues what has become a familiar theme in the NR. "Christianity," he writes, "if it is to be true to itself, will have to make ontological claims." But Stout continues by saying theology cannot defend those claims "in secular or philosophical terms."[20]

Stout refers to Kierkegaard and Barth as theologians who avoided Schliermacher's reduction to *Glaubenslehre* (a kind of Protestant scholasticism). Barth himself is an interesting example of theology's predicament. He is lauded on the one hand for his unwillingness to compromise the paradoxes of the Christian faith, and his instance that we cannot reason our way to faith for faith creates "a context of reasons within which theology as a rational endeavor can be undertaken."[21] Barth, nevertheless, is also disregarded because he leaves the impression of placing Christian-

---

flow" in developing a nonfoundational theology, but one that is founded not on empirical evidence but "from within the network of current Christian beliefs and practices" (Thiemann, *Revelation and Theology*, 81).

18. Stiver, "Theological Method," 174.

19. Stout, *The Flight from Authority*, 105, 147.

20. Ibid., 143.

21. Ibid., 144.

ity's most trusted truth-claims behind a fideistic zone of faith and grace; an unacceptable move if you intend to engage science and argue for a nonfoundational starting point for Christian apologetics.[22]

J. Wentzel van Huyssteen's answer to theology's postmodern predicament is both creative and telling. He sets forth to steer a course between foundational objectivism and nonfoundationalist relativism. The positive upshot is to position theology as sharing with science "resources and overlapping reasoning strategies."[23] The viability of rationality as the hardpan over which theology and science traverse is a discussion in itself (see below), but for the moment I am questioning the premise, so important for the NR, that science and theology have become objective enough to make the two commensurate. Van Huyssteen's carefully crafted mediating course may be very appropriate for theology but still be irrelevant for science because science hardly sees itself as sharing a common rationality with theology.

A tentative conclusion looks something like this. For the sake of credibility, and for theology's own good, it chooses to prioritize truth-claims that are not only cognitive (rational in the sense of meeting commonly held standards of coherence, consistency, and internal integrity) but also ontological in nature. For some theologians associated with the NR this means the kind of truth-claims that are referential and reality depicting; for others it means a rethinking of natural theology. Polkinghorne serves as a prime exemplar of the former and Stanley Hauerwas of the latter. The difference between the two "camps" turns on the "hardness" of the ontology. Polkinghorne, for instance, is looking for a symbiosis between Christian truth-claims and the way the universe actually is (those "scientifically disclosed features of our universe").[24] In his Gifford Lectures of 2000-2001, Stanley Hauerwas argues for a natural theology where the ontology is how we are to live life.[25] Because Hauerwas champions Barth over William James and Reinhold Niebuhr, this quote stands out.

---

22. After conceding that Barth did not withdraw from the political controversies of his time, Jeffrey Stout's perceptive critique is that Barth's unwillingness to argue the grounds of paradox and the irreducibility of God's word had the effect of undermining "the *preconditions* for genuine debate with secular thought" (*Flight from Authority*, 146; emphasis added). Paul Hinlicky likewise characterizes the importance of Barth's stand on theology "as a nonapologetic, nonspeculative, autonomous discipline" (*Paths Not Taken*, 3).

23. Van Huyssteen, *The Shaping of Rationality*, 8, 169.

24. Polkinghorne, *Science and the Trinity*, 62.

25. Hauerwas, *With the Grain of the Universe*, 22.

"Moreover, I will argue that Barth—in a way not unlike Aquinas—rightly assumes that the vindication of such a theological program is to be found in the way Christians must and should live."[26] We know that Hauerwas is thinking of a natural theology that differs from Polkinghorne or Alister McGrath when key elements of the NR are not considered and the physical universe does not play a prominent role. Hauerwas is content with a methodology where faith, witness, and church are key to knowing the truth about the way things actually are, while rendering secondary Polkinghorne's instance that theology be anchored in the way things actually are, thus making science indispensable.[27] The difference between the two is not insignificant because the validity of the NR hangs in the balance.

2. *Common Ground Premise*

The argument is persistently pursued: Science and theology find themselves in the same postmodern situation and therefore share common ground. But do they? The common ground assumption of the NR rests upon several premises. Each is overrated. The first premise is that theology and science share the same postmodern situation. If postmodernity is anything, it is a philosophical reaction to the Enlightenment. The gift and the burden of the Enlightenment is that truth can be rationally *constructed*, and as such, objectivity and universality are possible. Rational minds should be able to agree, and should be able to distinguish between truth and untruth. The NR works from the premise that scientific truth-claims are little different from other truth claims, such as theological ones, because they are constructed (not discovered or found). In making this assumption, theologians of the NR count on support from philosophers and historians of science. Even experimental scientists would concur that experimental data is theory laden. But the road is long and difficult from conceding the constructive nature of scientific truths to the argument that empirical truths and theological truths are weighed on the same scale, or that they share the same postmodern conditions. Arthur Peacocke, speaking as the scientist he is, asks if science has withstood

---

26. Ibid., 39.

27. See Polkinghorne, *Science and Christian Belief*, 8, 39, 191. Note also the substantial difference in how Hauerwas and Polkinghorne use words like "actual" and "real." For Hauerwas these words always have a philosophical-theological ring to them, while Polkinghorne gives them a scientific connotation, thus presenting us two different kinds of arguments.

the withering blows of postmodernity. Peacocke gives a common sense reply in the affirmative. We know philosophy has not, and we suspect theology has embraced postmodernism too readily. Peacocke believes scientific realism is still the majority view of practicing scientists. And while it is a qualified realism—not the least being the concession that scientific language cannot exhaustively describe an external world—science does proceed in a progressive and continuous way. "My conclusion, so far," he writes, "is that science has proved a bastion against the gales of postmodernism and serves to preserve . . . a conviction that the processes of human rational inquiry, infallible though they are, are not always fated to be engulfed in relativism, social contextualization, and even nihilism."[28]

J. Wentzel van Huyssteen advances the argument that while science is our best example of cognitive rationality, it is "unique only because of its history of success in coping with the problems of empirical reality."[29] His motivation is clear. He wants to establish a common ground for theology and science, and that common ground is the emergence of "methodological continuity" that exists across many disciplines. In particular, these disciplines share a common-ground rationality. Van Huyssteen advances the thesis that "the scientific method is not radically different from the rational attitude in everyday life or in other domains of knowing."[30] And yet there is this history of success that is the envy of every discipline, and that needs to be explained. It seems difficult to avoid the conclusion that apart from a kind of shared rationality that makes conversation possible, the sciences utilize a unique methodology, thus posing a significant qualification to the common-ground thesis of the NR.

Second is the common-ground presumption that both science and theology utilize "inference to the best argument." A certain amount of "leveling" happens when theologians and scientists make the best argument they can make with the hope of convincing others. As valid as this may be, it bypasses the question of whether empirical and theological arguments are of the same kind. I am not raising the issue of rationality per se or of rationality versus faith. One hopes it is not necessary to defend Thomas Aquinas as a rational person, or as someone who is as rational as Albert Einstein. Rationality is not the real issue in spite of the nuanced way it is handled by van Huyssteen (e.g., in *The Shaping of*

28. Peacocke, *Evolution: The Disguised Friend of Faith?*, 167.
29. Van Huyssteen, *Essays in Postfoundationalist Theology*, 264.
30. Van Huyssteen, *The Shaping of Rationality*, 39.

Rationality). While inference to the best argument or to the best explanation is practiced across a wide range of disciplines in the sciences and the humanities, it does not thereby guarantee that those diverse disciplines rely on a common pattern of justification and acceptability. Science and theology do come together and carry on very rational conversations based on "inference to the best conclusion." They may find that they agree or disagree but in doing so they are likely to ignore important shades of emphasis, kinds of evidence, ways of making a rational argument, diverse hermeneutical rules, and what they truly delight in doing. By blurring the distinction between "best argument" and "best explanation," the common-ground supposition conveniently ignores inherent differences between a discipline (theology) that is essentially about the best argument until another better argument is made and a discipline (science) that is committed to explaining a phenomenon until there is nothing left to explain or until empirical evidence says otherwise.

The NR strives for a common ground of "explanatory criteria" with science. Peacocke, for example, proffers these common-ground criteria: comprehensiveness, fruitfulness, general cogency and plausibility, internal coherence and consistency, and simplicity or elegance.[31] The question, again, is not whether these are common criteria among scientists and theologians, but whether, to utilize the language of van Huyssteen, in sharing "resources of rationality" science and theology become "equal partners in a democratic, interdisciplinary conversation."[32] This common-ground thesis falters on the assumption that a certain set of criteria for the sake of rationality and truth are equally important for doing science as they are for doing theology. Coherence and consistency play a much larger role if you are writing a multivolume systematic theology, fruitfulness is more important if you are proposing an explanatory theory, and elegance means one thing for a theologian and something different for a scientist.

In trying to decipher how Einstein achieved so much, physicist Lee Smolin writes, "He simply cared far more than most of his colleagues that the laws of physics have to explain everything in nature coherently and consistently."[33] By this example, coherence and consistency may be equally important to the scientist and the theologian, but that would fail to notice the very different ways they are applied to a written text or to

---

31. Peacocke, *Evolution: Disguised Friend of the Faith?*, 171–72.
32. Van Huyssteen, *The Shaping of Rationality*, 8–9.
33. Quoted in Isaacson, *Einstein*, 549–50.

Lingering Questions and Some Tentative Conclusions 121

a string of equations. Yet to be explored in the next two chapters is a description of the integrity of science and theology. And if my argument is convincing there, theology is par excellence a discipline that relies on verbal truths. Science, however, has other resources, such as mathematics and experimental data, and goes about making arguments that are appropriate to a methodology that directly (more or less) engages an independent reality.

Reference to nonfoundationalism litters the literature of the NR (and liberal theology in general).[34] It constitutes a third premise that interdisciplinary conversation requires science and theology to forego foundational principles because of their reliance on self-authenticating justifications. On one level, nonfoundationalism signals a willingness on the part of theology to relinquish absolute claims, or at least suspend them for the sake of public dialogue.[35] Ted Peters suggests that a "more peaceful cooperation" can take place around "hypothetical consonance."[36] Thus, a cross-disciplinary conversation requires that both science and theology forswear their respective claims for absoluteness, that is, the absoluteness of objective truth or the absoluteness of revelation. In practice, however, neither science nor theology can function without foundational principles. "All reasoning," David Bentley Hart writes, "presumes premises or intuitions or ultimate convictions that cannot be proved by any foundations or facts more basic than themselves" and "one always operates within boundaries established by one's first principles, and asks only the questions that those principles permit."[37] Taking the high ground of nonfoundationalism is a tricky business. You are castigated if you do and castigated if you don't; you can't do without foundational principles but you don't want to be caught espousing them.

---

34. For a more general introduction to nonfoundationalism, see John E. Thiel, *Nonfoundationalism* (Minneapolis: Fortress, 1994), and for a Roman Catholic perspective see Francis Schüssler Fiorenza, *Foundational Theology: Jesus and the Church* (New York: Crossroad, 1986). "Foundationalism," writes Nicholas Wolterstorff, "has been the reigning theory of theories in the West since the high Middle Ages." See his *Reason within the Bounds of Religion* (Grand Rapids: Eerdmans, 1976), 31. Philosophers and theologians agreed long ago that certain knowledge is grounded in noninferential, self-evident beliefs that can serve as foundation for other beliefs.

35. The public requirement of a nonfoundational theology is widespread and generally accepted by contemporary theologians. For instance, it is strongly advocated by theologians as diverse as David Tracy, Gordon Kaufman, and Edward Schillebeeckx.

36. Peters, *Science and Theology*, 1.

37. Hart, *Atheist Delusions*, 101.

It seems to me that one of the reasons why science and theology have a difficult time "getting on the same page" is the reality that both disciplines begin with, and depend on, a received set of principles, core understandings, and presuppositions that are highly resistant to compromise. In practice they are nonnegotiable. Keeping in mind Thomas Kuhn's highly influential book *The Structure of Scientific Revolutions*, one could point out that there are paradigm shifts when a foundational principle is thrown out. The most likely scenario is that a foundational principle is revised, and the discipline continues to hold onto core commitments. The history of theology demonstrates this as well, if not better, than science. Every discipline begins with and builds on a body of knowledge, a body every competent theologian and every competent scientist must master in order to be competent. Relinquishing it renders you incompetent. Theologians and scientists belong to truth-seeking communities and to that end both must demonstrate a willingness to accept criticism. But how does one do this if there are foundational principles and beliefs at the core of a discipline's identity and integrity? It happens internally when a belief or principle is found to be inadequate and a more comprehensive belief or principle proves to be richer and more comprehensive while exhibiting fundamental continuity with the tradition of inquiry as it had been understood up to this point.[38]

The recent move to nonfoundational theories is clearly a reflection of our postmodern condition. The reason consonance is easier to propose than to achieve is not that Christian beliefs and scientific principles function differently within their appropriate discipline, but rather is the way theology and science begin with incompatible foundations. Consonance presupposes boundaries that are more open than is the case when a rational tradition is constituted by foundational beliefs and principles.

Finally, lurking in the background is the supposition that science has moved just enough to the historical side of knowledge, while theology has moved just enough to the empirical side of knowledge (reason and experience) to make a new conversation fruitful. The historization of science, as I have noted, is a presumption the NR takes from the philosophers of science who have "relativized, historicized, and subjectivized the presumed objectivity of scientific research." From this Ted Peters draws the quintessential postmodern conclusion: "By relativizing alleged objectivity in science, the methodological discussion placed the natural

---

38. For how an epistemological crisis is resolved, leading to a new and richer conceptual framework, see Alasdair MacIntyre, *Whose Justice?*, 361–69.

sciences into conversation with other humanistic disciplines such as theology that were also wrestling with the relativity of human knowing."[39] The presumption, if it is not yet clear, rests with the notion that scientists have "bought into" the *alleged* relativity of their discipline, and the supposition that theology is thereby like the natural sciences. Without denying the transition from a perspective of hard science to soft science, has sufficient common ground been created? For example, is Geertz correct that Kuhn represents the nail in the coffin of any claim for epistemic privilege on the part of science?[40] The essential thrust of the argument that science and theology supposedly swim in the same postmodern ocean hinges on the rejection of the following Enlightenment-modern postulates: (1) universal truths are possible because a verifiable universe is within our reach, (2) individuals can transcend their place in class, culture, and history, and (3) truth is an inherent property of the universe. Postmodernists in turn accept the postulates that (a) all truth-claims are interpretations, (b) self-aware subjects acknowledge that all knowing is inherently contextual, and therefore it is impossible to express universal truths, and (c) truth is not an objective property but is constructed by what a particular community says it is. Kevin J. Vanhoozer nicely summarizes the postmodern situation when he writes, "it is interpretation 'all the way down.'"[41] From various quarters of science a contrary voice is heard saying, "this is not how we see it."[42]

The renowned physicist and astronomer Steven Weinberg makes a few distinctions we ought to consider before presuming all disciplines are in the same postmodern boat. He argues against the view that by examining the history of science one is justified in reaching the conclusion that scientific theories are basically social constructions. Weinberg counters that the laws of nature are different from, say, the rules of a game, because they are culture-free and permanent. The distinction he makes is between theories as they are being developed—that time of "negotiations" over what theory is going to be accepted—and their final form where "cultural

---

39. Peters, *Science and Theology*, 3.
40. Geertz, *Available Light*, 163.
41. Vanhoozer, ed., *The Cambridge Companion to Postmodern Theology*, 160.
42. See Gerald Holton, the distinguished historian of science at Harvard University, for a broader perspective on a postmodern backlash rooted in a Romanticism that threatens to undermine modern science. See Holton, *Einstein, History, and Other Passions*, 39.

influences are refined away."[43] Furthermore, even though the achievements of science pass through a process of "communal acceptance" they are nevertheless permanent in their mature form. Stated more bluntly, Weinberg asserts that he will even use the dangerous words "nothing but" and claim "the laws of physics as we understand them now are nothing but a description of reality."[44] Weinberg does not deny that a better understanding of relativity, for example, has taken place, but he remains unmoved regarding its permanence and objectivity (being culture-free) exclaiming "we just understand it better."

Scientists may argue among themselves regarding the degree of objectivity, but there is little or no argument that they are examining the same reality. David Deutsch, a physicist with impressive credentials, expresses both the negative and the positive: "As I have said, it is impossible literally to 'read' any shred of a theory in nature; that is the inductivist mistake. But what is genuinely out there is evidence, or, more precisely, a reality that will respond with evidence if we interact appropriately with it."[45] On the other hand, the presence of evidence—the same evidence for everyone who follows the same procedures—accounts for why it is possible to decide between competing theories. The lack of the same kind of consistent evidence resulting from a "fixed" physical reality is why theology struggles to build a body of interlocking, universally accepted truths. While everyone agrees that science makes softer truth-claims now, we must also affirm that science mines truths that adhere to a physical reality. If theology claimed to mine truths that adhere to the Trinity, it would be a very different kind of claim.

I can think of a number of parallels to Weinberg's argument in the historical development of theological truths, such as the process of ecumenical acceptance of creedal statements, but I am not comfortable if theology believes it is coming ever closer to universal truths by extending a body of accepted knowledge (which is exactly where Weinberg ends his argument). Certainly most scientist are uncomfortable if theology claims to stand on this same higher ground, and I doubt that many theologians see themselves as driven to *discover* the next truth destined to become a permanent part of human knowledge. While the argument can be made that theologians have reached a level of consensus regarding the cardinal

---

43. Weinberg, "Physics and History," 123.
44. Ibid., 123.
45. Deutsch, *The Fabric of Reality,* 94.

beliefs of Christianity (as found in creedal statements), this has not put an end to the bickering, divisions, stubborn and enduring disagreements over a considerable number of central doctrines. The impression that theologians spend their time and considerable intellectual abilities arguing about the same issues seemingly without an end in sight is not unfounded. As I will argue in the following two chapters, it is the nature of science to solve problems and move on, while it is the nature of theology to continue to reinterpret, endlessly, a deposit of truths.

Even if science and theology share a common ground of postmodern presuppositions, something is asked of theology that is not asked of science. Arthur Peacocke believes it is essential that theology "be subject to the same demands for epistemological warrant and intellectual integrity as other disciplines, especially science—and to relinquish the unestablished confidence of, for example, neo-orthodoxy, that it is divinely authorized."[46] Thus, theology finds itself in a quandary science does not; namely, the dilemma of how to join faith and reason, how to shed protective strategies associated with foundationalism and still protect those claims that are particular to theology. Meanwhile, scientists see themselves as withstanding the withering relativism of postmodernism in ways other disciplines have not, and as a consequence, they remain suspicious of a discipline that seems unable to free itself from the grip of cultural influences and parochial squabbles.

3. Critical Realism

Is critical realism the bridge that science and theology normally assume? The embrace of critical realism takes two forms. In the minds of many, critical realism is a methodological link between science and theology. Polkinghorne's bottom-up approach to doing theology is appealing because it shows that theologians can do the rigorous work of empiricism. Likewise, Nancey Murphy's *Theology in the Age of Scientific Reasoning* (1990) is the epitome of what a scientific methodology might look like when practiced by theologians.[47] But as a methodology, critical realism has not become normative for theology, which is not surprising since critical realism is not a methodology per se. The methodologies of sci-

---

46. Peacocke, *Evolution: Disguised Friend of the Faith?*, 173.
47. For a critique of Murphy's concept of theology as an empirical research program, see Gregersen's "Contextual Coherence" in *Rethinking Theology and Science*, 205–12.

ence and theology, yet to be discussed in the next two chapters, may operate in a climate of realism, but that does not make science and theology methodological allies.

Critical realism can also refer to a general outlook known as realism. Polkinghorne expresses a ruling sentiment of the NR: truth-claims made by critical realists are the same for scientists as they are for theologians in that both should be expected to make large swaths of experience intelligible, and that theologians and scientists "believe that there is a truth to be found or, more realistically, to be approximated to."[48] Polkinghorne does not make reference to speculative theology, but he has it in mind when he insists that internal coherence is not sufficient, nor are internalized symbols of our deepest commitments. For belief in God to be on solid ground requires truth-claims that have an ontological reference or bear some relation to the actuality of the world.

We can put this discussion about realism in perspective by looking at the important contribution of Alister E. McGrath, professor of historical theology at Oxford University with doctorates in both biology and theology. Like his mentor, Thomas F. Torrance, McGrath both breaks with and still maintains continuity with Karl Barth's distinctive approach to reality firmly grounded in Christology. In his three volumes *A Scientific Theology* (2001–2003), he is faithful to Barth while developing a vigorous apology for "a new appreciation of the role played by a Christian natural theology.[49] Following Barth, McGrath is careful to keep natural theology subordinate to revelation. He accepts the orthodox position that there are two modes of knowing God: one through the natural order and natural reason, and the other through Scripture and revelation; the second mode is clearer and fuller than the first. "There is thus a fundamental resonance—but nothing more—between nature and theology, with the latter offering a prism through which the former may be viewed and understood."[50]

---

48. Polkinghorne, *Belief in God in an Age of Science*, 45.

49. McGrath, *The Science of God*, 82ff. *The Science of God* is an abridged guide to McGrath's one thousand pages of closely set type, three-volume *A Scientific Theology: Nature, Reality, Theory* (Grand Rapids: Eerdmans, 2003). Notice should be taken of the prominent presence of "scientific" and "science" to the point that it becomes part of the theological vernacular. McGrath further elaborates his understanding of a new natural theology in his *The Open Secret: A New Vision for Natural Theology* (Malden, MA: Blackwell, 2008).

50. McGrath, *The Science of God*, 89.

By giving a prominent place to a "theological realism," McGrath finds himself swimming against the postmodern tide as espoused by George Lindbeck's influential *The Nature of Doctrine*. For instance, McGrath writes: "For Lindbeck, theology was about the *grammar* of faith; for Torrance, theology is about the *ground and grammar*—that is to say, the external foundation and internal coherence of Christian theology."[51] Lindbeck's grammar of faith is insufficient for McGrath because any theology that depends on coherence and consistency as its principal criteria for truth invites the inevitable charge of justifying one's claims by appeals to internal standards unique to one's discipline. Behind McGrath's critical statement is a concern that when doctrines are not grounded or related to reality they begin to sound like speculation. Nevertheless, both Lindbeck and McGrath are squarely in the postmodern camp because they want to distance theology from self-authenticating claims, and that in itself seems to justify their claim for critical realism.

Whether in the form of critical realism or a critical theological realism, theology needs to clarify for itself what place to give to empirical explanations of the universe.[52] Are they the core of what Christians believe, integral to what they believe, or tangential? Why are explanations of reality essential to Christianity? McGrath does not argue for making "explanatory aspects of theology" its primary task. Rather, it is only by virtue of theology's nature and scope that "a scientific theology cannot help but offer at least some explanation of the nature of things."[53] But in this move toward a "scientific theology," McGrath and the NR have at times appended the word "scientific," or espouse critical realism, with the expectation that theological truths will be regarded as being on the same level as empirical truths.

Within the framework of a science-theology dialogue, critical realism is a logical move. But let's be honest and admit that critical realism has been introduced into the conversation for the sake of theology. Science does not especially need it, and when it is discussed it becomes a debate among philosophers who are removed from what scientist do. Theology, too, has been able to function without it for many centuries. The core of Christian teachings, as well as the gospel itself, were formulated long before modern science. Something has changed, though,

---

51. Ibid., 157.

52. A helpful essay in this regard is Andreas Losch, "On the Origins of Critical Realism."

53. McGrath, *The Science of God*, 167–68.

and that something is the emergence of empiricism as the condition for what it means to be rationally relevant. I say it without being judgmental: theology needs to demonstrate that it is capable of critical, realist thinking. Polkinghorne says as much when he writes, "A defense of theology's claim to a place within the spectrum of rational inquiry into what is the case, must have an empirical aspect to it.[54]" The argument being reviewed here is not whether theologians can be critical realists testing their truth-claims against a mind-independent reality, but whether realism requires an empirical methodology, and if such a methodology is essential for doing sound and relevant theology.

To state the question crassly: Why should theology busy itself with making claims meant to explain physical reality? The NR has been consistent in stating that it has no desire to compete with science over empirical-type explanations. This in turn leads Niels Henrik Gregersen to make the distinction between causal and semantic explanations, keeping theology rooted only in the latter. The distinction is important because one can be a critical realist by aiming to explain the universe by building a network of causal explanations or by making sense of the universe by examining a broader swath of experience and observation using the tools of language. The conclusion Gregersen draws is this: Most theological explanations are actually semantic explanations, and the primary role of theology is "to form proposals about *the interrelations of meanings*, seen from the specific resources of Christian traditions, rather than offering *causal explanations* in competition with non-theological alternatives."[55] To balance his conclusion Gregersen reminds us that even though theology does not usually make predictions, "neither are theological explanations simple ad hoc explanations, since they explain persistent features of the universe."[56]

Critical realism, then, is not a *methodological* bridge between theology and science. Within the framework of a theology-science conversation, critical realism has scarcely escaped a critical look.[57] As a philosophical attitude about our ability to employ meaningfully language

54. Polkinghorne, *Reason and Reality*, 19.

55. Gregersen, "A Contextual Coherence," 211.

56. Gregersen, "Critical Realism," 84.

57. For an assessment of critical realism with the focus on Ian Barbour's groundbreaking contribution, see Russell, ed., *Fifty Years in Science*, chapters 2, 3, 4, and 5. See also Wesley Robbins, "Seriously, But Not Literally: Pragmatism and Realism in Religion and Science," *Zygon* 23 (September 1988) 229–45, as well as the responses generated by the article in the same issue of *Zygon*.

about our external world, critical realism serves to reinstate the importance of a mind-independent reality in the doing of theology. While critical realism is useful when theologians enter the discussion regarding the nature of the universe, it brings with it the potential of distorting theology by subjecting it to the standards of empiricism. Realism is good insofar as intelligibility requires everyone to be informed and liable for making absurd statements, but realism is a diversion insofar as it lures theologians into thinking they are relevant and viable if they can participate in the prevailing notion that the only truth that matters is truth associated with what is real. To anticipate a conclusion: If theology cannot rid itself of methodological envy, it will continue to languish in the shadow of an impoverished view of reality known as realism or naturalism. If we remember the cardinal rule laid down by Torrance and Polkinghorne that epistemology follows ontology, and remember the substantial difference between the reality science seeks to explain and the reality theology strives to elucidate, then critical realism is less important than usually assumed.

4. An Asymmetrical Conversation

Does the current state of affairs reflect an asymmetrical conversation? Given their interlocking histories, including a recent separation by consent, it should come as no surprise that each discipline approaches dialogue with different motivations. The interdisciplinary dialogue between theology and science is a hot ticket and the literature is liberally punctuated with the world "mutual," but can we assume science and theology have now, at long last, entered into an honest and mutually respectful dialogue? While different personal experiences will confirm or rebut my impression, the following indicators point in one direction.

Theologians of the NR agree that "scientific knowledge should inform and sharpen theological truth claims."[58] But where do we hear a corresponding acknowledgement from scientists that theological understandings should inform and sharpen their truth claims? Ted Peters expresses a widespread hopeful expectation: "Theology and science in concert provide greater illumination and understanding of the reality in which we live than we would have if we worked with one or the other

---

58. Peters, *Science and Theology*, 1.

discipline alone or with the two independently."[59] One does not, however, hear a similar sentiment from scientists but for a few exceptions. When scientists engage in self-criticism, they do not turn to theology but make it an in-house matter. Historians, philosophers, and sociologists of science have had more success than theology in engaging scientists in a process of critical self-examination. Truth be told, science has not bought into the "explanatory inadequacy" formulation proposed by theology in order to leverage parity with science.

For the most part, scientists have little motivation to go beyond the evidence and venture into more holistic interpretations. They are leery about thicker accounts that appear to be an excuse to include theological explanations. In *Science and the Trinity* Polkinghorne states his intention this way: "What I shall claim is not that we can infer the Trinity from nature, but that there are aspects of our scientific understanding of the universe that become more deeply intelligible to us if they are viewed in a Trinitarian perspective."[60] After reading *Science and the Trinity*, a Christian might be persuaded by Polkinghorne's argument that the Trinity provides a thicker, richer understanding of the universe than the thin, reductive understanding characteristic of contemporary science. But why should scientists read *Science and the Trinity*? Would they consider Polkinghorne's treatment a thicker understanding? Would they feel obligated to recommend it as a must-read to students on their way toward a profession in science? Apart from whether Polkinghorne makes his case, most scientists would demur starting with a large dose of skepticism concerning the premise that the Trinity could possibly be useful. "Using Trinitarian theology to provide an extended context within which to accommodate certain striking features of our current understanding of the cosmos" is a move Christian theologians can make. But what specifically does a Trinitarian theology add to scientific explanations of the nature of the universe?

Theologians are well aware of the impact of modern science, invigorating and shaping how they understand God in relationship to the universe, but the very same theologians are hard-pressed to cite a reciprocal energizing and informing. As a rule theologians do not contest empirical conclusions, nor do they involve themselves with intrascientific developments. Theologians are seldom competent in science, though there are

---

59. Ibid., 2.

60. Polkinghorne, *Science and the Trinity*, 61.

a few exceptions. For their part, scientists acknowledge they are rather amateurish theologians. There is, however, an important difference. Scientists have made it clear that they will not countenance the intrusion of dogmatic-theological tenets simply because they do not meet their empirical standards. Theologians (some but not all), on the other hand, have continually sought ways to accommodate science. They do not operate with a "rule" barring scientific conclusions. While reserving the right to receive or reject scientific accounts, they are motivated to take them seriously.

Much of the asymmetry, then, is caused by the fact that science has not understood itself as one methodology among others. In spite of a tempering of what science claims for its discipline, theology is not regarded by the broader scientific community as an important resource, and one suspects the reason is little more than the feeling on the part of scientists that theologians pursue a different kind of truth.

Time and time again we hear proponents of the NR challenge themselves to listen to what scientists are saying. Theologians of the NR have come to expect, if not rely on, science to challenge their presuppositions concerning God and the world. What I miss are theological questions intended to challenge not the science per se but the motivations and consequences embedded in the doing of the science. Ian Barbour begins *Nature, Human Nature, and God* with five challenges to religious thought posed by current scientific thinking. Regardless of the specifics, Barbour's argument follows the pattern of asking whether theology is up to these challenges. His methodology of compare and contrast is appropriate for identifying places where Christian and scientific teachings are similar and dissimilar. Amid Barbour's original fourfold classification of conflict, independence, dialogue, and integration, there is no mention of a dialogue that stirs the pot.[61] This leads me to believe that when reconciliation is the preferred model, it precludes the possibility of two disciplines in critical tension challenging each other to see what they cannot see from within their own methodology and conceptual framework.

In *Science and the Trinity* Polkinghorne writes, "The aim of this volume is to make a contribution to the science and religion dialogue in which it is largely theological concerns that are allowed to shape the argument and to set the agenda."[62] Ironically, setting the agenda is exactly

---

61. Barbour, *Religion in an Age of Science*, ch. 1.
62. Polkinghorne, *Science and the Trinity*, xiii.

what theology has not been able to achieve. When and where has theology set the agenda for what science does?

Barbour and Polkinghorne ask very little of science beyond a healthy dose of self-examination. This may have something to do with the fact that both are trained as scientists. If at work is an unspoken premise that theology is not equipped to pass judgment on scientific questions, then what does theology bring to the conversation? The traffic flows primarily in one direction; religious beliefs are reformulated in the light of scientific understanding and science is asked only to reconsider its reductive ways, which is no small matter except that theology does not press the issue very hard. Polkinghorne, for instance, will ask the question—Is science enough?—and conclude that it is not since it does not take into account ultimate questions or the "wider setting," and is limited by its own restrictive methodology.[63] This is a familiar refrain in NR circles, and while true enough, it seems to be a critique without serious consequences.

What is gained if science is theology's interlocutor—the one asking the hard questions? What difference does it make if creation and Christology are interpreted through the lens of ontology of becoming rather than the lens of a Hellenistic philosophy of being? Does it matter if the backdrop is modern science or the ancient Near East? The apparent answer is that it makes a world of difference. Theology can count the substantial gains resulting from listening to science, gains that go beyond just being relevant. Science has something to offer, and what it offers, besides a successful methodology, is a consistent and comprehensive account of why the universe is the way it is.

What theology wants is the kind of dialogue where the participants regard each other as truth-seekers with valid truth-claims generated by valid methodologies. Scientists are still inclined to consider theologians as defenders of a truth already deposited rather than like-minded explorers of truths yet to be discovered. I submit we have not reached mutuality and the work before us includes backtracking in order to prepare a better foundation.

---

63. Polkinghorne, *Beyond Science*, 2. An interesting contrast is Bill McKibben, who casts a critical eye on the "fruits of our new scientific understandings" by asking if this is enough, in his *Enough: Staying Human in an Engineered Age* (New York: Henry Holt and Company, 2003).

5. A Methodological Impasse

Science and theology are at a methodological impasse, whether they admit it or not. When I submitted a rejoinder to Richard Dawkins' column in *Free Inquiry,* "The Emptiness of Theology" and it was rejected, an interesting conversation commenced with the editor, Tom Flynn. My counter-arguments were not accepted on procedural grounds because the readership of *Inquiry,* according to the editor, is made of hardheaded rationalists who do not accept the principle that science and religion are complementary. And by complementary Flynn means "on some level epistemologically equal in stature despite their obvious differences." The stated inference is that "science occupies a unique position of epistemological privilege" (at least among secular humanists). Consequently, the conversation could not begin because religion/theology would need first to demonstrate that it is in any respect "a way of knowing."[64]

Likewise, this kind of negative sentiment is echoed by most of the scientists who contributed essays for *Science and Religion,* edited by Paul Kurtz. Steven Weinberg is forthright: "I am all in favor of a dialogue between science and religion, but not a constructive dialogue. One of the great achievements of science has been, if not to make it impossible for intelligent people to be religious, then at least to make it possible for them not to be religious. We should not retreat from this accomplishment."[65] And while it can be said that scientists such as Weinberg and Daniel Dennett, who also contributes an essay ("Why Getting It Right Matters: How Science Prevails"), are not representative of the wider scientific community (though I rather doubt it), they are the voice of science most people hear. Jacob Pandian, a professor of anthropology at California State University at Fullerton, matches Weinberg's sentiment when he writes: "The intellectual history of the past five hundred years has been one of religion attempting to preempt and/or incorporate scientific discoveries as religious truths."[66]

The NR leaves the impression that critical realism coupled with rational, nonfoundational strategies, leads to a methodology akin to what scientists utilize. Van Huyssteen, though, acknowledges "the fact that

---

64. Email correspondence with Dr. Flynn, August 6–10, 2002. Dawkins's op-ed piece, "The Emptiness of Theology," appeared in *Free Inquiry,* Spring 1998.

65. Paul Kurtz, ed., *Science and Religion: Are They Compatible?* (Amherst, NY: Prometheus, 2003), 40.

66. Ibid., 166.

theology and the sciences have different epistemic scopes, different experiential resources, and different heuristic structure" but then concludes that this "does not mean that they also have different rationalities."[67] This may well be true in the broader sense, otherwise science and theology would be incommensurate. But his conclusion is more optimistic than accurate because it overlooks the very real differences in the way rationality is applied. Even within various scientific disciplines, working distinctions are made regarding rational strategies, methodological values, kinds of evidence, and agreed-upon standards of what counts as a sufficient understanding.[68] But even the distinction between "epistemic scopes" (van Huyssteen) does not accurately describe the all-too-recognizable difference between an empirical methodology and a theological methodology.

Before leaving these five lingering questions a few generalizations are appropriate.

What should we make of the fact that the NR was initiated by a physicist and popularized by a physicist, Ian Barbour and John Polkinghorne, and has been driven primarily by a dialogue with the new physics and cosmology, notwithstanding the contribution of Peacocke and Haught? How would the conversation change if the principal interlocutors become representatives of the biological sciences, or the science of the brain, or the science of human nature, or robotics, or nanotechnology? What really sets these disciplines apart as different kinds of dialogical partners is the possibility of remaking ourselves as we learn to manipulate genes, molecules, and neurons. Puzzling metaphysical questions about "the God particle" and a multidimensional universe are replaced by complex ethical dilemmas. Even theological questions about the beginning of life morph into moral and legal issues of what constitutes human nature and legitimate genetic engineering. The tide has turned and environmental studies bring to the fore urgent issues that must be solved globally. Two examples come to mind of what is to come: *Sacred Cells? Why Christians Should Support Stem Cell Research* (2008), edited by Ted Peters, Karen Lebacqz, Karen Gaymon Bennett, and the multidisciplinary essays found in *In Search of Self: Interdisciplinary Perspectives on Personhood* (2011),

---

67. Van Huyssteen, *The Shaping of Rationality,* 2002.

68. See Peter Achinstein, *Scientific Evidence* (Baltimore: Johns Hopkins University Press, 2004), Evelyn Fox Keller, *Making Sense of Life: Explaining Biological Development with Models, Metaphors, and Machines* (Cambridge, MA: Harvard University Press, 2002), and Peter Galison's landmark book, *Image and Logic.*

edited by J. Wentzel van Huyssteen and Erik P. Wiebe. It remains to be seen if this kind of interdisciplinary dialogue moves beyond a collection of essays to a level cross-disciplinary *criticism* and sustained collaboration concerning our genetic and environmental future.

The traditional formulation of natural theology presumes the Book of Nature as a source of reliable evidence, even proof, of God's existence. Since Hume, this use of natural theology has been discarded because it requires too much from the argument from design, reading theistic conclusions where they are unjustified. Both Creationists and intelligent designers think otherwise and stand behind the argument from design by citing new scientific evidence meant to justify the existence of a Creator God. Even in the liberal tradition, natural theology becomes an argument from design dependent on the presumption that there are features of the universe that illumine our understanding of God. My question to all attempts to revive natural theology goes to the failure to look at nature and the universe in its actuality and totality. It is just too convenient to select certain features of the universe as revealing God's divine nature while turning a blind eye to those features that cause a peculiar kind of Christian heartburn. Critics of the argument from design and natural theology invariably confront theologians with inconvenient facts of nature: the wasteful and wandering character of evolution, the inconceivable destructiveness of cosmic forces, the role of chance and mutations in how the universe and life develops. If classic theodicy questions are about natural disasters, the contemporary issues are posed by a universe the biblical writers could never imagine. The argument from design at the heart of any natural theology is never far from defending a God who intervenes in history and nature.[69] Remove from God any obligation to sustain and intercede and the picture is a universe that in its raw actuality is a vast void of emptiness.[70] A Christian natural theology, then, is necessarily strung out between two seemingly untenable poles: defending

---

69. For example see Polkinghorne, *Science and The Trinity* (ch. 4), where new "scientifically disclosed features of our universe" become an apology for a Christian natural theology. Francis Collins, an Evangelical Christian but writing in the liberal tradition, is likewise committed to working out a theology where the transcendent Creator is subtly and indirectly present in a personal way (*The Language of God*).

70. I am remembering Carl Sagan's comment on the enormity of the space in which there is nothing, nothing: "There is a wide yawning black infinity. In every direction the extension is endless . . . and the darkness is immortal. Where light exists, it is pure, blazing, fierce; but light exists almost nowhere, and the blackness itself is also pure and blazing and fierce." See Joel Achenbach, "Star Power," *Smithsonian* (March 2014) 68–78.

the personal God of Abraham and Sarah who cares and refuses to stay removed, and accepting the cosmic framework of forces, which while law abiding, care naught if we live or die.

Some Tentative Conclusions

The NR has helped a generation of Christians, and others, to comprehend not only the new physics and evolutionary theory, but also to think of them in a positive fashion. Ted Peters simply and directly describes what has been taking place in the last sixty years as "the reasking of the God-question within the orbit of scientific discussion about the natural world."[71] The unique contribution of the NR is also precisely what Polkinghorne states it to be in his Gifford Lectures: "What I want to know is whether the strange and exciting claims of orthodox Christianity are tenable in a scientific age."[72] The dialogue with science, especially as it begins to assume its modern form after Darwin, has become the occasion for both rethinking old themes and for creative new thinking; and theology is the better for it. One needs only to consider the way contemporary theologians think about providence, creation, divine action, eschatology, the nature of God, evil in the world (theodicy), ecology, and most particularly, an intense questioning of its methodology.[73] The NR is to be commended for its steady commitment to the unity of truth, for its resistance to all forms of dualism, and for taking the initiative toward an integrated search for intelligibility. Theologians of the NR have faithfully modeled what it means to be conversant in more than one discipline; and while this seems obvious for interdisciplinary conversation, it is far from the norm on the part of scientists. Finally, its most important contribution may be the way it has turned theology toward a scientifically grounded realism.

---

71. Peters, *Science and Theology*, 11.

72. Polkinghorne, *Science and Christian Belief*, 7.

73. For additional readings of themes not specifically taken up in this book: for providence see Michael J. Langford, *Providence* (London: SCM, 1981) and Thomas F. Tracy, "Particular Providence and the God of the Gaps," in R. J. Russell et al., eds., *Chaos and Complexity*, 289–324; for eschatology see J. Polkinghorne and M. Welker, eds., *The End of the World and the Ends of God*; for the nature of God see Sallie McFague, *Metaphorical Theology* (Minneapolis: Fortress, 1982); for ecology see Sigurd Bergmann, *Creation Set Free* (Grand Rapids: Eerdmans, 1995); for methodology see Hans-George Gadmer, *Truth and Method* (New York: Crossroad, 1975).

Because the NR is so focused on furthering the theology-science dialogue, it is on the verge of forgetting a more radical critique of science. But by its very nature rapprochement slides toward accommodation, maximizing points of intersection at the expense of minimizing important areas of unresolved contention. James Gustafson not only points out that "accommodation, at best, maximizes coherence and minimizes incoherence," it also shapes the engagement so "the meaning of traffic from each is revised to achieve this."[74] Here I am not thinking of the usual critique of secular science as atheistic and materialistic, but the kind of broad analysis offered by Jacques Ellul, Hans Jonas, Albert Borgmann, Langdon Winner, Václav Havel, Leon Kass, Charles Taylor, Walter Brueggemann, Wendell Berry, Bill McKibben, and Ivan Illich.[75] This is not the place to summarize their body of work but to observe that the inclusion of their insights substantially changes the meaning of rapprochement. By mounting a broad philosophical critique of technology, the very notion of accommodation turns sour in one's mouth because of the missed opportunity on the part of theology to confront science as the predominant culture of the Western world. These thinkers take seriously the way technology creates its own culture. From their perspective technology, the handmaiden of science, is more than the principal *problem* of modern life, it is its principal *condition*.

Further evidence of a softening critique of science is the move to pare off atheistic and materialistic aspects of science in order to establish dialogue with a sanitized empiricism. No one should argue that science in its purest form is atheistic or that all scientists are closet atheists. And would it matter if they were? We take for granted that theologians are theists and that does not bar them from interdisciplinary dialogue. What concerns me is the propensity to let science off the atheistic-materialistic reductive hook by making a sharp distinction between a materialistic philosophy and scientific discoveries, as if they have little to do with materialistic philosophies. Historically speaking, there is ample evidence that Newton's science morphed into Newtonianism, which in turn made possible a materialistic way of thinking. Even those who rose to defend Christian orthodoxy against those who would misuse Newton, such as Samuel Clark's defense in his Boyle Lectures of 1704–1705, did

---

74. Gustafson, *An Examined Faith*, 83.

75. Ivan Illich is the lesser known among these social critics. A good introduction is *The Rivers North of the Future: The Testament of Ivan Illich*, as told to David Cayley (Toronto: Anansi, 2005).

not foresee "that in the heart of Newtonianism . . . lurked an entirely naturalistic, secular way of explaining the natural world."[76] And while I grant that materialism and atheism have lives of their own, both as philosophies and political ideologies, this does not constitute an argument against the inherent character of empiricism to give us a universe devoid of meaning and readily exploited for financial gain. In its zealousness to believe science and theology have become intellectual buddies, the NR also wants to believe we have entered an era where recent scientific discoveries serve to "confound the materialist's expectations and confirm those of the believer in God."[77]

The deeper issue in all of this is not whether theology can or should accommodate science but whether theology can or should accommodate itself to any culture. Polkinghorne mentions the fivefold typology of H. Richard Niebuhr and the five possibilities Hans Frei suggests.[78] It is significant, though, that Polkinghorne does not gravitate toward a model where Christianity is a counterculture faith. Rather than giving voice to the prophetic nature of Christianity, the NR is so absorbed with consonance and integration that the obligation of speaking truth to power falls away. It falls away because interdisciplinary conversation takes place at the level of sophisticated abstractions, and therefore at the expense of political decisions, economic priorities, and lived values. The mistake is to think of science has having little to do with these practicalities, as if scientific knowledge is value free while technology is not.[79]

It matters how one reads the history of science and theology as interlocutors. Polkinghorne proposes that they share a cousinly relationship: "These considerations suggest that, despite the differences in their subject matter, the sciences and theology share a cousinly relationship in the common search for truth about reality."[80] But this does not exactly clarify their relationship because theology and science have cycled between amity and sympathy, rivalry and partnership; and at times their relationship, like all intellectual parleys, stagnates or become stuck. It matters whether

---

76. See Dobbs and Jacob, *Newton and the Culture of Newtonianism*, 96, and 78–101.

77. The quote is Stephen Barr's, who adopts this argument as the principal thrust of his *Modern Physics and Ancient Faith*, esp. 26 and 29.

78. Polkinghorne, *Scientists as Theologians*, 84.

79. See Coleman, *Eden's Garden*, for a discussion of whether basic scientific knowledge is neutral (89 ff.).

80. Polkinghorne, *Science and Christian Belief*, 47; also *Reason and Reality*, 19 and, with Welker, *The End of the World and the Ends of God*, 5.

Lingering Questions and Some Tentative Conclusions 139

one takes a long view or a short view. Polkinghorne's reading of history, which is slim to begin with, seems simplistic and shortsighted. While I do think Polkinghorne's "common search" is a worthy goal, it ignores the degree to which the conversation is now asymmetrical, and when science is quite content to go it alone. The argument I make here, and explore further in the last chapter, is whether science and theology are enduring rivals because of irreconcilable differences, and are the better for it.[81] The NR does not want to talk about unresolvable differences, and ultimately they may not be, but science and theology cannot easily shed a history of substantial differences standing in the way of rapprochement.

Hanging around is the proposition that scientists do what scientists do separate from their personal beliefs and convictions, and that what counts as materialism or atheism is what happens after submission to journals and other forms of peer review. The distinction between what a scientist does and what his or her science becomes is even fuzzier if we acknowledge that scientific values and interests inevitably embody the culture at large, and that science in turn impacts and even transforms culture. Only an antiquated naïvety still thinks science and scientists do not engender their own matrix of values and interests.[82]

Submerged beneath the angst of wanting to be relevant and credible, theology in the twentieth century has been at a loss regarding how to become a viable and valuable discipline in a scientific milieu. The NR, however, has been clear sighted about what should be done. In a discussion of "Science and the Future of Theology: Critical Issues," Peacocke voices a familiar analysis that "for many decades now—and certainly during my adult life in academe—the Western intellectual world has not been convinced that theology is a pursuit that can be engaged in with intellectual

---

81. To understand theology and science as sibling rivals is the principal argument in my *Competing Truths*. By framing their historical relationship in this way, science is the upstart brother who overshadows his sister and establishes himself as an autonomous and superior sibling.

82. The literature is quite diverse but a starting place is Michael Heller who flat out writes, "rationality is undoubtedly a value" (*Creative Tension*, 48). Then there is the intertwining of science with the profit motive. See, for instance, Sheldon Krimsky, *Science in the Private Interest* (Lanham, MD: Rowan & Littlefield, 2003) and Daniel S. Greenberg, *Science, Money, and Politics* (Chicago: University of Chicago Press, 2001). Taking a broader, social-philosophical approach as mentioned above (Ellul, Jonas etc.), see the essays in M. Smith and L. Marx, eds., *Does Technology Drive History?* (Cambridge, MA: MIT Press, 1994) and Bill McKibben's *Enough: Staying Human in an Engineered Age*, which is quite accessible. Philip Kitcher may be the best source to demythologize "the myth of purity" that surrounds a science of pure knowledge. See his *Science, Truth, and Democracy* (Oxford: Oxford University Press, 2001), ch. 7.

honesty and integrity."[83] The remedy according to Peacocke is for theology to be subject to "the same demands for epistemological warrants and intellectual integrity as other disciplines, especially science.[84] Thus we have a rationale for Nancey Murphy's proposal in *Theology in an Age of Scientific Reasoning* to equip theology with an empirical-like methodology. The same can be said of van Huyssteen's *The Shaping of Rationality*, except that Murphy sees credibility resulting from the convergence of a shared methodology of competing research programs, while van Huyssteen envisions interdisciplinary dialogue made possible by shared epistemic strategies.[85] Both Murphy and van Huyssteen want very much to end theology's epistemic isolation in order to make theology a viable voice. The goal is worthy and needed. The NR, however, has been singularly devoted to just one course of action focused on the trajectory of "scientific." Is it possible that we are confusing rational strategies with epistemological parity? In other words, can theology have its own epistemological warrants, its own rational strategies, and its own intellectual integrity without being a methodology of explanation or a scientific methodology of ontological reference? The question is not easily answered.

The motivation behind pursuing cross-disciplinary conversations has had the salutary effect of compelling theology to disengage from epistemic protective strategies. But in the rush to meet postmodern standards of rationality, and in the requirement to become intellectually credible, theology is apt to neglect its own authentic voice and end up sounding like one among many voices. The apprehension that theology will continue to be regarded as "not quite up to the standards of empiricism" seems to override everything else.

Theology has not known what to do with a distinctive scientific methodology that claims to be superior. Theology has been unclear and hesitant about how to assert the validity of its own methodology without making its own claims of superiority. When theology did rule as queen, she made the same claim; namely, that her methodology was distinctive and superior, referring to the certainty of revealed truths and the

---

83. Peacocke, *Evolution: Disguised Friend of the Faith?*, 160.

84. Ibid., 173.

85. Van Huyssteen separates himself from Nancey Murphy in other important ways. See his critique of her *Theology in an Age of Scientific Reasoning* in "Is the Postmodernist Always a Postfoundationalist? Nancey Murphy's Lakatosian Model for Theology," *Theology Today* 50 (1993) 373–86; reprinted in van Huyssteen, *Essays in Postfoundationalist Theology*, 73–90.

inspiration of sacred texts. When science grew strong enough to disengage itself, it flourished and stubbornly refused to make accommodations. On the other hand, theology's "fall from power" occurred when its sacred texts were proving to be historically and culturally conditioned, and when faith and revelation as a source of authentic knowledge were becoming more of a liability than an asset. Science, on the other hand, kept its head above historical contingencies by demonstrating a methodology capable of generating universal truths. The prospects for rapprochement were rekindled when it could be argued that science and theology share a postmodern common ground. The anticipated parity, however, has not happened, both on methodological grounds and on theology's effort to convince scientists to incorporate a deeper and more comprehensive account of reality. But the latter argument is not necessarily invalid simply because science isn't buying it. Theology just hasn't found a way to convince the public that it is intellectually credible and vital because the basis of its understanding emanates from a unique perspective—a perspective that is unlike any other truth because its listening and thinking, its speaking and doing is done in the presence of God.[86]

---

86. In *An Examined Faith*, Gustafson comes to a similar conclusion: "The major contribution of theology and ethics in interactions with scientific and other secular accounts is to expand the received information by interpreting it from a different perspective" (82).

5

The Distinctiveness that Is Science

THE GOAL OF RAPPROCHEMENT is to find common ground and to establish an interdisciplinary dialogue. The very nature of rapprochement, however, underplays what makes each discipline unique and distinctive. If the pairing is religion and science, the difference between the two is patent, almost visceral. Religion is the subjective matter of the restless heart, while science is the pursuit of an objective (confirmable) explanation; the comparisons could go on. When theology and science are the dialogue partners, the parameters are drastically redefined. Both utilize critical reasoning in order to better understand what is true about the universe and ourselves. But even this similarity suggests an intuitive feeling that theologians and scientists engage in distinctively different practices. At the very least, the subject matter (ontology) and the method of knowing (epistemology) are brought together in a way unique to each discipline. I have already broached these issues and will return to them again in the last chapter. In this and the next chapter I will focus on what scientists and theologians actually do in order to identify the integrity of their disciplines. I have given myself the challenge of defining what is distinctive about science and theology in order to see what comes of it, and I do this eschewing an approach of comparing and contrasting popularized by Ian Barbour in favor of a straightforward narrative description.[1] Even though I am sincere in my intention to probe insightfully into the heart of the matter without the bias of selecting only what is congenial to my point of view, I confess that running in the background is an awareness of my central arguments concerning rapprochement and where I believe it has faltered.

---

1. See Barbour, *Issues in Science and Religion* and *Myths, Models and Paradigms*.

After pondering for some time and asking others what they think constitutes the integrity of science, my working conclusion is this: scientists measure just about everything, they reduce as far as they can go, they think mathematically and theoretically, they problem-solve, and they invent new things. The reader should note the emphasis on what is being done, rather than how it is being done; though this is just as important and will be addressed in the conclusion of this and the next chapter (methodology per se). Also, let it be said that there are other equally valid candidates for defining science. Scientists, for instance, are continually engaged in experimenting.[2] The choices I have made, therefore, are by no means absolute.

The Measure of All Things

Science seems to have intense periods of fascination with a particular matrix of questions: the starry skies above, exploring and mapping the Earth, the mystery of life, the human body, identifying fundamental laws, invisible things very small, or space and time very large. A scientist is someone who measures and studies the things that can help answer those questions: the orbits of celestial bodies, the circumference of the Earth, the fluctuation of the Earth's magnetic field, the mass of Jupiter, the resistance of conductors, blood pressure, surface tension, the gravitational bent of mass. Is there anything more scientific than the passion, the inveterate need, to measure; both the measuring of things and the making of instruments necessary to measure? It seems that we have been measuring things for as long as someone first made a mental note of how far they had walked or why all days are not the same duration. To ask what is the distance, or the weight, or the potential of something is to ask how one goes about measuring it. When Von Humboldt set sail in 1799 to map, track, catalogue, and otherwise dissect the New World (Latin America), he brought with him a barometer to determine air pressure, a hypsometer to measure the boiling point of water, a theodolite to survey angles, a sextant to calculate distances, a magnetic needle to establish the force of Earth's magnetism, a hydrometer to discern the dampness of the air, a eudiometer to measure the oxygen levels in the air, a Leyden jar to capture electrical charges, a cyanometer to ascertain the blue of the sky,

---

2. See George Johnson, *The Ten Most Beautiful Experiments* (New York: Alfred A. Knopf, 2008).

and a portable clock to not only measure time but to fix the degree of longitude.[3]

I personally have no idea how to weigh the Earth. When I want to weigh something I look for a scale. Of course, it is not possible to actually weigh the Earth on a scale, so there must be another way (e.g., by measuring the gravitational pull of the Earth's mass). How does one measure the distance from the Earth to the Sun, the circumference of the Earth, or the mass of an electron? Not only is the math beyond me, I also lack the theoretical tools necessary to frame the problem.

The eighteenth century had a maniac preoccupation with the desire to understand the Earth by measuring it, and as such, overflows with wonderful stories of scientists enduring great hardships in order to measure the impossible. Every measurement, it seems, is a story in itself. In order to settle one of the greatest scientific questions of the day—What is the precise size and shape of the Earth?—the French Royal Academy of Science commissioned an expedition to Peru in 1735. Pierre Bouguer and Charles Marie de La Condamine surmised correctly that the Earth is "fatter" along the equator and so they set sail for the Andes, also thinking the mountains would provide them with better sight lines. Their approach would rely on the tried-and-true method of triangulation, and to do this they needed to establish an imaginary line of about 200 miles across the Andes. They, unfortunately, selected one of the most nearly impossible terrains on Earth, where cloud cover meant waiting for weeks in order to make a sighting. Their difficulties were just beginning for they were also chased out of town by a mob armed with stones, avoided death by disease, endured eight months waiting for permits, scaled some of the world's most challenging mountains, and hacked their way through mostly uncharted jungle. Bouguer and La Condamine demonstrated a French trait for tenacity and stuck with it for nine and a half long, grim years.[4]

Dava Sobel tells an equally fascinating story of the quest to solve one of the most pressing scientific questions of the day—longitude. Any seaworthy sailor could determine latitude because zero degree parallel of latitude is fixed by the laws of nature. Longitude, on the

---

3. See Daniel Kehlmann's best seller in Europe and now translated from the German, *Measuring the World*, 29.

4. See Bill Bryson, *A Short History of Nearly Everything* (New York: Broadway, 2003), 43–44, 52–62; and the historical fiction account by Robert Whitaker, *The Mapmaker's Wife* (New York: Basic, 2004).

other hand, shifts like the sands of time because its determination requires either complicated astronomical observations and mathematics or a very precise timepiece. If reckoned by time, then a portable clock would have to be made, for nothing existed that even came close to the required accuracy. Sobel describes what was involved: "This means it could not lose or gain more than three seconds in a twenty-four hour period. The arithmetic makes the point: Half a degree of longitude equals two minutes of time—the maximum allowable mistake over the course of a six-week voyage from England to the Caribbean. An error of only three seconds a day, compounded every day at sea for forty days, adds up to two minutes by journey's end."[5] Sobel notes that when the H. M. S. Beagle set sail in 1831, with Charles Darwin on board, it carried twenty-two chronometers just to be on the safe side. On July 8, 1714 the British Parliament voted in the Longitude Act establishing criteria and the monetary award for solving the greatest technological challenge of the age. The eventual winner was a London clock maker who "faded into his workshop and was hardly heard from during the nearly twenty years he devoted to the competition of his 'curious third machine.'"[6] It was not until 1759 that John Harrison finished the timekeeper that ultimately won the prize; a clock more like a large pocket watch than the kind you would buy for a fireplace mantel. But even claiming the prize of 20,000 pounds (worth millions of dollars today) proved difficult for Harrison. Since everyone believed it couldn't be done, the review process dragged on for years, requiring many sea trials.

When writing about certainty (and uncertainty) as the anchor of the physical sciences, winner of the Nobel Prize in Physics Robert B. Laughlin remarks that the discussion always comes down to precise measurement. "Deep inside every physical scientist is the belief that measurement accuracy is the only fail-safe means of distinguishing what is true from what one imagines, and even of defining what true means."[7] By this standard, truth is inextricably linked to measurement and accuracy, and both are inextricably linked with universals or fundamental constants. This being said, my favorite account of undying devotion to measurement is the story told by Ken Alder of Jean-Baptiste-Joseph Delambre (1749–1822) and Pierre-François-André Méchain (1744–1804). These two Frenchmen set forth in opposite directions from Paris in June of 1792. Their mission

---

5. Sobel, *Longitude*, 58–59.

6. Ibid., 86.

7. Laughlin, *A Different Universe*, 14.

was to establish a universal standard of measure—the meter—as one ten-millionth of the distance from the North Pole to the equator (or a quarter of the total meridian encircling the planet; a degree of meridian being an imaginary north-south line encircling the globe and passing through the poles or 1/360 of the distance around the planet).

Both were astronomers and regarded as preeminent thinkers of the Enlightenment. These savants, as they were known before the term "scientist" stuck, imagined a universal language of measurement that would bring order and reason to the exchange of both goods and information. But not just any measure would do. A babel of measures was already in existence, such as the copper *toise* of Paris, which equaled, by definition, six times the length of the royal *pied* (foot), and was actually a bar of iron mortised into the wall at the foot of the staircase of the great Châtelet courthouse. But neither Delambre nor Méchain, nor those who commissioned them, would settle for anything less than a unit derived from nature's truth. In order to be universal, and universally accepted, they would use as a standard a measure from the world itself.

Their method was to measure a meridian arc from Dunkerque to the north and from Barcelona to the south in order to extrapolate an even longer arc from the equator to the North Pole. The principal method would again be triangulation, requiring them to establish at least three visible reference points as the "corners" of a triangle—church steeples, open hilltops, even the summits of domed volcanoes, and even building their own constructed towers when everything else failed—and then to measure the horizontal angles separating adjacent stations as well as measuring the actual length of one side of one of the triangles. From this one could determine the distance along the meridian arc from its northernmost to its southernmost station. I abbreviate this process, for doing this as a paper exercise is a long, long way from actually doing it, and doing it precisely. Practical difficulties interceded at every point (what else is new). First, there was the difficulty of finding an appropriate visible reference point. Weather was often a problem, and sometimes months passed before conditions were adequate. Corrections had to be made to adjust all values to a common surface-level triangle. All angles had to be adjusted to take into account the atmospheric refraction of light. Even the simple matter of finding a "perfectly" level place to sight—setting up a sextant—became a vexing task.

If I do not have all the details of this exercise exactly correct, may the reader excuse me as it is beyond my limited mathematical abilities, and equally beyond my comprehension as to why such a utopian mission would even be attempted. Compounding their difficulties was the circumstance that it was undertaken during the dying days of the French monarchy when their equipment was repeatedly impounded, their motives questioned, and their lives threatened. We should not be surprised, then, that Delambre and Méchain worked at this for seven years, nearly causing the death of Méchain.[8]

Within Adler's account is a second story of modern science: the distinction between precision and error, or more simply, how does a science that strives for absolute accuracy settle for less? Remember that error is the great enemy of both the Enlightenment and empiricism, for the very definition of what it meant to be enlightened was to replace uncertainty with certainty and reliability.[9] Time and time again, Delambre and Méchain butted their heads against the question of how close is close enough. Early on, Méchain was aware that he had mismeasured, and for that unpardonable sin he tormented himself and everyone around him with a mountain of regrets and doubts.[10] The picture Alder paints is of a burgeoning science wrapped in idealism. The ruling premise dictated that humans would become rational and consistent if they learned to trust a methodology that is rational and consistent. In the instance of establishing the meter, science would provide a universal measure derived from nature's truth that would in turn produce a world of equality, order, and reason. This idealism was not entirely misplaced, for we find in their stories an extraordinary devotion to the common good by savants with an uncommon allegiance to science over allegiance to nation. According to Alder, the lessons to be learned include these: science cannot help but avoid the politics of power, there is no absolute objective point of reference, and the one doing the measuring is always a factor in the act of measurement. During the acrid debate about the meter's universality and its acceptance, many pointed out that the decision to base the meter on the Earth's meridian arc was itself arbitrary. Why not the circumference of the equator? Why is the *toise* itself inferior? Did not the designation

---

8. In *The Measure of All Things*, Alder includes numerous subplots detailing the many trials and tribulations encountered by Delambre and Méchain. Among my favorite are those found pp. 102, 119, 217.

9. From the perspective of modern science, another paradigm shift was necessary, namely, the accommodation of probability. See Jeffrey Stout, *The Flight From Authority* and Paul Jerome Croce, *Science and Religion in the Era of William James*.

10. Alder, *The Measure of All Things*, 213–14, 251.

"universal" have as much to do with its general acceptance as its supposed naturalness? And ironically as we in the United States know, the meter never did gain universal acceptance.

At least in the physical sciences truth and objectivity are a matter of accuracy in measurement. For Laughlin the physicist, the ten to twenty experiments credited with establishing the fundamental constants of the universe constitute our extricable link with truth. "A universal constant," he explains, "is a measurement that comes out the same every time" and "a physical law is a *relationship* between measurements that comes out the same every time."[11] The astonishing reliability of the atomic clock, accurate to one part in one hundred trillion, depends on the quantization of light wavelengths emitted from dilute atomic vapors, and like other universal constants, is the backbone of science. Similarly, the ability to measure the speed of light in a vacuum, known to be an accuracy of one part in ten trillion, is the reason scientists claim we can distinguish between what is true from what is imagined. Scientific knowledge, as Laughlin points out, "is just as susceptible to political whim as any other kind of knowledge, and it is only the anchor of certainty that gives science its special status and authority."[12]

Radical Reductionism

The word "reductionism" is like a hornets' nest: poke it and you can be sure to stir up a swarm of intense feelings. Adding the adjective "radical" only inflames the situation. Even among scientists, who are presumed to be advocates for reductionism, the word is controversial. No matter what one's opinion, it helps to make a basic distinction between reductionism as a program for scientific research and reductionism as a view of the world. The former is what interests me. The workable definition of radical reductionism that I will reference is any research intended to reduce the world of physical phenomena to a finite set of fundamental principles or equations. Only by association and extrapolation does it become a world view where the universe is understood to be nothing more or less than its physical or material properties.

In an essay entitled "The Great Reduction: Physics in the Twentieth Century," elder statesmen Steven Weinberg takes the reader on a short

11. Laughlin, *A Different Universe*, 30.
12. Ibid., 21.

tour of "the remarkable success in the past century of physics in the reductive mode."[13] He works from a historical perspective, and physics is his subject matter. Weinberg is something of an "in-your-face" kind of guy, taking on all who pooh-pooh the idea of scientific progress and scientific reductionism. He is quite aware of all the usual arguments against an objective science but still presses what he considers to be a valid approach.[14] In a remarkably short time, the physical universe is understood by science as consisting of subatomic particles, the rules of chemistry are subsumed under the dynamics of electrons and atomic nuclei, the mechanism of heredity is translated into molecular terms, the strong nuclear force and the weak electromagnetic force are joined along with chromodynamics, and everything comes together to form the Standard Model of elementary particles by the mid 1970s. A similar story can be told about Newton's understanding of gravity and Einstein's more comprehensive understanding of it, and the progressive line of development from Darwin's observations of how natural selection works to the contemporary reliance on genes and mitochondrial DNA. Reductionism is not the total story of science, but anyone looking at the history of science sees what Weinberg sees: "the rules that we discover become increasingly coherent and universal."[15]

In a book that is part autobiography, part history of the science of the mind, and part narrative of his own scientific journey, Eric R. Kandel leads us through the steps culminating in his Nobel Prize in Physiology or Medicine in 2000. Initially trained in psychoanalysis, Kandel never loses his fascination with how Freud's ego, id, and superego (the unconscious manifestations of the mind) might have a biochemical basis. After years of doing a variety of research projects, Kandel adopts the mission to understand how the mind creates memories. On the occasion of his Noble Prize ceremony, Kandel summarized the significance of what had been achieved. "We three [with Arvid Carlsson and Paul Greengard] have taken the first steps in linking mind to molecules by determining how the

---

13. Weinberg, *Facing Up*, 210.

14. A prime example of a contrary point of view is Larry Laudan's *Progress and Its Problems* (Berkeley, CA: University of California Press, 1977). The two views of Weinberg and Laudan may not be necessarily incompatible if we understand that Laudan is thinking about the dynamics of science (anticipating Thomas Kuhn) while Weinberg is looking at the historical development of a specific scientific problem.

15. Weinberg, *Facing Up*, 24.

biochemistry of signaling within and between nerve cells is related to mental processes and to mental disorders."[16]

Kandel does not engage in lengthy discussions about his methodology but his modus operandi is transparent. He writes of his nighttime work of theorizing (defining the problem), and his daytime work of confirming or disconfirming by way of experimentation. Guiding his research is the conviction that the biological basis of memory and learning should be studied first at the level of individual cells and, moreover, that the approach most likely to succeed needs to focus on the simplest behavior of a simple animal.[17] His organism of choice is the giant marine snail *Aplysia* because some of its cells are the largest in the animal kingdom, making it relatively easy to measure electrical activity.

Kendal's methodology is to reduce a complex problem to a series of definable problems. How and where is memory stored in the brain? How are synapses modified by carefully controlled electrical stimuli that mimic sensory stimuli? How is short-term memory transferred into long-term memory? In what way are neurons and their synaptic connections invariant? How do chemical signals change into electrical ones? How does the mind represent space (location) and how is the representation modified by attention? How does electrical activity in neurons gives rise to the meaning we ascribe to color or emotions? How does the brain (maybe here it is appropriate to speak of the mind) receive dispersed signals and present to consciousness a unified whole?

Radical reductionism, at its best, seeks to comprehend the universe in terms of simple and universal principles, and to reduce the world of physical phenomena to its fundamental states and entities. The very notion of reductionism leaves a bitter taste in the mouths of many theologians, and even some scientists. Freeman Dyson boldly asserts that he has "a low opinion of reductionism." One of several of Dyson's examples is Einstein's lonely attempt to reduce physics to a finite set of marks on paper and thereby "his extraordinary hostility to the idea of black holes."[18] Yet, it is clear that what Dyson has in mind is a "philosophy of reductionism" that by attempting to reduce everything (the whole of physics or the whole of mathematics) to a finite set of fundamental equations,

---

16. Kandel, *In Search of Memory*, 403.

17. Ibid., 144.

18. Dyson, *The Scientist as Rebel*, 11. Weinberg replies explicitly to Freeman, whose essay originally appeared in *The New York Review of Books*, May 25, 1995, 31–33. See Weinberg, "Reductionist Redux," *The New York Review of Book*, October 5, 1995, 39–42.

can lead scientists astray and blind them to other realities. Everything Dyson argues is perfectly valid but his critique does little to invalidate the immense value of reductionism as a methodological tool put into practice every day by scientists around the world.

To Think Mathematically—
A Universe of Numbers and Imagination

For no other reason than what he accomplished in 1905, Albert Einstein is the epitome of thinking mathematically. He promised his friend four papers, which he would produce in his spare time, and he delivered all four, including a fifth paper as a short appendix to the fourth. Those five papers, encompassing the vast sweep of modern science from the infinite to the infinitesimal, proved to be so revolutionary because they represent thinking outside the box in its truest form. Einstein was supremely confident that by pure thought we could discover the deepest truths about the nature of reality. In a 1933 lecture given by Einstein at Oxford University, he postulated that the "creative principle resides in mathematics. In a certain sense, therefore, I hold it true that pure thought can grasp reality, as the ancients dreamed."[19] This commonly held belief among scientists that there is a special relationship between mathematics and the physical world is difficult to explain. Yet it happens again and again that mathematics anticipates an experimental discovery, or an experimental discovery is better understood because it can be expressed mathematically.

Perhaps not for his entire scientific life, but clearly in the latter part, Einstein did his thinking mathematically. Isaacson reports that in his waning days, often as he slowly ambled from his Mercer Street home to the Institute for Advanced Studies, Einstein would be seen clutching scraps of paper on which he had scribbled equations the night before. At his bedside when he died were "twelve pages of tightly written equations, littered with cross-outs and corrections."[20] Like the scientist who constructs a universe using mathematical ideas, the musician passes the day lost in melodies and lyrics, the poet tosses about different plays on words, and the theologian mulls over the intersection of several theological concepts. Even on his last day of work, literally on his deathbed,

---

19. Quoted from Lightman, *A Sense of the Mysterious*, 66.
20. Isaacson, *Einstein*, 537 and 543.

Einstein laments to his son, "If only I had more mathematics."[21] For my discussion it is not important to explore the various explanations for this seemingly perfect fit between mind and universe, except to say it exists and it persists.[22]

In his acclaimed biography of Einstein, *Einstein: His Life and Universe*, Walter Isaacson reveals Einstein to be a nonconformist in all aspects of his life. Being the contrarian he was, Einstein imagined gravity to be the warping of space and time resulting from the interplay of matter, motion, and energy. He imagined what it would be like to roll a bowling ball onto the two-dimensional surface of an infinite trampoline. Then add some billiard balls. They move toward the bowling ball not because of some mysterious attraction but because of the way the trampoline bends. Now imagine this happening in the four-dimensional fabric of space and time. You can't, but that's why we're not Einstein and he was.[23]

The genius of Einstein is rightly associated with his fondness for thought experiments. Einstein employed thought experiments both to help himself think and to help others to understand very abstract conjectures. In order to get a handle on the general theory of relativity, Einstein invites you to picture yourself in an enclosed elevator accelerating through space. The effect you'd feel would be indistinguishable from the experience of gravity. Equally baffling is the constancy of the velocity of light. In this instance, Einstein resorted to a number of illustrations involving a train passenger relative to the motion of the train and a flash of light. My favorite is the perfectly simple visual experiment meant to help one comprehend a finite universe without boundaries. Imagine an explorer traversing the surface of an inflating balloon. His entire universe could be infinitely expanding, and nevertheless still be a universe with boundaries. When you are thinking outside the normalized box, in this instance the Newtonian world view of an absolute grid of space and time, it is absolutely necessary to imagine a universe that is actually quite different from that paradigm. Once you free yourself from thinking of space and time, matter and energy as independent absolutes, you are ready to begin to contemplate a universe where everything is interdependent.

21. Ibid., 542.

22. Lightman offers four explanations in *A Sense of the Mysterious*, 80–86. Johns Hopkins astrophysicist Mario Livio also explores the powerful way mathematics lends itself to explaining the universe in *Is God a Mathematician?* (New York: Simon & Schuster, 2009).

23. Isaacson, *Einstein*, 4.

The distinction made between pure mathematics and applied mathematics is not absolute but useful. Pure math is abstraction for its own sake while applied math is done to solve a specific problem. Physicists are known to deride pure mathematics, castigating it as merely a game with rules made up by those who play it. The rivalry between theorists and experimenters becomes a little testy at times and Murray Gell-Mann, in a moment of disdain for a "science" that spurns the connection with reality, let it be known that "mathematics bore the same sort of relationship to science that masturbation does to sex."[24] It's a statement that Gell-Mann has retracted, noting the fruitful interaction between mathematicians and physicists in formulating the Standard Model. Notwithstanding the way the language of math abides by its own rules, a good proof, writes theoretical physicist Alan Lightman, is a self-evident statement that helps us to understand clearly and deeply.[25] The analogy that comes to mind is the poet who with words alone creates "a world unto itself," complete and self-constituting. Here too is "a way into" truth that sustains itself, not by describing an independent reality, but by abstracting a new reality from an existing one.

The train of thought in this section leads us to ask whether there is a mathematical reasoning that some of us possess and others do not. The same could be asked about a gift for matters theological. Michael Guillen, ABC-TV's award-winning science editor and instructor of physics and mathematics at Harvard University, is enamored by the poetry of mathematics. With this in mind he selected "five equations that changed the world" (the title of his book). They include Isaac Newton's universal law of gravity, Daniel Bernoulli's law of hydrodynamic pressure, Michael Faraday's law of electronic induction, Rudolf Clausius's second law of thermodynamics, and Albert Einstein's theory of special relativity. The beauty and elegance of each equation is how much is expressed in such brevity. Each equation is a description of a particular set of relationships that just seems right, as if there could be no other way to say it better. Even to the extent that these equations represent a moment of creative

---

24. Quoted from Peter Woit, *Not Even Wrong: The Failure of String Theory and the Search for Unity in Physical Law* (New York: Basic), 189. Woit's book is no less than a stab at scientists who are content with theory alone, such as the current pursuit of superstring theory, something Woit does not consider a theory because it makes no predictions, right or wrong.

25. Lightman, *Sense of the Mysterious*, 73.

insight or reasoning, they also represent years of tedious and arduous preparation (mostly in a laboratory).

What will undoubtedly become one of the classic examples of what mathematical physicist Eugene Wigner referred to as "the unreasonable effectiveness of mathematics in describing the physical universe," is the discovery of the Higgs boson. It's a story that has been rehearsed many times, and includes the possibility of black holes that emerged from the mathematical analyses of German physicist Karl Schwarzchild, and the subsequent observational confirmation of the concept of antimatter that emerged from the mathematical analyses of quantum physicist Paul Dirac. When physicist Peter Higgs submitted a paper in 1964, he was proposing a mathematical idea for an invisible something permeating space in order to answer several unresolved questions. Now, after many years of anticipation and a year of analysis of data coming from the Large Hadron Collider straddling Switzerland and France, scientists are willing to assert that the Higgs field does indeed provide insight into a new form of matter, and accounts for what drove space to start expanding in the first place.[26]

Tinker, Inventor, and Engineer

By juxtaposing the intrepid explorer Alexander von Humboldt (1769–1859) and the genius mathematician Carl Friedrich Gauss (1777–1855), Daniel Kehlmann not only gets to tell a more interesting story but also helps us to think about two very different way of doing science. Humboldt may be the epitome of the kind of person who cannot help but record everything and miss nothing. In order to assuage his greatest fear, boredom, Humboldt is never at rest: traveling down the Orinoco to find a channel linking it with the Amazon, tasting poisons, ascending the highest mountain known to man, descending into volcanoes, exploring every hole in the ground, everywhere collecting plants, always determining his exact position, carting with him a box of human bones, enduring extreme hardships of heat, mosquitoes, and cold. Kehlmann writes this of Humboldt's obsession with facts: "Facts . . . he would write them all down, a vast work full of facts, every fact in the world, contained in a

---

26. Writing with his usual clarity about matters very complex, Brian Greene interprets what the Higgs particle/field means for science in "Mind Over Matter," *Smithsonian* (July-August 2013) 25–96. Wigner's quote is found p. 91.

single book, all facts and nothing but facts, the entire cosmos all over again, but stripped of error, fantasy, dream, and fog; facts and numbers, he said in an uncertain voice, they were maybe what could save one."[27]

Professor Gauss, often referred to as the "Prince of Mathematicians," complains bitterly whenever he is compelled to leave home for any reason. In Kehlmann's fictional account, Humboldt asks what is science and shows us by what he does. Gauss, in sharp contrast, believes that science is a man alone at his desk with a sheet of paper in front of him. Written at the young age of twenty-two, Friedrich Gauss's defining work is a treatise on number theory. Humboldt writes both a twenty-three-volume encyclopedia of his New World adventure and a five-volume *Kosmos*, a complete description of the universe. To ask who was the greatest scientist misses the point that science is both doing and thinking, but in the shadow of Einstein the humble thinker is often slighted.

In the persons of Humboldt and Gauss we meet two very distinctive styles of doing science. The contrast by no means implies an either-or dichotomy, for the best science is normally the marriage of the theoretical and the experimental, someone to theorize and someone to experiment, and someone who can do both. But the latter is fast becoming an anomaly as science grows ever more complex. It could be argued that science is fundamentally the testing of a hypothesis concerning the nature of the universe. But by temperament and circumstance, scientists are usually thinkers or doers. Those with a passion for their machines are quite different from those who lose themselves in the beauty of an equation and can spend hours, even days, in a realm of thought where both body and ego fall away (compare Lightman's description of "a state of pure exhilaration").[28]

In America a strong tradition of scientist-inventor is joined with the needs of a growing nation. The tireless Thomas Edison may be the embodiment of the versatile genius who theorized, tinkered, created, and engineered; but others, such as Benjamin Franklin, Samuel Morse, and Eli Whitney are cut from the same cloth of doing it all. The tradition is of course much longer, extending back to Galileo, who not only

27. Kehlman, *Measuring the World*, 251–52. Charles Darwin also needs to be entered into the hall of fame for always wanting more facts. Acclaimed biographers Adrian Desmond and James Moore, in their most recent and "new" portrait of Darwin as a tireless antislavery protagonist, write: "Facts: he always needed more facts. He never stopped collecting them." See their *Darwin's Sacred Cause* (Boston: Houghton Mifflin Harcourt, 2009), 289.

28. Lightman, *A Sense of the Mysterious*, 16.

theorized about the structure of the universe but also shaped his own glass to make a better telescope; or Michael Faraday, who, like many of his peers, was largely self-educated and discovered both benzene and the properties of electromagnetism by the tried-and-true method of hands-on experimenting.

Peter Galison in his ground-breaking *Image and Logic* turns another page in the history of science. The increasing complexity of doing physics requires distinct communities of experimentalists—engineers, theorists, and mathematicians—and as a consequence Galison speaks of a "trading zone" where the heterogeneity of practices and mind-sets can communicate with each other. If in the past the theorist was prepared to work it out by himself, the theorist must now trust the instruments and the instrument makers. "A colliding beam experimenter," writes Galison, needs "to learn not only about rare decays and Higgs searches but about computer and electronic problems associated with an environment of intense radiation."[29] Furthermore, Galison distinguishes between a tradition of image and logic; the former being the production of "images of such clarity that a single picture can serve as evidence for a new entity or effect," and the latter which depends upon "electronic counters coupled in electronic logic circuits."[30] Not to be passed over lightly is the way particular communities think about science. For the image experimenters the passivity of their systems is a virtue since it represents the dampening of human intervention. By contrast, the logic experimenters revel in controlling what is happening, thus setting up a dichotomy between "the objectivity of passive registration versus the persuasiveness of experimental control, vision versus numbers, and photography versus electronics."[31]

In the early 1930s the most vexing problem was the nature of the atom. By 1927 the atomic weight of various elements was known, as was the general structure of a nucleus encircled by electrons. The next step was obvious to everyone: explore the dynamics of the nucleus. Are there more electrons to be found? Finding protons with a positive charge exactly equal to that of an electron would suggest that there were more elements to be found. James Chadwick closed in on the existence of neutrons, weighing about the same as a proton but with no charge. And could there be other elusive particles to be found within the nucleus that defy all expectations? Here was a catch-22 if ever there was one. If an

29. Galison, *Image and Logic*, 8.
30. Ibid., 19.
31. Ibid., 25.

entirely new element existed inside the nucleus, how does one go about detecting it when it eludes all known measuring devices? In order to create a suitable measuring device you would need to have some idea of what you are measuring. But the more immediate problem was to find a way to bombard the nucleus and dislodge something to measure.

Now that the problem was identified, the race was on. By the latter part of 1931 teams in Cambridge, England (John Cockcroft and Ernest Walton), Washington, D.C. (Merle Tuve), and at Princeton University (Robert Van de Graaff) labored on, while Ernest Lawrence and Stanley Livingston were putting their money on the creation of a cyclotron. At the Cavendish laboratory in Cambridge under the supervision of Ernest Rutherford, John Cockcroft, and Ernest Walton, a team tinkered for years improvising vacuum systems, sealing leaks, and trying out various devices for handling high voltages. As Brian Cathcart tells the story, "after three years and four months of work here finally was the laboratory tool that Rutherford had called for in 1927, and it did just what he asked."[32] They had achieved the remarkable feat of making (inventing/creating) the first artificial acceleration of particles (the energy of about half a million volts) sufficient to penetrate the nucleus of an atom. While what they actually saw was "a twinkle of scintillations on a zinc sulphite screen," it was the beginning of a new era in science. For this scientific breakthrough Watson and Cockcroft received the Nobel Prize for physics in 1951. Cathcart asks that we not lose sight of the fact that "the successful experimental physicist . . . was a rare creature who needed the skills of the hand as well as the mind, and the right temperament to boot."[33] By the end of the twentieth century, science reached a point where expertise in accelerator design, particle interaction, general relativity, and string theory became pieces of the same puzzle.

It will not suffice to omit the newest cadre of tinkerers and creators—those who manipulate genetic material. Unlike all the talk about "the machine"—the five-story tall, multibillion-dollar Hadron Collider with its mind-boggling microelectronics required to accelerate a proton to near the speed of light—a gene splicer is a modest necessity for every lab doing genetic research. Is the mentality or the process fundamentally different because accelerators are replaced with gene splicers? Probably not, since the science involved demands the same integration of theory

---

32. Cathcart, *The Fly in the Cathedral*, 228.
33. Ibid., 143.

and practice, creations of the mind and creations of tinkerers.[34] Nevertheless, across this nation and around the globe, in laboratories small and large, the science that matters is the same as it has always been—the patient manipulation of some physical apparatus in order to affect some result that can be measured.

Problem Solving

Alan Lightman remembers well his first research problem. He was a graduate student in physics at the California Institute of Technology and his thesis adviser was Professor Kip Thorne. A great part of science, as Lightman learned, starts with a well-posed problem, that is, a problem that can be stated with enough clarity and definiteness to be solvable. The challenge before him concerned the nature of gravity; namely, to show by mathematical calculation that gravity is truly geometrical (that gravity could be described completely as a warping of space). In the early 1970s, some theories of gravity, such as Einstein's general relativity, were geometrical, while others were not. After months of frustration, Lightman woke up at 5 a.m. with a feeling of rightness. "I had a strong sensation of seeing deeply into the problem and understanding it and knowing that I was right—a certain kind of inevitability."[35]

I am not so much interested in the parallels Lightman and others might draw between his experience of being "completely without ego" or being grasped by the problem as if it is a mystical experience. My attention, instead, is drawn to Lightman's repeated remarks of the feeling of having solved the problem, "a kind of inevitability," or knowing when you have arrived. Now an adjunct professor of humanities at MIT, Lightman writes essays and novels. Gaining what we call a "critical distance," Lightman reflects on what he misses about doing physics: "I miss the purity . . . I miss the answers . . . I miss the rooms I could enter [where 'a physicist can imagine a weight hung from a spring bouncing up and down and

---

34. Two examples of what this blending of theory and practice looks like at the biological level is Francis Crick's *What Mad Pursuit* (New York: Basic, 1990) and at the subatomic level is Michael Riordan's *The Hunting of the Quark*.

35. Lightman, *A Sense of the Mysterious*, 17. For a similar kind of experience read Laughlin's account of John Bardeen, considered by some to be the greatest theoretical physicist who ever lived, who solved the problem of heat capacity over dinner (*A Different Universe*, ch. 8, "I Solved It at Dinner"); and Francis Crick, who describes a flash of enlightenment clearing away a mistaken assumption about RNA as the messenger for DNA in *What Mad Pursuit*, 120, 141.

fix this mental image with an equation'], and I miss the language that sounded clear as a struck bell."[36]

Who doesn't remember high school homework with pages of problems to be solved: geometry, algebra, chemistry, and physics? The tests, too, with only one correct answer. My experience of teaching a required religion course to high school juniors was completely different. I was always being asked how anyone could grade students on what they believe (or didn't believe) since there can be no correct answer. The point I am making is obvious. Science explains by distilling the process of explaining until it has literally explained away the problem at hand. Theology does not so much explain as seek an ever-deeper understanding of a deposit of truth. Nothing of significance is ever explained away. The nature of the Trinity may be construed as a problem to be solved, but theologians are more likely to consider it a mystery that will forever be a mystery.[37] In whatever sense theologians problem-solve, they do so by using the veracity of words. When asked how one decides the question of what one should do with one's life, the poet Rainer Maria Rilke advises the student to love the questions themselves. And it isn't that scientists don't love their questions and find them to be, at times, all consuming. The questions, though, are meant to have a natural end so that the next set of questions can be pursued.

Methodology Per Se

What is the nature of science? Some would say, and I would concur, that it lies in the character of its methodology. In the heyday of Descartes, Newton, William Whewell, and John Stuart Mill, the focus of debate was squarely about induction vs. deduction, and the validity of hypothetico-deductivism.[38] And while much has been settled, methodological ques-

---

36. Lightman, *A Sense of the Mysterious*, 178-79.

37. The internal discussion among scientists should be noted. In his review of Steven Weinberg's book, *Lake Views: The World and the Universe* (Cambridge, MA: Belknap, 2010), Freeman Dyson chafes at the idea of a Final Theory because it diminishes both the richness of nature and the richness of human destiny. "I prefer," he writes, "to live in a universe full of inexhaustible mysteries, and to belong to a species destined for inexhaustible intellectual growth" (*The New York Review of Books*, June 12, 2010, 12).

38. See Peter Achinstein, *Science Rules: A Historical Introduction to Scientific Methods* (Baltimore: The Johns Hopkins Press, 2004). Let us also keep in mind that Newton and Darwin were acutely aware of what they were doing methodologically. See Hull, *Darwin and His Critics*, ch. 2.

tions linger. Falling into the category of the latter is an array of questions generated by the intersection of theory and experiment, including the distinction between the generation of phenomena, the role of the crucial experiment, and the necessity of experimental confirmation in instances of highly theoretical propositions such as string theory.[39] In hindsight we can see how the twentieth century ushered in a broader category of philosophical issues pertaining to the nature of scientific reality, the correspondence model of truth, realism and anti-realism, objectivity and subjectivism, the growth of knowledge, and what constitutes normal science.[40] The infusion of philosophers and historians has stirred the water to no end. The likes of Paul Feyerabend, Russell Hanson, Mary Hesse, Larry Laudan, Imre Lakatos, Thomas Kuhn, along with a few sociologists such as Harry Collins, Trevor Pinch, and Andrew Pickering, represent a new perspective on just about everything heretofore taken for granted about science itself. In his introduction to *Image and Logic*, for example, Galison highlights the way the once reigning positivist program has been turned on its head by the antipositivists: ". . . instead of starting with observation and treating theory as its superstructure, the antipositivists took theory as primary and observation as subordinate."[41] Writing about some of the same metaphysical issues confronting science, Ian Hacking speaks of the harm that "comes from a single-minded obsession with representation and thinking and theory, at the expense of intervention and action and experiment."[42] No matter which way you look, scientists have crossed a contemporary threshold realizing that methodological issues are not going away in the near future.

A discussion of methodology per se inevitably leads to question whether science can be identified by its methodology when "science" is a term we use for disciplines within disciplines. Emeritus Professor of the History and Philosophy of Science at MIT, Evelyn Fox Keller speaks of a myriad of scientific communities each with its own "epistemological culture." These subcultures are distinguishable by their own agreed-upon

39. See Peter Woit, *Not Even Wrong*, where the author examines a number of methodological questions, including the falsifiability criterion when applied to more general theoretical frameworks such as superstring theory.

40. For a brief discussion of metaphysical issues, see Hacking, *Representing and Intervening*, ch. 8. There is no better reflection of what the issues have been than the collected papers of Hilary Putnam, *Philosophy in an Age of Science: Physics, Mathematics, and Skepticism* (Cambridge, MA: Harvard University Press, 2012).

41. Galison, *Image and Logic*, 11.

42. Hacking, *Representing and Intervening*, 131.

standards of what counts as a sufficient understanding of a natural phenomenon. Developmental biology, for instance, with its interest in the mechanisms of inheritance and mutation, the effect of population size, and the operation of natural selection through differential survivorship and fertility, requires its own unique set of criteria.[43] The eminent Harvard biologist, Ernst Mayr, argues even more broadly that the biological sciences do science their own way. The physical sciences are satisfied with no less than universal laws that are both mathematically elegant and logically simple. The biological sciences, on the other hand, study organisms that are characterized by their changeability over time. Among the special characteristics of living organisms not found, or not found in the same manner, in inanimate objects, Mayr mentions complexity and organization, uniqueness and variability, a genetic program, the continuous interplay of random and selective processes, emergence, branching and hierarchies, and historical narrative. In the instance of evolutionary biology or astronomy, we cannot neatly provide hypotheses that are "immediately" testable because the history of a species or a star can never be replicated and can never be directly accessible. Scientists can study the functions of genes and molecules and extrapolate backwards, and they can do this quite convincingly utilizing circumstantial evidence.[44] Astronomers now believe they have an accurate account of how stars are formed, not because they can replicate the process but rather because they can observe such a large number of stars at different stages of their lives.

In spite of distinctive subcultures across a diversity of disciplines, it can nevertheless be argued that science operates with a distinguishable methodology. Combing through the journals at the Science and Engineering Library of Boston University one afternoon yielded a surprising discovery. From a somewhat randomly selected sample—*Medical & Biological Engineering & Computing*; *Physica D*; *Nonlinear Phenomena*; *Tissue & Cell*; *Journal of Bacteriology*; *Journal of Insect Physiology*—the following format seemed to hold across disciplines:

43. Keller, *Making Sense of Life: Explaining Biological Development with Models, Metaphors, and Machines* (Cambridge, MA: Harvard University Press, 2002).

44. See Ernst Mayr, *The Growth of Biological Thought* (Cambridge, MA: Harvard University Press, 1982), esp. 51–76. Francis Crick of DNA fame has some insightful reflections from someone who was trained initially in physics, devised weapons during World War II for the British, and then transitioned into biology. "All this," he summarizes, "makes it very difficult for physicists to adapt to most biological research" (*What Mad Pursuit*, 139).

Introduction—includes a statement or definition of the problem, background information, and the purpose of the paper

Materials and Methods—includes a description of the physical apparatus, the set up of the experiment, and an explanation of the methodology being used

Results—includes findings and data

Conclusion and Discussion—includes any conclusions that can be drawn and where specific conclusions are not appropriate

Scientific papers usually end with acknowledgements and references, including grants, organizations, and other scientists and nonscientists instrumental to the research project.

In comparison with articles written for theological journals, I was struck by the sheer physicality of both the physical objects being studied (living and nonliving) and the physicality of the materials involved to conduct the study. The use of diagrams, pictures, tables, and mathematics is without parallel in theological journals. The frequency of collaboration among scientists is commonplace. To cite a specific example, the largest study of African genetic diversity includes data taken over a decade from 113 African populations. Lead researcher Sarah Tishkoff, geneticist at the University of Pennsylvania, tells of hauling centrifuges for processing blood samples into rugged terrain in four-wheel drive vehicles and running her instruments by connecting them to her truck battery.[45] Without fail, and certainly a prerequisite for publication in the first place, is a definable problem. The problem is not always resolved but the authors are convinced that progress has been made toward a resolution, otherwise they would not be submitting an article for review.

While I am willing to give credence to the point of view that science is "historically evolved, culturally located, and collectively produced," (Geertz), I resist the conclusion that the history of science is like every other history. Whether we should grant science a privileged position is another matter.[46] I am inclined, though, to follow Steven Weinberg's ac-

---

45. Tishkoff's paper is coauthored by twenty-five collaborators forming an international team of researches (the paper appeared in the May 1, 2009 issue of *Science*). The ground-breaking paper, "The Sequence of the Human Genome," appearing in *Science* (February 16, 2000) had 283 coauthors, and features a five-foot color-coded foldout map of the genome.

46. For the quote see Geertz, *Available Light*, 161. The issue of epistemic privilege is ongoing but without a clear definition of "privileged in what way." My uncomplicated

count of science because it just seems right to me, and because it represents the way most scientists regard their discipline. Regarded as one of the premier physicists of our time and the winner of the Nobel Prize in Physics in 1979, Weinberg professes an interest in the history of science. While willing to tip his hat to the argument that scientific theories are social constructions, he resists the conclusion that they are nothing but social constructions. Weinberg concurs with Kuhn's assessment that science is driven from behind, rather than pulled toward some fixed goal to which it moves ever closer. But if you push this logic too far—that one paradigm (explanatory model) is relatively better but not objectively better than another—you end up adopting the fallacy "that in science we are not in fact moving toward objective truth." Weinberg counters, "I do not see why the fact that we are discovering not only the laws of nature in detail, but what kinds of laws are worth discovering, should mean that we are not making objective progress."[47] Scientists have reason to believe that they are making *objective progress* because most scientists are convinced there is an objective reality to be understood. This objective truth, though, is not measured by some absolute standard—because there are no objectively valid norms of empirical reasoning—but by results that are accepted across cultures and that are permanent. Weinberg does add one important proviso: laws of nature are culture-free and permanent "not as they are being developed, not as they were in the mind of the scientist who first discovers them, not in the course of what Bruno Latour and Steve Woolgar call 'negotiations' over what theory is going to be accepted—but in their final form, in which cultural influences are refined away."[48]

The argument for permanence requires another qualification because the history of science is one in which it is impossible to ascertain when a particular theory has reached its final form. Whether it is the Standard Model of particle physics, the Periodic Table, the exact

---

argument is to say science is methodologically privileged to the degree it transcends history and culture in ways other disciplines do not. The other question is whether science should be granted certain privileges because of its methodological uniqueness. On that score I am sorely guarded, and my reasons are put forth in *Eden's Garden*, and go to my contention that science, in its practice and technology in contrast to its abstract theories, does not transcend the way humans embody their essential human nature in whatever they do and create.

47. Weinberg, *Facing Up*, 85, 86.

48. In Jay A. Labinger and Harry Collins, eds., *The One Culture: A Conversation about Science* (Chicago: University of Chicago Press, 2001), 123.

symmetry in nature between left and right, the double helix shape of DNA, or Einstein's theory of general relativity, Weinberg does not foresee a time when any of these conclusions becomes invalid. What we do see is how our understanding of permanent theory is deepened and expanded, just as we now understand that the law of exact symmetry is "only true in certain contexts and to a certain degree of approximation." Weinberg also adds the distinction that "approximate theories are not merely approximately true." Even though an equation, such as Maxwell's equation regarding magnetic fields, can only give an *approximate* answer, the equation or theory is *precisely* true.[49]

The claim for a truth that is culture-free and permanent (precisely true, never to be overturned) goes hand and hand with a discipline that measures things, reduces to the most fundamental level, solves problems, tinkers and creates in order to discover something new. To say that science has been historicized is not a reason to say it has "just now" become more subjective or just as subjective as other non-science disciplines, but rather is an admission that science is *practiced* in a historical context; and this invariably means scientists are selective about what they discover, what conceptual framework they will utilize, and how knowledge will be utilized.

Bringing together the themes of this conclusion, the following characteristics of a methodology distinctively scientific can be asserted:

Falsifiability—Scientific knowledge consists of a body of observations and ideas that have been accepted as working hypotheses about the universe. Some hypotheses have matured to the point of being accepted as "settled." This is to say, a hypothesis is proposed in such a way that it is at least potentially falsifiable. The principle of falsifiability is associated with the early twentieth century British philosopher of science, Karl Popper, who cut through a number of other competing ideas, such as induction and deduction. Popper argued that unless you can at least imagine an experiment that might falsify a theory, that theory is not scientific.

In the disputed question whether the transmission between nerve cells and muscle cells is chemical or electrical, each side was required to construct a testable hypothesis, that is, one which could be confirmed by others and at the same time shown to have the greater explanatory power. At a moment when John Eccles was locked into a fierce debate with Katz and Kuffler about just this question, and was beginning to doubt his

---

49. Weinberg, *Facing Up,* 208.

research (i.e., he might be on the losing side of a fundamental issue), he had a transforming encounter with the famed philosopher Karl Popper. Eccles writes, "I learned from Popper what for me is the essence of scientific investigation—how to be speculative and imaginative in the creation of hypotheses, and then to challenge them with the utmost rigor.... In fact I learned from him even to rejoice in the refutation of a cherished hypothesis, because that, too, is a scientific achievement and because much has been learned by the refutation."[50]

In a notable article by the philosopher Anthony Flew, theologians were challenged to restate their truth-claims in such way that they could be falsified. Flew asks provocatively for theologians to at least cite theoretically what evidence could be produced that would disprove the existence of God, or the divinity of Christ, and so forth.[51] The quandary this raises for theologians is immediately recognized. Essential articles of faith are not going to suddenly be reduced to provisional hypotheses. If asked about other theological claims, a theologian might say, "it depends." Theological claims, just like empirical claims, go through a process of development and negotiations before some are generally accepted as permanent.[52] But Flew's model is not one of historical development but of confirmation and falsification. Theologians, however, are not scientists and work at their profession by applying the "rules" of theological logic until consensus is reached (see next chapter). Flew was simply misguided, and thinking like a positivist, when he held up falsifiability as a suitable standard for theological claims.

A Collective Enterprise—Science is a collective enterprise for a number of reasons. First is the way scientific results become accepted and added to a body of previously accepted knowledge. Until consensus is reached, a conjecture is truly hypothetical or provisional. It is one person's best guess or best argument or best test result, and remains so until it passes through a process of replication, verification or falsification, and peer review leading to acceptance. While individuals practice the scientific

50. Quoted in Kandel, *In Search of Memory*, 96–97.
51. Flew, "Theology and Falsification," in A. Flew and Alasdair MacIntyre, eds., *New Essays in Philosophical Theology* (London: SCM, 1955), 98–99. Compare Barbour's discussion of Flew in *Myths, Models and Paradigms*, 126–33.
52. Jaroslav Pelikan's *The Christian Tradition: A History of the Development of Doctrine*, 5 vols. (Chicago: University of Chicago Press, 1975–1991) fully exemplifies the process of historical development inherent in the church's continuous understanding of what it believes and teaches.

method, sometimes separately and sometimes cooperatively, the permanent conclusions are the result of a community of scientists. Second is the trait of collaboration. From the regular gathering of the savants who founded London's Royal Society to the myriad of symposiums held each year, scientists gather to report and learn from each other. Even though at times science may be a one-person show, it is more and more a collaboration of minds. There were, for instance, 439 names on the paper announcing the discovery of the top quark. When scientific papers are submitted for review, they are often the result of a team approach to problem solving, and they always represent standing on the shoulders of those who went before. How often does a theological submission bear several names?

Knowledge That Accrues—No less than a giant himself, Newton gave credit to all the giants who preceded him in this well known statement that "if I have seen further than others, it is by standing upon the shoulders of giants" (Letter to Robert Hooke, February 5, 1675). Ian Hacking reminds us that the "Michaelson-Morley experiment" denotes a sequence of intermittent work beginning with Michaelson's initial success in 1881 and concluding with Miller's work of the 1920s. "One could say," Hacking writes, "that the experiment lasted half a century, while the [actual experimental] observations lasted maybe a day and a half."[53] And one could cite any number of similar instances, and it may be next to impossible to think of an example of a permanent theory that isn't the result of progress over time.

All science starts from an integrated body of knowledge that has been accumulating over decades, even centuries. The something "new" must be a better explanation, that is, it must account for previous explanations and show how they are deficient while proposing a more accurate or more comprehensive account. Demure about the designation "scientific progress," science in all its various subdisciplines depends on integrating the old with the new and then moving forward. Newton's theories of motion and gravity improves on Galileo's laws of motion, and Einstein transcends Newton. A theory or an account is superior because it transcends the limitation of its predecessors by proving to be more fruitful (answering a wider spectrum of questions). We can debate whether there is an end to the process—a final theory of something—but the process itself is one of accruement and advancement.

53. Hacking, *Representing and Intervening*, 174.

All three of these essential qualities converge to give us a kind of knowledge that reaches a point of universal acceptance after a history of progress. Scientists have reasons to believe there is an ontological factor that cannot be ignored. The reason scientific knowledge accrues is the consequence of studying a reality that is not only independent of the knower, but also everywhere the same. Additionally, it is a reality that "kicks back" when it is probed. Something as ephemeral as shadow photons kick back by interfering with the photons when seen through instrumentation. The significance of this fact is that scientists can study a cause and effect relationship and infer some conclusions. The probing itself can be anything from stirring a beaker, aiming a beam of light, or observing the results from administering a drug. Thus science is built on establishing a link between cognition (theorizing) and manipulation, and it is this link that sets science apart from other disciplines.[54]

While I encourage my reader to make his or her own comparisons between science and theology as the integrity of each is explored, this opportunity must be seized. It is quite reasonable to argue that theology is a discipline with a body of knowledge that accrues as a consequence of a collective or conciliar process. The creeds of the church are prima facie the best example. The argument for a body of knowledge that is subject to replication and verification, that proceeds by a process of discovery and theorizing, and is refined by a process of radical reductionism and problem solving, is much more difficult to sustain.

My own way of stating what is special about empiricism as a methodology is to emphasize the way science builds (incorporates) on the past. The philosopher Alasdair MacIntyre, who has taken a long, hard look at the issues associated with historical and social contextualism,[55] makes eminent sense by simply claiming that what enables us to make a rational choice between competing theories (regardless of their kind, whether moral or scientific) "is *not* by applying absolute standards, but

---

54. While his book is now a dated resource, Morris Berman clearly saw the paradigm shift when humans understood that it would be necessary to "vex nature" (Bacon) in order to understand nature, thus preparing the way for the next paradigm shift from man's *intrusion* into sacred territory (usually ritualized) to the outright *manipulation* of a sanitized nature, with manipulation carrying the connotation of creating something not found in nature. See Berman, *The Reenchantment of the World* (Toronto: Bantam, 1984), 17, 54, 78, 87.

55. Certainly, but not exclusively, Alasdair MacIntyre, (Notre Dame, IN: University of Notre Dame Press, 1981), followed by his *Whose Justice? Which Rationality?* (1988) and *Three Rival Versions of Moral Enquiry* (Notre Dame, IN: University of Notre Dame, 1990).

only historical ones: namely, whether or not the theory represents an advance on its predecessors compared to its rivals, by more successfully overcoming the problems which the previous theory had faced."[56] At this level of increasing historical awareness, theology advances in a way not unlike empiricism. But can we say a theological problem (difficulty) is sufficiently like an empirical problem to warrant the conclusion that theology advances in a progressive manner? The answer, I believe, is "no," especially if we add progressive in a patent way. The Nicene Creed, for example, represents advancement in our understanding of the Trinity found in the New Testament but never seems to reach a point where theologians can say "problem solved." The reason theology never leaves the past, so to speak, is the same reason it is unfair to say theology is mired in the past for the past is never a dead past since it possesses the potential for ever more meaning. This being said, the historical past for science is not the same historical past for theology. For the former, the past is an accumulation of distilled knowledge, sufficiently settled to be trusted, while for theology the past is a particular assortment of historical events pregnant with meaning, narratively connected and interpreted.

Theological truth-claims face the same daunting postmodern challenge of historization as do all truth claims. Within the Catholic tradition the "crisis" is acute because of the burden of infallibility and permanence. On one level, the parallel with science stands out. Writing about the need for theology to develop "new, ontologically appropriate notions of rationality and truth," Thomas G. Guarino is equally cognizant that such a notion of truth must also take into account "our historically, linguistically, and socioculturally embedded life and thought—a notion of truth that avoids the inappropriate 'objectivism' of metaphysics but one that is equally chary of an anarchistic and unruly relativism."[57] The reader should note Guarino's reference to "ontologically appropriate" as yet another indicator that here in the Catholic tradition is a prime example of theology's turn to the ontological, or the felt necessity to make ontological-like claims. Fundamentally, Guarino is making an argument that theology is not a subjective reading of history or revelation. He argues that there are teachings of the Church about God (the triune God), Jesus Christ (both human and divine), and human nature and reality (we

---

56. Robert Stern, "MacIntyre and Historicism," in John Horton and Susan Mendus, eds., *After MacIntyre* (Notre Dame, IN: University of Notre Press, 1994), 153.

57. Guarino, *Foundations of Systematic Theology* (New York: T & T Clark International, 2005), 96.

are made in the image of God and God's creation is good) that "while always existing within history, resist a total historicization."[58] He bolsters his case by using the terminology of normative, perduring, largely identical and selfsame, , universal and continuous. In summary fashion Guarino speaks of two kinds of changes that fundamental beliefs undergo: (1) changes required in conceptual construction due to the moment in time or the culture at hand (the task of reinterpretation); and (2) the organic development "continuing the fundamental thrust of the original doctrine or idea but now extending and amplifying it in consonance with the original meaning."[59] What Guarino argues concerning the "material continuity and identity" of the Christian faith throughout history sounds very much like Weinberg's argument. Does this mean, then, that science and theology are methodologically similar or compatible?

Guarino begins his book with a discussion of revelation, which is the most difficult issue to tackle. The one consistent argument Christian theologians have made from the beginning is that what we know about matters of faith, universally true and abidingly valid, are "nothing less than God's unveiledness, his free, gratuitous self-manifestation to us."[60] Even though God's self-revelation is the source of what we know of God's nature and God's intention for human life, revelation does not obliterate the unavoidable fact that this manifestation "is always filtered, by necessity, through human concepts, symbols, linguistic conventions, and historically and culturally conditioned perspectives."[61] But herein lies the conundrum uniquely theological: how to reconcile a timeless revelation with its timely reception. Science does not carry this burden because there is no self-revealing Subject, and there is no timeless deposit (manifestation) of truth.

To conclude: There are various ways to understand the methodology of empiricism, and each perspective reflects an ulterior motive. Scientific methodology is no less than a continuum from a "hard" understanding to a "soft" understanding. The level of hardness falls along the line presented by Steven Weinberg. We should keep in mind that he speaks as a physicist, and a physicist who works in a field where very exact results are normative. Reductionism is often associated with hardness because the goal is to problem-solve until there is nothing left to solve. Softness

58. Ibid., 59.
59. Ibid., 194.
60. Ibid., 1.
61. Ibid.

is a value that highlights holism, connectedness, and contextualism. The conceptual clusters for hardness are realism, rationalism, objectivism versus interconnectedness, constructivism, and subjectivism. It makes perfect sense that the NR favors a softer science because of the difficulties associated with thinking of theology as a hard science. It may be that my ulterior motive to favor a hard interpretation of science is due to my need to emphasize what makes theology and science distinctive (sibling rivals rather than compatible cousins). However biased my approach, it does put us in a position to understand the limits of rapprochement.

When all is said and done, the decisive question is whether there is a scientific methodology that is sufficiently distinctive and unique, and whether that methodology leads to a kind of knowledge that is distinctive and unique. The same question could be asked of philosophy and theology, and the answer would depend on an examination of how philosophers or theologians go about doing what philosophers and theologians do. The next chapter will defend the position that theology employs a distinct and unique methodology resulting in a particular kind of knowledge associated with word truth.

6

The Distinctiveness that Is Christian Theology

What Counts as Theologizing

GIVEN THE CENTURIES THAT theology has had to develop into a mature discipline, it has become an enigma to those looking in from the outside. As with other mature disciplines, theology consists of various subdisciplines. My aim is not so much to describe each and every facet of theology but the characteristics that set Christian theology apart from other disciplines. Is there something we can identify as doing theology (theologizing)? Is there a definable theological methodology? What is its integrity?

There are a number of ways to identify the subdisciplines. At colleges, universities, and seminaries we find professional theologians who teach dogmatics, systematics, apologetics, patristics, biblical theology (Old and New Testament theology), hermeneutics, historical and practical theology, and Christian ethics.[1] In some instances theology is a matter of style, such as the subtle difference between polemics and apologetics. Some would see themselves as teaching constructive, problematic, or exploratory theology where disciplinary boundaries are bypassed in order to pursue a particular theme. Other theologians specialize in Christian theology as it intersects with the arts, sciences, societies, and religions of the world. Theologies are developed in order to address a particular

---

1. Roger Shinn's statement about Reinhold Niebuhr's unique style of doing practical theology is irresistible: "Niebuhr aimed not to write about problems of theology but to write theologically about human problems." Quoted from Daniel F. Rice, ed., *Reinhold Niebuhr Revisited* (Grand Rapids: Eerdmans, 2009), xx.

historical moment, such as feminist theology and liberation theology. Writing from a Roman Catholic perspective, R. R. Reno contrasts theologians committed to developing and sustaining a normative theology in order to build up the faithful and those devoted to an exploratory and critical theology that serves the church in ways that leaven and enrich her theological culture.[2]

We might put ourselves in the position of an editor of a prominent theological journal as a way of getting a handle on what we mean by theologizing. The deciding factor for publication is not going to be whether a submitted article contains many good arguments or develops a well-thought-out thesis, for that is a given. Near the top of an editor's criteria would be an explication that demonstrates a depth and breadth of knowledge, and that the author is familiar with the relevant material. Relevancy is only a starting point because an editor is hoping to see a meaningful conversation with other theologians and thinkers, living and dead. Saying something fresh and relevant is also important. Publishers are probably not going to print something that is considered heretical. They are more likely to be concerned with good or bad theologizing. And during the process of peer review the essay's readers will ask whether a theological conversation is taking place between the author, Scripture, and tradition (Tradition if you are Roman Catholic); and if the author is saying something new in the sense of adding to or deepening the understanding of Christian faith and doctrine.

I made reference above to good and bad theologizing. A good editor knows the difference but may be hard-pressed to define just how he or she knows. It will take the rest of this chapter to clarify what exactly theologians do and demystify the distinction between "good" and "bad" theologizing. In trying to make himself clear, Miroslav Volf makes this interesting comment in a footnote: "in the last part of the book, I am engaging in what from one angle might be described as a 'thought experiment'—not a straightforward argument for a position but an argumentative exploration of a possibility that is very much in sync with what Christian tradition claims about redemption, both now and in the future."[3] Not only is the phrase "an argumentative exploration of a possibility" revealing, but also Volf adds, not incidentally, that all of this takes place "in sync" with what Christian tradition claims about redemp-

---

2. R. R. Reno, "Theology After the Revolution," *First Things,* May 2007, 15–21.
3. Volf, *The End of Memory* (Grand Rapids: Eerdmans, 2006), 142 n.34.

tion. Furthermore, this is an argument that not only looks backward (anamnesis) but also anticipates what needs to be said in order to open a new and future understanding. In his popular book, *The Doors of the Sea*, David Bentley Hart uses the equally thoughtful terminology "the inexorable logic of absolute divine sovereignty."[4] For Hart, good theology does not compromise in any way the absolute sovereignty of God; to do so results in logical absurdity, and "we become guilty of both an infantile anthropomorphism and a philosophical catachresis."[5] For both Volf and Hart, good theology is not so much a matter of being relevant as it is remembering what the church remembers about the truths she holds dear and practicing "the very rationality" required by the gospel (another phrase from Hart).[6]

Good theology, worthy of publication, hinges on the criterion of a persuasive argument that is theologically informed and relevant. The theologically informed caveat means many things: a depth of understanding, knowledge of the pertinent resources, an awareness of Scripture and tradition, as well as the particulars of a specific tradition (such as the Reformed or Russian Orthodox or Roman Catholic). At times the academic theologian is primarily interested in good scholarship, which is often an effort to recover and explain. The measure of relevancy is particular to theology in that truth is personal, life-changing, and perennial. Augustine is just as relevant today as in the fourth century because he writes of enduring truths about our human condition and our relationship to God. Yet, not everything Augustine wrote is equally relevant to a twenty-first-century American. The task of the theology is to identify and amplify, to criticize and commend, those facets of truth that matter to us now.

Theologizing would be less complicated if the rubric of good scholarship and making a good argument were sufficient. It is not. The theological word is related to its author in a very unique way. Here are *words we can stand by, even die for*. The idea of standing by one's words is of particular interest to the eclectic Wendell Berry. A sign of our times, according to Berry, is the way we are taught to speak in a manner that precludes assuming ownership of our words. He abhors the way we have retreated to worlds of subjectivity, objectivity, abstraction, and specialization, as well as all the ways we have severed the connection between

---

4. Hart, *The Doors of the Sea*, 90.
5. Ibid., 76.
6. Ibid.

language and community. He deplores language that refers to nothing in particular, and language that tries to be so objective that it means nothing. Absent from this use of language is what Berry calls "community speech," where there is a direct reference or designation for which the speaker can be held accountable.[7]

Being a theologian is different from being a preacher, though both are a form of Christian witness. James H. Cone, reflecting on his vocation as a theologian, clarifies the difference. "The motivation for theological reflection is like the motivation to preach the gospel. They both arise from faith itself. In preaching, one experiences the urgency to proclaim. . . . In theology, one experiences the urgency to understand, to reflect upon what the gospel means in a world that is ever-changing, complex, and oppressive."[8] Theology, then, is faith demanding to be understood, while proclamation is faith demanding to be made known.

Coming at this same quality from another direction, Michael Welker finds that at least two things must be present before an utterance can be counted as theological. "Thus we can call statements about God and other contents of faith theological if they show an existential seriousness in the speaker and/or in the subject matter, and if at the same time they are comprehensible, communicable and capable of material development."[9] Those who are speaking and their subject matter are such that they evidence an existential seriousness. One thinks of Martin Luther at the Diet of Worms: "My conscience is captive to the Word of God. Thus I cannot and will not recant, for going against my conscience is neither safer nor salutary. I can do no other, here I stand, God help me."[10]

---

7. From a 1979 essay, "Standing by Words," in a book with the same title, 24–63. In particular, Berry examines the language of the technocrats during the meltdown at Three Mile Island. From the perspective of linguistic and literary theory, George Steiner identifies as a critical problem in our late modern world: the dissolution of trust between word and world. The consequence is "the nihilism of deconstructionism," "the abrogations of meaning," and the dissolution of "truth seeking." See his *Real Presences* (Chicago: University of Chicago Press, 1989), *passim* and esp. 93. Interestingly, James Davison Hunter agrees with Steiner and finds that we are living in a culture where words can mean anything because they are "no longer answerable to the world. " See Hunter, *To Change the World* (New York: Oxford University Press, 2010), 238 and 205–10.

8. James H. Cone, "The Vocation of a Theologian," in M. Douglas Meeks, J. Moltmann, and F. R. Trost, eds., *Theology and Corporate Conscience: Essays in Honor of Frederick Herzog* (Minneapolis: Kirk House, 1999), 67.

9. Welker in Polkinghorne and Welker, *Faith in the Living God*, 141.

10. Quoted in Roland H. Bainton, *Here I Stand: A Life of Martin Luther* (New York: Mentor, 1955), 145.

Welker also insists that theological utterances be capable of material development. This requirement, in turn, stands in contrast to theological statements that are self-enclosed not only in attitude but also in a way that is definitive, thus closing the door on further development. Welker may not be thinking so much of creeds and confessional statements as the ongoing work of theologizing. The NR is a fine example of both criteria: engaging science with a positive *openness* in order to understand anew and *develop* more fully what is already a core Christian belief.

"Words to stand by" and "existential seriousness" are not far from a more familiar refrain in Christian circles, namely, the evangelical notion that theological statements bear witness. Martin Luther certainly understood himself as bearing witness, and I dare say he felt that way about everything he wrote (and that was quite a lot!). Nor did Luther retreat from making a persuasive argument or entering into debate with anyone. To read him is to hear an evangelical ring arising from one who practices theology in order to bear witness. David Hart, in his breathtaking *The Beauty of the Infinite*, speaks of where theologizing must begin. "Christian theology has no stake in the myth of disinterested rationality: the church has no arguments for its faith more convincing than the form of Christ; enjoined by Christ to preach the gospel, Christians must proclaim, exhort, bear witness, persuade—before other forms of reason can be marshaled."[11]

Theologians have something distinctive to say not because of some uncommon erudition, but rather because their faith is such an uncommon thing. Theologians also have something to say about everything. Nicholas Lash, a Roman Catholic theologian at Cambridge University who has earned a respect that spans the English-speaking world, reflects on what it is that theologians do: "to think as a Christian is to try to understand the stellar spaces, the arrangements of micro-organisms and DNA molecules, the history of Tibet, the operation of economic markets, toothache, King Lear, the CIA, and grandma's cooking—or, as Aquinas put it, 'all things.'"[12]

Theologians do not have something important to say about "all things." They have something to say uniquely about important things. If they are going to commit themselves to words worth standing by, then theologians will choose to theologize "about everything that counts in

---

11. Hart, *The Beauty of the Infinite*, 3.

12. Interview with Professor Lash, "Performing Scripture," *The Christian Century*, December 11, 2007, 30.

life."[13] But the scope of theology is only part of the picture. Lash points to a motif that has been around for a long time. Quite dear to him is a remark of Gerald O'Collins, the Australian Jesuit, made forty years ago—"A theologian is someone who watches his/her language in the presence of God."[14] The same could be said about prayer. And is there a better way to understand the biblical witness, from Abraham to John of the book of Revelation?

Part of the enigma of Christian theology is the distinction between apologetics, dogmatics, and systematic theology. If dogmatics is the church's dialogue with itself, apologetics represent theology's dialogue with the world, and systematics is some of both with an eye toward coherence and thematization. No one should think of the separation as absolute because while the church is addressing the world it is also pursuing its own dogmatics, and while the church is narrating and renarrating its core beliefs, it is also mindful of the culture and history it is engaging. In other words, good theology is a conversation with many partners, some of whom are believers and some of whom are skeptics.

A dogmatic theologian is simply someone who understands his or her task to be one of clarifying the speech and acts of the triune God as they are found in gospel, Scripture, and tradition. Kevin J. Vanhoozer provides a less formal definition of doctrine and it works very well for my purpose: Doctrine is "the reward that faith finds at the end of its search for the meaning of the apostolic testimony to what God was doing in the event of Jesus Christ."[15] So, rather than typecasting dogmatics as official teaching, think of it as theology working its way up until it reaches the level of consensus doctrine. In the ongoing process of interpreting the Christian message for a new situation, the church must come to a new understanding of something it holds to be true. This, of course, is a search that never ends, and it continues in part because meaning is not something extracted from the past and merely passed along to the next generation. When Bonhoeffer asks, "Who is Christ for us today?," the church does not have a reply except to rethink accepted doctrine cast in a new light.

---

13. For instance, see Gilbert Meilaender's essays gathered around the theme *Things That Count* (Wilmington, DE: ISI Books, 2000).

14. *The Christian Century*, December 11, 2007, 30.

15. Quoted in a review of his book, *The Drama of Doctrine: A Canonical-Linguistic Approach to Christian Theology* (Louisville: Westminster, 2005), in *The Christian Century*, February 12, 2008, 41.

When one mentions apologetics a number of negative associations come to mind, and most revolve around the church defending its theological terrain. In explicating the classic statements of the Nicene and Apostles' Creeds, Archbishop Rowan Williams picks up on the phrase "taking responsibility for making God credible in the world."[16] This seems a more than apt way to describe what theologians do—*they take responsibility for making God credible in the world*. We tend to assign this role to those who have been trained theologically. But this cannot be the entire story. All Christians bear this responsibility, both to themselves and to all they engage. Williams informs his reader that he owes the phrase to Etty Hillesum, a young Jewish woman living in Holland when the Germans invaded. Imprisoned in the transit camp at Westerbork before being shipped off to Auschwitz, Hillesum wrote, "there must be someone to live through it all and bear witness to the fact that God lived, even in these times. And why should I not be that witness?"[17] Etty Hillesum did not survive, but her heroic witness does.

If dogmatics and apologetics play out the church's dialogue with itself and the world, systematic theology makes both possible. There is ample evidence that systematic theologians see themselves as doing more than just writing primers for students. A systematic theology does more than meet theology's need for coherence, more than a *summa theologiae*. Beginning with the development of one or more theological trajectories, something new is produced. The systematic theologians' methodology becomes their theology and their theology becomes their methodology. Every systematic theologian is writing for his or her moment in history. Aquinas, for example, found himself at the juncture of a significant cultural transition from ecclesiastical scholasticism to an Aristotelian secularism.[18] Karl Barth precipitated his own crisis in theology with the publication of his commentary on The Epistle to the Romans, and then continued writing a revolutionary theology while Hitler's tank divisions were terrorizing most of Europe. What makes this kind of theologizing special is the unique blending of the timely with the timeless.

The last characteristic of doing theology is the one I regard as most important. To do theology is to learn and practice a peculiar kind of

16. Williams, *Tokens of Trust*, 22.
17. Quoted in ibid.
18. I found Thomas F. O'Meara especially helpful in placing Aquinas in his historical context. See his *Thomas Aquinas, Theologian* (Notre Dame, IN: University of Notre Dame Press, 1997).

logic—a *theological logic*. Theologians seldom reflect on this aspect of what they do; they just do it. We catch a glimpse of what I mean when Hart writes that good theology does not compromise in any way the absolute sovereignty of God, and to think otherwise will result in a logical absurdity. Hart has his own "take" on what this means, but so does almost every theologian.[19] In the instance of God's sovereignty, a theologian begins with a certain premise, which includes that God is, in "his" nature, impassible, and proceeds to extend the implications of the premise (something Thomas Aquinas did without equal), or in some instances to challenge the premise. But in spite of their agreements and disagreements, one discovers that they are all practicing the same theological logic; that is, they are trying to understand the nature of God while being faithful to Scripture and tradition.

Modern theology is yet another facet in the ever-changing landscape of doing theology. Regardless of the theological premise and its logical implications, faithfulness to Scripture and tradition are no longer sufficient. What changed was making experience normative for theology in the sense that authentic theologizing must pass the test of existential verification. In other words, a valid theological interpretation needs to be true to life or reality or what all humans experience, otherwise it is suspect. Theology was never likely to ignore experience. From St. Augustine's soul searching in his *Confessions* to John Wesley's emphasis on "experiential faith," theologians continued to return to the personal nature of faith and religious experience. Making religious experience an essential component of religious studies can make a strong argument that William James represents a decisive turning point in the turn to experience.[20] The NR played its part by expanding the meaning of "experience" to include our experience of the physical universe, principally as it is discovered and understood by science.

---

19. A snippet of what this looks like is Hart's understanding of God's impassibility over against a contrary understanding by a theologian he greatly respects, namely Robert Jenson. See David Bentley Hart, *In the Aftermath: Provocations and Laments* (Grand Rapids: Eerdmans, 2009), ch. 18.

20. See for instance Taylor, *A Secular Age*, 730 and Hauerwas, *With the Grain*, ch. 3 and passim. Known as the "father of modern theology," Friedrich Schleiermacher is often credited with changing the direction of theology, and he did so by reclaiming the centrality of religious experience. James, however, is thoroughly modern in the way he gave experience depth, breadth, and universality.

Theology's Faith Factor

It goes without saying that theology is more than reason, that it is somehow, and in some way, an act of faith. But what exactly does faith bring to the reasoning process? Theology's faith factor draws it into a conundrum of misplaced but nevertheless persistent presumptions, including the assertions that faith leads to speculation, that it condones intellectual dishonesty by ignoring the evidence, and that it emboldens theology to claim the higher ground.

The rediscovery of Aristotle's writings during the thirteenth century ignited a slumbering issue regarding the relationship between faith and reason. While Aristotle's revolutionary move was to embrace the application of natural knowledge to a wide spectrum of experience, Aquinas's daring move was to pursue a positive course via Aristotle so "the study of the humblest of fact will lead to the study of the highest truth."[21] Aquinas was not the only extraordinary mind at work. Along with Peter Abelard, Giovanni Bonaventura, and Roger Bacon, a momentous intellectual struggle was set in motion, which reached a pragmatic climax when a decision needed to be made about the inclusion of Aristotle into a curriculum dominated by theology. The question was not whether reason was useful in discerning the natural world, but whether it was sufficient, and whether it represented a threat to theology as a superior way of knowing.[22] Despite Aquinas's two-handed approach that characterized theology henceforth—a clear distinction between faith and reason, conceding to each its own particular integrity, yet granting to faith and revelation an upper hand—he did not win the day. In the process of establishing autonomous universities (The University of Bologna in about 1150, The University of Paris in 1200, and Oxford University in 1220), knowledge was partitioned into independent departments, thus setting a course that still dominates where reason and faith are considered incompatible at best, and more likely mutually exclusive.

When it was proposed that a course entitled "Faith and Reason" be added to the core curriculum at Harvard University, Steven Pinker reacted by writing an editorial for the *Harvard Crimson Magazine* arguing that the "juxtaposition of the two words makes it seem like 'faith and reason' are parallel," when faith as "believing something without good reasons to

---

21. G. K. Chesterton, *St. Thomas Aquinas* (New York: Sheed and Ward, 1933), 99.

22. See Rubenstein, *Aristotle's Children*, ch. 6 ("The Great Debate at the University of Paris").

do so has no place in anything but a religious institution."[23] The proposal did not make it past the science department faculty.

Besides the historical evidence (above), humans have a natural inclination to distinguish between two kinds of truths: truth that is proper to reason, and truth that is peculiar to faith. This goes a long way toward explaining why we have two disciplines, theology and science, instead of one. But demarking a distinction between matters of faith and reason only makes a modicum of sense if each kind of knowledge is attached to a specific kind of methodology. Empirical knowledge is the consequence of experimentation and measurement, while faith knowledge is the outcome of revelation and faith. And while this may be a common-sense approach to a thorny dilemma, it serves to lend credence to the presumption that faith and reason are indeed at odds with each other. And such is not necessarily the case.[24]

In his encyclical letter *Fides et Ratio*, John Paul II shows no hesitancy to affirm "different faces of human truth," "two modes of knowledge," "two orders of knowledge, distinct not only in their point of departure, but also in their object."[25] With a ring of eloquence John Paul II also writes that faith and reason are like two wings on which the human spirit rises to the contemplation of truth. Speaking from a long history of theology's alliance with philosophy, John Paul recognizes the potential conflict between the order of natural reason (most notably philosophy and science) and truth conferred by revelation, yet affirms his confidence such a conflict is overshadowed by the unity of truth (First Vatican Council), the principle of noncontradiction, and the human desire to discover ultimate truth. Declaring the unity of truth, however, does not make it so. A more cynical view is Michael Shermer's complaint that insofar as God himself is the guarantor of truth, then that order of truth does not meet the criteria of universal reason.[26] Shermer, the founding publisher of *Skeptic* magazine, finds that once again theology is asking for a special dispensation when the Pope declares that "reason in fact is not asked to

23. Steven Pinker, *Harvard Crimson*, October 27, 2006. www.thecrimson.com/article/2006/10/27/less-faith-more-reason-there-is.

24. See the helpful discussion by Charles Taylor, "A Philosopher's Postscript: Engaging the Citadel of Secular Reason," in Paul J. Griffiths and Reinhard Hütter, eds., *Reason and The Reasons of Faith* (New York: T & T Clark, 2005), 339–53, and Terry Eagleton, *Reason, Faith, and Revolution*, ch. 3 ("Faith and Reason"). Together these writers make many helpful distinctions that are usually not even considered.

25. John Paul II, *Fides et Ratio*, 41, 47, 70.

26. Shermer, *How We Believe*, 136.

pass judgment on the contents of faith, something of which it would be incapable, since this is not its function."[27] For skeptics like Shermer, and many others, that is exactly the function of reason—to question everything with no exceptions. (Such is the thrust of Daniel Dennett's *Breaking the Spell* where religious belief doesn't measure up to the standard of universal reason).

The chasm between faith and reason, however, is not as wide as Shermer makes it. He has it all wrong when he writes, "the whole point of faith in fact is to believe regardless of the evidence, which is the very antithesis of science."[28] Faith, as practiced by theologians, hardly makes them delusional, unreasonable, intellectually dishonest, less curious, or more likely to ignore evidence. Aquinas is no less rational than Aristotle, Karl Barth no less rational than Stephen Hawking. The tradition the NR emulates is an understanding of faith as an inducement to know what we would not otherwise ever know.[29] Could it be that theology, by the way of word *truth* (see below), brings to the table a form of logic (reason), faithfulness, authenticity, and existential seriousness worthy of our attention and respect?

On many levels Anselm's celebrated formulation—*fides quaerens intellectum* or "faith seeking understanding"—is inscrutable to most scientists. For Anselm, faith is a precursor necessary for full understanding. To simplify, let us say that in matters of a theological nature reason is not sufficient. But notice that the sphere of knowledge is knowledge of God, and that makes all the difference. Faith leads the way not by leaving reason behind but by stretching it. Jeffrey Pugh's insight into Anselm's "faith seeking understanding" is helpful: "For Anselm, the determination of faith establishes the origins as well as the limit of knowledge given by God."[30] Faith, then, determines the origin of what we know about God as it is given by God, and at the same time posits the limits of faith as knowledge of the unknowable. Terry Eagleton takes a different tack by pointing out that a deeper level of understanding requires a loving commitment. In other words, acts of commitment open up a new order of

---

27. John Paul II, *Fides et Ratio*, 56.

28. Shermer, *How We Believe*, 123.

29. Compare Bruce Marshall, "Putting Shadows to Flight: The Trinity, Faith, and Reason," in Paul J. Griffiths and Reinhard Hütter, eds., *Reason and the Reasons of Faith*, (New York: T & T Clark, 2005).

30. Jeffrey C. Pugh, "Fides Quaerens Intellectum—Anslem as Contemporary," *Theology Today* 55 (April 1998), 38.

truth. Under this rubric, faith commits you before a full account of how the way things are is possible. Without this loving commitment reason would never go as far as it could.[31] Eagleton appropriately refers to Pascal: "As Pascal writes, the saints maintain that we must love things before we can know them, presumably because only through our attraction to them can we come to know them fully."[32] Eagleton is quite good at dissecting why "reason does not go all the way down."

It can be said of faith that it goes where reason hesitates to tread, and thus creates an air of speculation. There was a time when theologians spoke openly and positively of speculation. But now the word is tarred with negativity. How many angels can dance on the head of a pin is of course irrelevant, yet speculation about angels continues within contemporary theology. Are angels disembodied spirits, can they assume human form and converse with mortals, are they "poetic symbols of the structures or powers of being" (Tillich)? Regarding angels, John Calvin urges us such moderation as God commands us and to therefore not speculate more highly than is expedient, lest the reader be led away from the simplicity of faith. But Calvin, nevertheless, unable to restrain himself, engages in a lengthy exposition on angels.[33]

Theologians speculate because theology cannot help but be metaphysical. Theologians are drawn to take up a variety of metaphysical questions: What is the nature of the Trinity? How can Christ be both human and divine at the same time? What does it mean to be resurrected? And we are left wondering at what point the haunt of speculation forecloses the plausibility of theology as a truth-seeking discipline. And yet it is the nature of theological inquiry to exceed the normal boundaries of reason and to engage in what Hart calls "the richness of an irreducibility that calls out for a constant energy of addition and deferral, an eruption of analogical additions proportionate to and determined by its intensity."[34]

Individual scientists may or may not profess a faith. When they do it is usually privately, and nearly all are skeptical of the argument that faith is a faculty necessary or even helpful in the quest for authentic knowledge. For those scientists who profess to be theists, faith is operative when

---

31. Eagleton, *Reason, Faith, and Revolution*, 119–20.

32. Ibid., 120.

33. Angelology is not dead. Besides the pop versions of angelology, serious theological attention is still being paid to angelology. See articles in *Theology Today*, October 1994.

34. Hart, *The Beauty of the Infinite*, 304.

matters turn theological. Such is the road taken by Owen Gingerich, Professor emeritus of Astronomy and the History of Science at Harvard University. Concluding a lecture on "Dare a Scientist Believe in Design?" Gingerich humbly states, "And I think my belief makes me no less of a scientist."[35] Though to be honest, Gingerich has done a little parsing. When wearing his scientific hat, he attempts to confine empiricism to a "neutral way of explaining things." His faith—Amish in the Anabaptist tradition—comes into play when science becomes metaphysical. Metaphysics, he reminds us, is a term that literally means "beyond physics." The beyond is not whether the structure of the universe is purposeful, for that can be defended empirically, but whether a designing mind and a designer's hand is empirically defensible and necessary. For Gingerich, faith in a God of purpose and design is not a ticket to self-delusion, but he does leave us hanging on the question of whether faith makes him a better scientist rather than "no less of a scientist."

The rapprochement between theology and science has given rise to various arguments intended to overturn the presumption that faith and reason are opposed because one is subjective and the other is objective. For the most part I have no difficulty with such arguments, for they are necessary to dispel harmful and distorted caricatures of both science and theology. (A primary text is van Huyssteen's *The Shape of Rationality*.) It seems, though, that no matter how persuasive these arguments are they always fall short of overcoming a history of associating religion with subjectivity and identifying science with objectivity. Confusion reigns first by mistaking theology for religion and second by associating subjectivity with irrationality. By all accounts, religious experiences are personal, and even a little arbitrary, and in this regard are subjective. But as religious experience is brought to expression, given theological substance, then joined with the voices of Christians in every place and time, the personal-subjective character of religion gives way to the ecumenical character of theology. The NR has done yeoman work to show that theology is not as subjective as normally presumed, and science is not as objective as one might first think. Theologians find themselves in the bind of claiming for theology an objectivity that is free from personal prejudices and arbitrariness, but they know at the same time their truth-claims do not meet the other aspect of objectivity, namely, that the same conclusion can be arrived at and confirmed by anyone under the same conditions.

35. Gingerich, *God's Universe*, 76.

When theologians and scientists begin with the same information, concurrence is a reasonable expectation. But data or information is only the starting point. What theologians do with that information, such as explore its theological implications, is exactly what makes scientists feel uncomfortable.

Trying to *reconcile* faith and reason increases the burden of expectation. Why not just ask what faith adds to reason or what reason adds to faith? The latter can be simply answered in the words of John Paul II: "the truth conferred by revelation is a truth to be understood in the light of reason."[36] Theologians have always known that reason adds something to theologizing and have never doubted that they are being rational. Scientists, on the other hand, are content to practice empiricism without faith because they do not see how faith makes their science any better. The sticky wicket begins with clarifying what faith adds to the reasoning process. We can begin by asking, what is the epistemological value of faith when theologians inquire into the nature of reality? Notice that the question is not about inquiring into "a saving faith" (that faith required to be saved), or faith that enables the believer to understand "what no eye has seen, nor ear heard" (1 Cor 2:9). The issue is the epistemic value of faith exercised by theologians in conjunction with reason in order to achieve a better understanding of the nature of the universe.

Faith is not a separate faculty tucked away some place in the brain. Nor is it a methodological procedure such as the historical-critical method. But sticking with Anselm, faith partners with reason in order go deeper, especially in regard to all things mysterious. In contrast to empiricism, the epistemological value of faith is to remain still and ponder rather than to continually move on to the next thing. More so, faith is a contemplating in the presence of God. When theologians speak of a thicker, fuller explanation, it is in opposition to an epistemology that deconstructs reality to its barest fundamentals. Faith is not about proving supernatural explanations in order to convince the skeptical, but neither is it satisfied with naturalistic explanations of equations, formulas, and confirmable conclusions. Theologians seldom think of themselves as explaining much of anything since explaining implies closure. They do think of themselves as engaged in a continual process of interpreting, elucidating, and understanding because the universe is mysterious, ineffable, and indefinable.

---

36. John Paul II, *Fides et Ratio*, 48.

The Real that Really Matters

We have reached a historical juncture when theology feels the full force of not being sufficiently ontological or grounded in the empirical real. In short, theology is thought to be in trouble if it cannot make ontological truth claims. Such claims are necessary if theology expects to be to taken seriously as a public truth.[37] Ontological truth-claims are considered crucial in order to keep theology from falling into the abyss of speculation and the irrelevancy of internalism. Swimming against that stream, I would like to suggest that ontological claims are not as important as the NR believes. Ontological claims are by no means incidental but they are only "minimally" important in regard to the integrity of theology. All of this will be clarified as I develop the importance of word *truth* for a theology that is committed to knowing the true nature of reality.

The real does really matter, but not for the usual reasons. First, we need to clarify what is meant by ontological truth-claims and why they are important to Christian theology. The turn to reality has a history we should keep in mind. The underlying premise of natural theology is the conviction that the universe reveals the nature of God because it is an incarnation of the divine, and because it can be established by reason. During the centuries when science was coming into its own, Christians were motivated by a genuine fascination with doing science—conducting experiments, closely observing nature, collecting facts, charting the course of celestial bodies, contemplating the design of the cosmos, measuring the world, testing hypotheses, and developing theories. Both cosmos and nature were the object of study for the love of it, and for reading the hand of God. These were the naturalist-savant-gentlemen scientists[38] whose names are familiar to us: Kepler, Galileo, Boyle, Newton, Mendel, and Agassiz. But when we turn to Darwin, Einstein, Heisenberg, and Thomas Kuhn, science begins to look very different. The default assumption that revelation and reason could advance the knowledge of God begins to falter.

The advent of the Gifford Lectures in 1890, dedicated to "a lively and perpetual debate on science and 'all questions about man's conception of God or the Infinite,'" is the embodiment of how this discourse would play

---

37. See Peacocke, *Evolution: The Disguised Friend of Faith?*, 187.

38. See Steven Shapin, *A Social History of Truth: Civility and Science in Seventeenth-Century England* (Chicago: University of Chicago Press, 1994). Shapin pays special attention to Robert Boyle as illustrative of the of the gentleman scientist.

out over the next century.[39] Larry Witham's book, *The Measure of God: Our Century-Long Struggle to Reconcile Science and Religion (The Story of the Gifford Lectures)*, displays not only a diversity of approaches, but also a variety of disciplines, including anthropology, psychology, physics, and sociology. Witham rightly notes that from the 1920s through the 1960s theology was occupied with two movements that showered their influence across Europe and, later, North America; namely, existentialism and neo-orthodoxy.[40] If any generalization applies, it is the observation that these notable great minds of the Gifford lectures chose to deal with generalities rather than relating specific theological doctrines with specific scientific details. Their engagement with science is with a metaphysical reality, a debate about abstractions, and at times, but not always, an apologetic for God. Heisenberg's Gifford Lecture in 1955, published as *Physics and Philosophy*, and a very different kind of study by the Benedictine priest and physicist Stanley Jaki, *The Road of Science and the Ways to God*, exemplify a failure to distinguish between a natural theology and a Christian natural theology. When Stanley Hauerwas initiated his Gifford Lectures in 2000-2001, he did not make that mistake, for he practically pits neo-orthodoxy over against existentialism by saying, "Yet the heart of the argument I develop in these lectures is that natural theology divorced from the full doctrine of God cannot help but distort the character of God and, accordingly, of the world in which we find ourselves."[41]

By focusing on rapprochement there is a real possibility of forgetting that science was not the paramount issue for modern theology. During different periods the historical-critical method, historicism, biblical theology, existentialism, hermeneutics, the turn to linguistics, liberation theology, and feminism all took center stage. Alongside the various "turns" in theology, the turn to experience is paramount. In 1975 the Roman Catholic theologian David Tracy writes that "a widely accepted dictum of contemporary theological thought holds that all theological statements involve an existential dimension, indeed a dimension which includes a claim to universal existential relevance."[42] In order to invoke their own principle of verification, theologians looked to the religious dimension of our common experience, such as Tracy's "boundary situations" and Peter Berger's "signals of transcendence." H. Paul Santmire

39. Quoted in Witham, *The Measure of God*, 1.
40. Ibid., 200–201.
41. Hauerwas, *With the Grain*, 15.
42. Tracy, *Blessed Rage for Order* (Minneapolis: Seabury, 1975), 47.

makes an even broader judgment that during the Reformation (namely Luther), and built into Reformation theology, is a preference for *hearing* over *seeing*, and so theological discourse about the nature we see was marginalized by the word we hear. "Many of Luther's successors," Santmire concludes, "had nothing, or next to nothing, to say about nature."[43]

Apart from the New Rapprochement's engagement with physical science, theology chose to engage science at the level of existential reality. That is, theology's ontological claims essentially ignore the science of scientific journals. When, for instance, are they quoted or referred to in the normal course of theologizing? The turn to reality, such as it was and is, stems from a "reality" of theology's own choosing. It is the reality of ultimate questions and ultimate answers. It is an embrace of empiricism in the form of methodological foreplay for the sake of credibility. The inclusion of ecological issues and moral issues arising from the biological-genetic revolution is genuine enough, but it still stands on the periphery. Don't misjudge what I am saying. In any recent era, the nature of universe counts for something. Nevertheless and speaking generally, what theology chooses is an acquaintance with science rather than a critical interrogation of empirical science.

Now, to be specific. Stanley Hauerwas is invited to give the 2000-2001 Gifford Lectures and chooses to recharge natural theology by examining William James, Reinhold Niebuhr, and Karl Barth. He goes about developing a natural theology by mounting an apologia for the centrality of the cross and resurrection of Jesus Christ, and by giving an account of the moral life as a true understanding of the way things are.[44] As his argument unfolds it becomes evident that for Hauerwas natural theology explicates "the way the world is," and "the way things are."[45] And in his estimation no one does this better than Karl Barth. And while the case can be made, as Hauerwas does, that this approach is in keeping with Lord Gifford's interpretation of natural theology in "the widest sense of that term," it is an interpretation and approach that is quite a distance from

---

43. See Santmire, "A Reformation Theology of Nature Transfigured," *Theology Today* 61 (January 2005), 519. A close reading of Luther, as Santmire conducts, finds his views about nature to be ambiguous and overpowered by a theology of the word.

44. Hauerwas, *With the Grain*, 17-18. I agree with Gabriel Fackre in his assessment that Hauerwas is misreading Niebuhr, and to read him correctly would place him at the center of a realism much needed for our times. See Fackre, "Was Reinhold Niebuhr a Christian?," *First Things*, October 2002, www.firstthingscom/article/2002/10/was-reinhold-niebuhr-a-christian.

45. Hauerwas, *With the Grain*, 21.

a natural theology dependent on the premise that to know something of God's creation as it truly is, is to know God as God truly is. Barth's approach is to see ultimate reality through the eyes of revelation, as opposed to understanding nature to be a legitimate form of revelation. This rather tired argument about natural revelation versus special revelation gets us nowhere insofar as we stick to the old paradigm of simply trying to read off nature some confirmation of the biblical witness or the Trinity. Barth is absolutely correct in his theological logic. Ultimate truth is always a gift of God. At the same time, this logic dampens our capacity to truly see the universe for what it is; namely, something reflective of its Creator. And to the degree that revelation is a dislocating truth—a truth we don't want to hear and a truth we cannot imagine (see below)—the universe in all its immensity and complexity is immensely disconcerting in its own way. Hauerwas is entitled to his understanding of natural theology in terms of Christian ethics, but we should be aware that it does little to encourage Christians to love science for what it teaches us about the universe, or to heed Calvin's admonition to see the physical universe as a school where Christians go to be instructed.

Ronald Thiemann, who agrees with George Lindbeck and quotes him, argues that "'Christian ontological truth-claims' are made 'in the activities of adoration, proclamation, obedience, promise-hearing, and promise-keeping which shape individuals and communities into conformity with the mind of Christ.'"[46] The move here is to grant to certain linguistic practices with performative effect the status of "ontological." These are essentially illocutionary acts that result in an observable behavior, behavior that demarcates what it means to be Christian. Obeying, singing, praying, hoping, celebrating (the Lord's Supper), and sanctifying (marriage) are ontological to the extent that words are used to point to some happening, and thereby meet the criteria of verification. Similar to the way Hauerwas reformulates natural theology, Thiemann and Lindbeck are content with an existential ontology, that is, a reality of Christian conduct and practice (and certainly for Hauerwas practices that are countercultural) that has little to do with looking through a microscope or painstakingly observing an ant colony.

The pattern I discern is that theologians will refer to the *real* when they say they are inquiring into the *real* meaning of this or that. The use of "real" is meant to carry the weight of "ontological," but it is limited

---

46. Thiemann, *Revelation and Theology*, 94.

to referencing the ontologically real in the sense of *ultimate* meaning or purpose. The implication is that Christian theologians are the only ones who know the way things actually are. I am not disputing theology's right to claim this as its province. What bothers me is the way science is shuffled aside as if knowing the real universe of atoms and molecules, deep space and galaxies is of inconsequential importance.

If theology is to share ontological truth-claims with science, those claims will need to be about the physical universe. Here the tethering of words to reality is distinct from using words to express your love of the universe. While words of endearment may effect a new reality—someone who is called brother may begin at that moment to feel a special kinship—they are not describing a causal relationship. Philosopher John Searle differentiates between "features of the world that are *intrinsic*, in the sense that they exist independent of any observer, and those features that are *observer relative*, in the sense that they only exist relative to some outside observer or user."[47] If all observers cease to exist, the world will still contain mass, gravitational attraction, and molecules. Because of the way evidence is gathered, we are confident the periodic table conveys the truth about chemical elements arranged according to their atomic number; and even though this is an arbitrary organizational decision, it is dependent on, and not independent of, the intrinsic character of the world. While the choice to understand chemical elements according to their atomic structure is observer relative, the actual structure is not. Once this differentiation is acknowledged, a distinction can be made between truths meant to explicate intrinsic qualities of the physical universe, and truths that have nothing to do with the former but everything to do with how words are put together.

So, are ontological truth-claims just about the intrinsic features of the physical universe or do they include claims about the meaning of those very same features? A narrowly defined empiricism is only interested in discovering the fundamental causal relationship between entities with definable properties. A scientist of this ilk only asks for the most elegant equation or the most direct explanation (Occam's razor). At this level the conversation between theology and science has no place to go except to inform theologians who believe good theology needs to be cognizant of good science. But what happens when the ontological spreads out to include our evolutionary history and becomes a prominent factor

---

47. Searle, *The Rediscovery of the Mind* (Cambridge, MA: MIT Press, 1992), xiii.

in how we *understand* ourselves (the human condition), the *significance* of a particular gene for a particular disease and the ethical *implications* that ensue, the *value* we place on genetic engineering, or the *distinction* between a very specific arrangements of cells and what we call life? Significant questions about meaning, motivation, and value can be both observer relative and attached to the intrinsic features of the physical world. Good science and good theology, it would seem, not only find mutual exchange compelling, but also necessary.

Every language-in-use draws our attention to certain aspects of the world; or to phrase it differently, any description of reality requires a particular way of lighting it up, of making some of its features more "visible" than others.[48] Disciplines have their own technical languages because they light up particular aspects of reality using a particular language. The question arises, then, *what* aspect of reality does theological language light up and *what* is particular about its language? Several traditional answers come to mind concerning the "what": the goodness of creation, the providential character of time (including history), our sinful (self-destructive) behavior, the power of love, and the experience of the holy. We have yet to discuss the language particular to theology (next section) but we can suggest that it is language that pays attention to questions that cannot be settled empirically, and to the potency of language to form *a universe of truth*. Jacques Ellul writes eloquently of the latter: "I am certain that since the beginning, human beings have felt a pressing need to frame for themselves something different from the verifiable universe, and we have formed it through language. This universe is what we call truth."[49]

The physical real, then, is vitally important for theology because the physical universe is God's creation. As humans, we look to the starry skies and unravel the structure of DNA because we cannot help but do otherwise. We are insatiably curious and profoundly inquisitive, and we find ourselves inexplicably drawn to ponder the hand of the One who could have made us this way. In a typical David Bentley Hart flourish, he writes of how theologians respond to what God has created: "God's speech in creation does not, then, invite a speculative nisus toward silence—the silence of pure knowledge or of absolute saying—but doxology, an overabundance of words, hymnody, prayer, and then, within this

---

48. Steven Pinker, *The Stuff of Thought: Language as a Window into Human Nature* (New York: Viking, 2007), 131–33.

49. Ellul, *The Humiliation of the Word*, 22.

discipline of gratitude and liturgy, a speculative discourse obedient to the gratuity of existence . . . or a contemplative silence whose secret is not poverty but plentitude."[50] Lastly, we come to what truly sets theology apart. Whether science concurs or not, theology proceeds on the basis that the physical universe signifies something, and that something is available most uniquely by way of theological interpretation, and this reading or redescription of reality is not possible without reference to text, tradition, faith, and revelation.

Word Truth

Stated overly simplistically, but nevertheless accurately, theologizing is what one does with words in the presence of God, and this more than anything else sets theology apart from science. On the surface, theologians write a lot of words. They pile words upon words. Every well-known theologian from Augustine to Barth to Schillebeeckx wrote volume after volume. What gives them the confidence to rely so heavily on words is the conviction that words themselves can generate meaning, and that there is such a thing as theological meaning that penetrates to the truth of the matter. This chapter began with describing the distinctiveness of theology as that use of language requiring a level of ownership (existential seriousness) and communal participation not found in other disciplines. Broadly speaking, theology is that peculiar use of words that comes from standing in the presence of God and listening to what God speaks (in text, tradition, creed, witness) in order to speak a living word.

In *The Humiliation of the Word* (1985), Jacques Ellul makes two astute observations. The first is his argument that the distinctive value of language lies in *truth*: to ask questions and attempt to answer them as only words can. Ellul scarcely needs to remind us—but maybe he does—that we derive meaning and understanding from language, and that unlike the empirical or literal word, "the blessed uncertainty of language is the source of all its richness because it allows us to go beyond the reality of our lives to enter another universe."[51] Second, Ellul believes that in a

---

50. Hart, *The Beauty of the Infinite*, 298. Hauerwas says as much: "At best, theology is but a series of reminders to help Christians pray faithfully" (*With the Grain*, 10).

51. Ellul, *The Humiliation of the Word*, 22. Literary critic George Steiner matches Ellul in many ways by writing effusively of a transformative cosmos of discourse: "It is within the language system alone that we possess liberties of construction and of deconstruction, of remembrance and of futurity, so boundless, so dynamic, so proper

post-Enlightenment culture we have misidentified truth with *reality* and made reality—its description, explanation, and image—the source of all truth. Thus, Ellul directs our attention to a distinction between truth and reality, and the predominance of reality over truth. At odds with many postmodern philosophers, Ellul refuses to join the rush to make every question about truth a question about reality and how it can be represented or explained accurately. The humiliation of the word—the word that is so central to doing theology—is what we should expect of a culture skeptical of the power of words to access truth, or a truth that is so much more than asking which description of reality is the best.

How can humans know God if not through words? For Judaism, Christianity, and Islam the word is primary. They share an understanding of a creation story where God creates human beings and endows this creature, and this creature alone, with the capacity to converse with God using the language of words. In many and diverse ways all creation sings the glory of God, but only humans are addressed by God and thereby blessed as bearing the image of their Creator. From here arises a distinctive understanding of God who speaks and is heard, of speaking in the name of God and being deputized to speak on behalf of God,[52] and of inscription. Each of the three religions are replete with references to word power, the power of the word to bring life out of death, to create where there was nothing, to empower and sustain the human spirit with hope when hope is not to be found. A classic example in the Hebrew tradition is Psalm 33.

> By the word of the Lord the heavens were made,
> and all their host by the breath of his mouth (v. 6).
> Yahweh spoke, and it came to be; Yahweh commanded, and it stood forth (v. 9).

The Christian faith, though, has a unique tradition flowing from the belief in the Word made flesh (John 1:14). No only is this a revelation that one can witness to, as John reports ("John bore witness to him"), but it is an entire theology, an incarnation theology, where Christ is fully human

---

to the evident uniqueness of human thought and imaging that, in comparison, external reality, whatever that might or might not be, is little more than brute intractability and deprivation" (*Real Presences*, 97). Steiner, however, would not have us break the covenant of trust between discourse and world since it is that tradition of discourse that provides access to intelligibility and coherence (narrative) (92–93).

52. See Wolterstorff, who is very lucid on this point, *Divine Discourse*, 45–51. Also, see Thiemann's discussion of revelation in *Revelation and Theology*, 94–96.

in a world that will be redeemed as well. It is not only the physicality of the world that bears witness to its Creator, for when the Word became incarnate in Jesus Christ, words and testimony become revelatory.

My principal arguments are twofold. First, theology is preeminently about word truth. Theologians use words to get at truth, and that truth is the ultimate meaning of life, the universe, and the nature of God. Second, there is no one model of language that is entirely appropriate for theology. Even though there is an inner logic peculiar to theology, theology is not wedded to one linguistic form. Even if theology is a peculiar language or a peculiar way to language reality, no single model of truth can claim theology's heart. And the reason is straightforward. Theologians are confronted by a diversity of media through which Yahweh speaks and acts: history, narrative, wisdom, lament, proverb, parable, epistle, biography, autobiography, vision, and created universe. Perhaps each medium deserves its own criteria of truthfulness: propositional, historical, confessional, narrative, mystical, metaphysical, authentic-to-life, and fact-assertive. Each is an attempt to connect with a dimension of reality, and in each instance, whether the intent is to be realistic or autobiographically revealing, the rendering is a theological one.

In *Words with Power*, Northrop Frye points to the almost obvious, "It soon becomes clear that language is a means of intensifying consciousness."[53] But language does not merely bring-to-expression; it makes something more of that experience. In acquiring a language a child first learns how to name things—assigning the right words to physical realities and inner emotions. During this process of intensifying consciousness, children begin to bring-to-expression and manipulate words in order to organize their world. Does the mind impose order on the world or does the world impose order on the mind? It would seem, some of both. Language prepares us to act on the world, and this includes gathering information about the physical world, organizing our thoughts, and getting in touch with our beliefs, desires, and intentions. The very young child at play may be hardly aware of either the physical world or the state of its mind, for that will come later as the brain develops and the mind clarifies a stream of consciousness. What comes last is learning how to use language to breach the world of meaning and to think abstractly and reflectively.

---

53. Northrop Frye, *Words with Power: Being a Second Study of the Bible and Literature* (San Diego: Harcourt Brace Jovanovich, 1990), 28.

This very brief and inadequate outline of language development is meant to track the three classic ideal types of language theory: representing, expressing, and performing. Into this mix is also the language of love: the use of words, whether spoken or signed to form and sustain relationships. This use of language is the stronghold of religion. But in the juxtaposition of theology and science, the overriding concern is the relationship of language to world. Correspondence theories of truth rely on an establishable correlation between an object (Kant's thing-in-itself) and its signification. Correspondence or representation language does not let go of its ontological reference and thus strives to eliminate ambiguity and uncertainty. The ontological is preserved because there is something independent of the mind that has intrinsic meaning in itself. In the *The Stuff of Thought*, Steven Pinker reminds us that in the case of snow and words for snow, "not only did the snow come first, but when people change their attention to snow, they change their words as a result."[54] Critical realists argue that language explicates and expands signification but does not create the source of that signification. We are all realists to some degree, and our everyday use of language includes words, signs, and grammar to portray and communicate how things are in the world. Practically and ultimately we use language to get what we want.[55]

Few would dispute the fundamental difference between the use of language by empiricists and theologians. Scientists and theologians do use language in much the same way when writing an article for a professional journal in which they are trying to convince the reader of something. Nevertheless, we can say that for the scientist language is direct and minimal, and it is almost always reductive in the sense of saying no more than is required to get at a fundamental truth. For theologians language is often indirect and boundless, and is almost always expansive in the sense there is always something more to say in order to get at some deeper understanding. If scientists believe there is a definitive solution, a conclusion that is anything but arbitrary, there comes a point when words

---

54. Pinker, *The Stuff of Thought*, 127.

55. The corollary is that we use language to "know everything" and that is the intent of the serpent's temptation to take and eat and be like God, "knowing good and evil" (Gen 3:5); "good and evil" being a Hebraic formula referring to "all things." And to follow through with this line of thought—"to know everything" is paramount "to getting everything we want." In its technological manifestation, science ferments the quest to know all things so that we can control all things, and therefore get everything we want. To see how this plays how in our expectations for the future, see Coleman, *Eden's Garden*, ch. 6 ("Science as the New Occasion for Sin: When Humans Overreach").

(and equations) can say everything that needs to be said (at least for the foreseeable future). But when it comes to understanding the Creator of all things, the Creator who exists beyond and before the universe, there will never be enough words. One is committed to pile words upon words.

In *The Subtler Language*, Earl Wasserman writes, "language, then, flies simultaneously in two directions, centrifugally towards its references and centripetally toward its own organizational form as language."[56] The spectrum of language, then, rests on these two functions. "At one end is the customary discourse, in which the reference function of language predominates, and the syntactical function is minimal; its purpose is to direct us as modestly as possible to something outside itself. At the other end is poetry, in which reference values are assimilated into the constitutive act of language; its primary purpose is to trap us in itself as independent reality."[57] The language of theology is neither empirical nor is it poetry. A great deal of theology, influenced by postmodern poetics and language theory, wants to place truth nearer to poetry than to universal objectivity. It finds considerable sympathy with the conclusion that since the universe does not have a necessary or transparent meaning, and since empiricism owes too much to the naiveté that reductionism can explain reality, theology should remember that it is not served well by the hubris of empirical rationality.

If theologians commit themselves to a language like no other, then it becomes necessary for them to be self-conscious and critical about the word truths they wield. The suggestive title of a book of essays by Walter Brueggemann, *The Word that Redescribes the World*, invites the question: Which "word"? Brueggemann has persisted in calling out attention to a text (word) that offers "a different narrative account of reality that is in profound contrast to the dominant account of reality into which we are all summarily inducted."[58] Here we are in Ellul's universe where we are obligated to ask questions and attempt to answer them as only words can do. We also enter the world of Scripture and a Hebrew understanding of language where the word (text) has the power to transform.

A synthesis of Anthony Thiselton, Paul Ricoeur, and John Searle gives us this dichotomy between word and world: words that are matched to the world (*words-to-world*) and words meant to get the world to match

---

56. Wasserman, *The Subtler Language*, 6.
57. Ibid., 7.
58. Brueggemann, *The Word that Redescribes the World*, 95.

the words (*world-to-words*).[59] The context of words-to-world is that of explaining, as in explaining causal connections, while the context of world-to-word functions in a context of transformation and promise. At every turn in Scripture one is confronted by transforming texts; words spoken and enacted so that you pack up your belongings and leave your homeland of Ur (Abraham and Sarah), so that sins are forgiven (Matt 9:21), so that the sick are healed, lepers cleansed, and the dead raised (Matt 10:8), so that you might believe (John 20:30). These are words that send, invite, commission, promise, empower. Thiselton and Ricoeur also draw this comparison: the language of description and explanation "stifles the passion for the possible by confining us within the limits of the present and by closing our imagination to the future."[60] For science, the future is always about a new discovery. For theology the eschatological future—forcefully present in both the Old and New Testaments—impinges on the present by way of promise interwoven with themes of covenant and eschatology, creating a tension between what "is" and what "ought to be."[61] Absent this tension everything falls flat, everything thins out, everything collapses into the present moment.

We can affirm the importance of a theology informed by the best science without committing theology to a referential view of language, or to the demands for empirical verification. And yet theology is indebted to science for showing it the raw physicality of the universe, especially when such a reality unsettles and challenges theological normalcy. Theology is necessarily caught in the time-honored question of where to locate truth. The literary critic James Wood quotes George Eliot that "art is the nearest thing to life: it is a mode of amplifying experience and extending our contact with our fellow men beyond the bounds of our personal lot."[62] Following Wood's lead, if art is the nearest thing to life, what is the nearest thing to truth? The distinction between life and truth returns us to the crucial distinction between religion and theology. Even though we might say that religion is about truth in life, theology is inescapably about truth itself.

Unlike the scientist, the theologian answers to an authority (sets of interlocking authorities) that lies beyond the physical evidence. No apology is needed. Because theology operates from a frame of meaning that is

59. Thiselton, *New Horizons,* 294.
60. Thiselton, referring to Ricoeur, ibid., 357.
61. Ibid., 300.
62. Wood, *How Fiction Works* (New York: Farrar, Straus and Giroux, 2008), 241.

not drawn directly or explicitly from the physical universe, and because it concerns itself with ontological categories requiring theological insight, its methodology must be a little bit odd. Given the fact that the universe itself is neither entirely mute nor fully transparent, it will require words that allow us to access a universe inclusive of purpose, design, obligations, and promise in order to understand it rightly.

Methodology Per Se

By common agreement a method is definable, repeatable, and teachable. Empiricism has its own history of coming to terms with a definable methodology.[63] Nevertheless, the doing of science proceeds as if it knows what it is doing methodologically, notwithstanding those who demur.[64] The plain fact that there are competent theologians, century after century, testifies to a teachable theological methodology. Read enough theology, hear enough preaching, be guided by enough tutors, and students learn to think theologically. But have they learned a method? Can theology even claim a definable methodology? Historical criticism, textual criticism, literary criticism, historical studies, and comparative religious studies are all definable, teachable, and operable within established procedures; but doing theology is something else or something more. In the opening discussion I spoke of a number of characteristics: existential seriousness, material development, words to stand by, the faith factor, word truth, a theological logic, a willingness to put yourself in the presence of God. But these too do not constitute a definable, agreed upon, methodology. Even though theologians seem to know what is good theology (we know it when we hear it), compared to science, theology is a methodological fuzz ball. Could it be that theology employs a variety of methodologies, and that is a prima facie reason why it is so frustrating to hold up a definite methodology?

Theology's thorn in the flesh is how to give revelation and faith their due. It should come as no surprise that theology's rapprochement with science has conveniently sidestepped this thorn. An outsider and critic such as Michael Sherman repeats a familiar refrain: "Science and religion

---

63. A technical and historical treatment is Peter Achinstein, ed., *Science Rules: A Historical Introduction to Scientific Methods* (Baltimore: Johns Hopkins Press, 2004).

64. In spite of Steven Weinberg's assertion that "most scientists have very little idea of what the scientific method is" (*Facing Up*, 85), they do learn a teachable methodology.

are, at present, largely separate spheres of knowledge divided by, more than anything else, a difference in methodologies."[65] Theologians do not know how to respond to such a statement because they are still trying to decide if their discipline is a science or merely scientific-like, or whether it has little or much in common with empiricism. Along with others I have noted how theology seems preoccupied with epistemological issues. Unlike science, theology must deal with the collapse of its epistemological girders, otherwise known as its turn away from foundationalism, or those assumptions that guarantee its truth claims. In so far as theology rebuffs a foundational epistemology—the reliance on a set of self-evident, God-revealed truths coupled with its own rules of justification—it complicates and blurs the opportunity to distinguish itself. At times empiricism looks attractive, and at other times it seems inappropriate. Theology's epistemological crisis is only partly a struggle to define its own methodology. The linchpin has always been what to do with revelation and faith.

What if revelation and faith are presumed to be critical for theology? Of course neither revelation nor faith is a methodology, far from it. On the other hand, theology is vacated without either. Revelation and faith have no parallel in the world of empiricism. Revelation and faith posit something given by the Wholly Other. What exactly that something is entangles theology. Empiricism operates on the premise that something is discovered, a connection is drawn, data confirms a hypothesis, an equation satisfies the factors. For science nothing is given that is not already there or constructed by the human mind. There is no Other to reveal or inspire, only the feeling of exhilaration when a problem is solved.

Ronald Thiemann begins where theology needs to begin: "Theology's object differs from the object of every other scientific discipline in that it is 'not a mute fact' but a self-disclosing, self-communicating subject."[66] Dupré elaborates by pointing to "the unique dialectic between the essential receptivity of the religious act with respect to a transcendent revelation and, on the other side, the active role the believer plays in creating symbols, theories, and norms within which he receives that revelation."[67] Within a religious context the knowing subject quiets his or her own ego in order to make space for the Other to disclose and inspire. Expressed theologically, what is known of the divine Subject is known through the inquiring subject, but at the same time what is revealed is

---

65. Shermer, *How We Believe*, 123.
66. Thiemann, *Revelation and Theology*, 37.
67. Dupré, *Religious Mystery and Rational Reflection*, 9.

more than the self. While other cognitive acts bring their object into the focus of self-consciousness, the religious act allows something to be given, and that giving is always in association with the Spirit. In its radical form, as Barth would have it, God's self-revelation is always a free act of God, and always a word that "cannot then be taken into possession as an object of human cognition apart from the God who speaks and the God who is heard."[68] Thus, there can be no Word without the Spirit, for the Spirit prepares the heart for what otherwise cannot be heard.

All of this is standard fare for theologians. But questions abound, especially for the empirical skeptic: If what you say about revelation and faith is true for our salvation, is it also true for knowledge which is not particular to salvation? Is religious inspiration different from other occasions of inspiration when the individual is lifted to a different level of consciousness to do and say extraordinary things? What exactly is being disclosed? Is there even a distinct religious cognitive act? To ease the discomfort this kind of questioning evokes, and in the end to write better theology, a gradual process of rethinking and refining has taken place since the Reformation regarding revelation and faith. Whether as a necessary accommodation to modern language theory or to accommodate science, theology did not stand pat. The trajectory of modern theology is essentially the struggle to find new grounds or justifications (not necessarily a new foundation) for Christians to continue to believe:

- A distinction between the experience of faith and the content of faith.[69]
- A reluctance to identify revelation with an *antecedent* event to which faith is a *subsequent* response.[70]

---

68. Quoted in Hinlicky, *Paths Not Taken*, 55. Karl Barth's radicalization of how Christians should understand revelation is fully developed by Hinlicky, 44–60 and ch. 3.

69. The distinction may not have its origin with Wilhelm Hermann but does come into prominence as Rudolf Bultmann incorporates it from his teacher and makes it basic to his theology. See Wilhelm Hermann, *The Communion of the Christian with God* (Minneapolis: Fortress, 1971), and for Rudolf Bultmann, *Jesus Christ and Mythology* (New York: Charles Scribner's Sons, 1958).

70. Once the distinction is made between revelation as something that happens prior to its reception, and prior to its interpretation by the faith community, then revelation is split between historical event and its contingent interpretation. James Barr's critique of such a view is to say that by attempting to establish the authority of Scripture upon such an antecedent revelation we end up explaining one event by a series of subsequent interpretations, and that leads to an unacceptable level of ambiguity. Barr is hoping we will see the question: "How can the historically conditioned truth of one generation be the basis for that of another generation?" See James Barr, *Bible in the*

- A shifting of the authority of Scripture from the written text to the Spirit who speaks through the text. Shifting may be too strong of a description since Reformation theology consistently reacted negatively to any identification of human words with the very word of God and preferred to think of divine inspiration as occurring when the same Spirit who was present to the one who wrote is present to the one who reads (or hears or proclaims).

- A view that asserts "Christianity is not a message which has to be believed, but an experience of faith that becomes a message."[71]

Schillebeeckx's protestation that revelation is not a message but "an experience that becomes a message" represents a diversity of arguments by a number of theologians who seek a creative approach to a host of long-standing difficulties associated with propositional revelation and its companion, verbal inspiration. Pivotal to this discussion of revelation is Karl Barth's position that since Jesus Christ is the only objective self-manifestation of God, all other forms of divine discourse, such as the word of God preached and the word of God written, are derivative and indirect.[72] The implication of Barth's uncoupling of revelation from written text opens several avenues of understanding. "Finding" the historical Jesus loses its urgency since the texts themselves are a witness to Jesus Christ without requiring a uniformity of interpretation.[73] The second implication of shifting the focus from the content of revelation to the experience of revelation is to alter how we understand revelation itself. In his inquiry into Barth's theology, George Hunsinger writes, "The God who is wholly other and therefore wholly incomprehensible posits, in the

---

Modern World (New York: Harper & Row, 1973), 120–23. Louis Dupré gives this question considerable attention in *Religious Mystery and Rational Reflection*, 108ff.

71. See Edward Schillebeeckx, *Interim Report on the Books of Jesus and Christ* (New York: Crossroad, 1981), 12. Schillebeeckx takes care to clear up any misunderstanding here. Experience here is not itself revelation, but the self-revelation of God *through* experience. Since it is quite possible for someone to be wrong about "an experience of God," and since all experience contains elements of interpretation both in the experiencing itself and its subsequent reflection, the cognitive dimension of revelation belongs to, and is defined by, the community of faith (the church).

72. Cf. Thiemann, who takes issue with Barth when he argues that "there can be no linguistic or logical connection between God's revelation and human language" (*Revelation and Theology*, 95).

73. See Beverly Roberts Gaventa and Richard B. Hays, eds., *Seeking the Identity of Jesus* (Grand Rapids: Eerdmans, 2008), where a fresh accent is placed on the identity of Jesus as revealed in the continuing re-presentation of Jesus and in the continuity of the church's testimony to Jesus; and the considerably earlier but ground-breaking work of Ernst Käsemann, *New Testament Questions of Today* (Minneapolis: Fortress, 1969).

event of self-revelation, an incomprehensible analogical relation between human word and divine referent."[74] In other words, a revelatory "event" of God is a self-revealing that cannot be anything less than disruptive of everything that is human. The inescapable relationship between two ontologically distinct beings—God the Creator and human beings the creature—requires it. By definition (theological logic demands it), revelation questions us in a way that only God can question us, and thus it is theologically sound to say that revelation is less a transfer of information or the disclosure of a message and more an experience that causes us to reexamine everything we thought we knew about God and ourselves. Revelation, then, is not a linguistic or conceptual event, but a "disruptive happening" where nothing is the same afterwards, where "everything has a special luminosity."[75]

Revelation is foremost an act of revealing or disclosing as it impinges upon the knowing subject. But something, nevertheless, is revealed. Nicholas Wolterstorff, retired Professor of Philosophical Theology at Yale University and scheduled Gifford Lecturer at St. Andrew's University, introduces a number of distinctions meant to open up "a whole new way of thinking about God speaking."[76] He begins with the distinction made by J. L. Austin between *locutionary acts* of ordinary acts of speaking and writing, and *illocutionary acts* performed by way of locutionary acts, such as asking, asserting, commanding, promising, and so forth. Wolterstorff in turn highlights the illocutionary act of deputizing when someone is authorized to speak on behalf of someone else. In the Old Testament, prophets are regularly deputized to speak in the name of God by virtue of having been authorized to speak for God. The locus classicus is Deuteronomy 16, when Moses is deputized: "and I will put my words in his mouth and he shall speak to them all that I command him." Likewise in the New Testament, a divine commissioning takes place when the disciples are sent into the world to baptize and teach "all that I have commanded" (Matt 28:16ff.). On the illocutionary side of the total speech act, what matters most is that someone is authorized, someone is sent,

---

74. Hunsinger, *Disruptive Grace*, 220.

75. In Thomas Keneally's *Three Cheers for the Paraclete*, a young nun is being examined for alleged heresy. She is asked bluntly, "Have you *seen* God?" Discovering a sudden resolve, she replies: "One knows by the results. Nothing is the same afterwards. Everything has a special luminosity. You are able to see, well, *existence* shining in things." Quoted in Rowan Williams, *Christ on Trial* (Grand Rapids: Eerdmans, 2000), 91.

76. Wolterstorff, *Divine Discourse*, 13.

and some text is being set aside (canonized). Grace must first disrupt the messenger before he or she is authorized to disrupt others with a message they did not expect to hear, and in most cases, did not want to hear.

As Wolterstorff points out, shifting the emphasis away from locutionary acts—what someone actually said—does not relieve the interpreter of deciding whether a particular locutionary acts is literal or metaphorical, and so forth. "It may well be the case," Wolterstorff cautions, "that a great deal of God's discourse is accomplished by way of deputation and appropriation, [but] it can't all be like that. At some point God must Godself do things which generate God's acts of discourse."[77] Dupré and Hunsinger also think it is necessary to affirm the adequation of words.[78] The straightforward approach is to say God provided the words, syntax, metaphors, narratives, and so forth, that were sufficient to convey the meaning God desired; nevertheless, "straightforward" is encumbered with many difficulties all of which have to do with how language is shaped by culture and history. The way a sentence frames a linguistic "event" will affect the way the listener will construe it. While calling, sending, and promising are very much what revelation accomplishes, communication between Being and being includes the transfer of particulars. Isaiah 6:1–9 is often held up as "pure" call, but it quickly becomes specific ("in the days of Ahaz"), and the word "the Lord has sent" is made explicit ("against Jacob and upon Israel"). Disturbed by Yahweh, Jonah, who does not want to go to Nineveh, is commissioned to go to Nineveh and no other place; and Jonah, who does not want to bring a message of grace to the idol-worshipping Ninevites, is not authorized to speak his own message of divine retribution.

Again the contrast with an empirical way of coming to know is striking. The difference does not rest with some kind of "exception clause" for theology. For the most part theology has come to terms with the historicization and contextualization of all truth. Dupré says what is now almost commonplace. "First, revelation can be received only in and through human experience." Furthermore, "all experience contains elements of interpretation, not only in the subsequent reflection but already in the experiencing act itself."[79] Thus, revelation and faith do not exempt

---

77. Ibid., 116–17.

78. Hunsinger, *Disruptive Grace*, ch. 9; Dupré, *Religious Mystery and Rational Reflection*, 107–17.

79. *Religious Mystery and Rational Reflection*, 109; here Dupré is following Edward Schillebeeckx's *Interim Report on the Books of Jesus and Christ*.

the knowing subject from the rule of experience and interpretation, the constraints of culture and language. Thiemann retorts, "Theology remains rational as long as it constructs a vigorous disciplined method appropriate to the nature of that object."[80] So, the difference must rest some place else.

Remembering the historic turn to the knowing self as someone who constructs truth and does so objectively, theology holds on to a countertradition where the knowing self is always suspect, not so much because of the intrusion of subjectivity but rather for the fact of original sin.[81] If the subject as knower-constructor is the legacy of the Enlightenment, Christian theology has stood its ground and refuses to lift its suspicion of all things rational. Speaking to that theological tradition, Augustine took note that when he looked within himself to find God, he indeed found God, but intolerably "against" himself. Even though Augustine shifts the focus from the field of objects to know thyself, he does so with a new twist. This turn to the self is not meant to light up a dichotomy between the subjectivity of faith and the objectivity of reason. Rather, Augustine's language of inwardness calls attention to belief that authentic knowledge is never divorced from the knowing of oneself, and the knowing of oneself is always a perilous journey because of sin.

For an approach so devoted to word truth, theology looks like it would easily fall into subjectivism, confusing the word of God with human thoughts. The possibility is real and distresses scientists. But remember that for Augustine sin is more about the will and the possibility of not doing the good I intend, even when I desire to do what is right.[82] In the tradition of Socrates, Plato, and Aristotle, reason is the most excellent faculty, and all human imperfection and deficiency is correctable by education or re-education. Reason is independently motivating; it has its own ends and it inclines those who possess it toward them. By contrast,

---

80. Thiemann, *Revelation and Theology*, 37.

81. For a postmodern defense of original sin, see Richard J. Coleman, "Saving Original Sin from the Secularists." *Theology Today* 70 (January 2014) 374-406.

82. Ibid. According to MacIntyre, prior to Augustine there is no vocabulary for any conception of the will. He writes, "For both Plato and Aristotle reason is independently motivating; it has its own ends and it inclines those who possess it toward them, even if it is also necessary that the higher desires be educated into rationality and that the bodily appetites be subordinated to it." For Augustine, MacIntyre concludes, "the human will is then the ultimate determinant of human action, and the human will is systematically misdirected and misdirected in such a way that it is not within its own power to redirect itself." See *Whose Justice?*, 156–57.

Augustine proposed that the will is distinct, anterior, and more fundamental than reason. Reason, then, is vulnerable, for the intellect needs to be moved to activity by will. Because human will is the ultimate determinant of human action, knowing is secondary. Thus salvation requires a turning of the will, and so revelation is foremost a disturbance of the will. When Christians confess they do not repent of correctable algorithms but of a will that needs to be made right with God. This is where theology and science take a different turn, since the issue of subjectivity is very different for the theologian than for the scientist.

What may seem to have been a digression is not, because an understanding of revelation defines the distinctiveness that is theology. Revelation seems to place theology at odds with science. Whether that is true is a different discussion and depends on what one means by "at odds with." The tension, though, is real but mitigated if we think of contemplation as a long, loving look at what is *real*. When contemplation is directed at what is real, that makes it nothing like navel gazing. Pulitzer Prize winner David McCullough retells the wonderful story of Louis Agassiz's unorthodox method of selecting students. The Harvard professor would ask the student when he would like to begin. If he responded "now," the student was immediately presented with a dead fish and told to look at the fish whereupon Agassiz would leave the room, not to return until later in the day, if at all. The professor only seemed to be satisfied when the student responded, after an afternoon or more of examining the fish upside and downside, to the question, "Do you see it yet?," with "No, I am certain I do not, but I see how little I saw before."[83] Theologizing is something like that, only words are the instrument and God's creation is the fish. For empiricism, knowing is a doing, a discovering, a solving, a manipulating, while in all traditions of contemplation the believing knower has to let "the things of the world" fall away in order to listen and receive.

Finally, it is said that Christian faith is really a decision before all the facts are in, and that beliefs turn into understanding over time. Since the most any individual can do is claim a truth that is true for him, the language of revelation and faith belong in the context of faith communities where the authentic work of theologizing takes place.[84] This journey of

---

83. David McCullough, *Brave Companions: Portraits in History* (New York: Simon & Schuster, 1992), 25.

84. Stanley Hauerwas is forthrightly critical of both the notion that "each person in the church thereby is given the right to interpret the Scripture," and the notion that Scripture can be self-interpreting. The reason for his judgment rests with his belief that

faith, as Augustine understood it, requires guidance from God, not from within. The soul needs to be enlightened, Augustine insisted, by light from outside itself. The Augustinian tradition of Western Christianity does not isolate the individual in the manner of a Jacob wrestling with God but sets the self within a community of believers. The saving grace of God (*sola gratia*) pierces one's heart but is sustained by real people, a physical universe, actual texts, specific institutions, and enduring rituals.

---

interpretation is properly done only in the midst of a disciplined community of people where the gospel is actually lived out. See Hauerwas, *Unleashing the Scripture* (Nashville: Abingdon, 1993), 16, 23.

7

Where Do We Go from Here?

BEGINNING IN THE 1960s the NR represents a new era of constructive dialogue and interaction between what had become quite separate and divorced fields of inquiry. The primary beneficiaries of the rapprochement so admirably advocated by Ian Barbour, Arthur Peacocke, and John Polkinghorne are Christians who find the world of science bewildering and distressingly difficult to reconcile with Christian beliefs. To a large degree it succeeds by crafting a coherent world view that accommodates contemporary science while remaining faithful to Christian orthodoxy. Just as important is the way the NR shows us how to do theology that is no longer reactive or defensive but positive and innovative. It could even be said that by steering clear of the extremes of materialism, idealism, dualism, vitalism, reductionism, and religious fundamentalism, the NR establishes and sets a new standard.

More than half a century later the time has come to assess the NR. Undoubtedly, there is value in continuing a dialogue respectful of the integrity of each partner. And yet something is missing in this present asymmetrical "arrangement" of accommodation and conciliation on the part of theology. In addition, the present status quo is looking more and more like the same old, same old. By shying away from and minimizing a history of dissonance—if not irreconcilable differences—theology stands to lose its unique and prophetic voice. For whatever reasons, science has not followed theology's lead in a process of mutual enrichment and interdisciplinary awareness, and it remains stubbornly set in its "better fences make better neighbors" mentality. This indicates to me that some fundamental spadework is required. There are basic methodological issues to attend to. Theology needs to find alternative ways of being taken seriously, and that might well begin with a forceful apologia for why a distinctive theological perspective is relevant and credible. The other rapprochement waiting backstage is the respect due to truth-seekers who remain at some level rivals.

The reference to irreconcilable differences may be a little rhetorical, but it serves to emphasize that if we take seriously the integrity of each discipline (chapters 5 and 6), the NR is perpetuating a distorted picture. Whether rhetoric or hype, this last chapter asks that we look at these stubbornly difficult-to-resolve issues as benefits rather than liabilities. Irreconcilable differences do not have to create enemies; nor do they even make theology and science rivals in the sense that one must lose for the other to win. If scientists and theologians can be truly honest with each other, avoid defensive measures, affirm the places where their interests converge, and dispute everything else, a more fruitful conversation will ensue.

Zygon: Journal of Religion and Science celebrated its fortieth anniversary with an issue devoted to the question, "What Is the Future of the Science-Religion Dialogue?"[1] According to philosopher John C. Caiazza the science-religion dialogue has stalled, while scientist-theologian John Polkinghorne believes the dialogue is entering a "new and creative phase." The reason for Caiazza's pessimistic assessment is the inability of both religion and science to render a "knockdown argument."[2] At one point Caiazza speaks of an inconclusive draw, but it is clear that he is more inclined to conclude that at a cultural level "science has won and religion is discounted as irrelevant."[3] Consider, he says, the way science has changed from "a form of praise of God's creation by such early giants as Galileo and Newton into an aggressive competitor of religious faith"[4] The tripping point in this long process of displacement, according to Caiazza, is the publication in 1902 of William James's Gifford Lectures, *The Varieties of Religious Experience*, marking "a transition from a science whose purpose was to reflect the glory of God to a science whose intent is to replace religion with the glorification of the human intellect."[5] Caiazza

---

1. *Zygon* 40 (March 2005). An update to the discussion of the future of the debate is found in "Symposium: *Zygon* and the Future of Religion-and-Science," *Zygon* 45 (June 2010) 419–522.
2. *Zygon* 40 (March 2005), 14.
3. Ibid., 12.
4. Ibid., 15.
5. Ibid.

concludes that we have arrived at an era of "techno-secularism" where scientific reason simply overshadows revealed knowledge.

Polkinghorne, on the other hand, is optimistic and confident for a number of reasons. He is correct, as I have fully noted, that the contemporary conversation has moved beyond the usual historical studies (Galileo, Newton, Darwin etc.), and beyond an agenda set by scientific discoveries (cosmology, evolutionary biology) where theologians are merely responsive or just defensive. Polkinghorne foresees a time when theology becomes more proactive by choosing issues to place on the agenda. He then names a few topics "ripe for engagement" (essentially topics Polkinghorne has been exploring for the last decade or more).

Apart from whether we should be pessimistic or optimistic about the future of a meaningful dialogue between theology and science, what is needed is a fair-handed appraisal of the NR. Caiazza seems to sense something Polkinghorne does not, namely, a growing frustration with religion and the inability or unwillingness of scientists to regard theology as a form of genuine knowledge. Polkinghorne, on the one hand, knows intimately how respectful dialogue between science and theology (not religion) stirs the creative juices and opens a world of new possibilities. Caiazza does not seem to appreciate a perspective where theology and science are not competitors requiring knockdown arguments, while Polkinghorne does not appreciate how predictable and irrelevant a one-sided "dialogue" has become.

In chapter 4 of this book I reached some tentative conclusions arising from lingering questions. The next two chapters described what scientists and theologians actually do in their professional roles. We are now in a position to take seriously what is distinctive about both science and theology and ask what the future would look like if theologians and scientists were to engage each other with less concern for rapprochement and with greater attention to places where dissonance is strongest. Can we revive and benefit from an older and neglected form of disputation?

Level the Playing Field—A Good Clean Fight

A level playing field implies the players (participants) are of equal status, understand and accept the rules of engagement, and want a good, clean game. In chapter 4 I touched on the asymmetrical character of the science-theology dialogue as it has taken place thus far. The most glaring shortcoming is the lack of interest, and in turn a lack of preparedness, on the part of scientists to commit to sustained and substantial dialogue. Scientists tend to see such invitations as a disguised effort to co-opt science for religious purposes; a feeling that is both a residue from a bygone era, but also very contemporary. Science operates with a home field advantage, giving science a take-it-or-leave-it attitude. A few scientists take a metaphysical turn, usually in their statesman-like later years, but scientists writing with theological acuity are rare. There is very little appreciation for, or acquaintance with, Augustine, Aquinas, Luther, Barth, Pannenberg, McGrath, or the conciliar tradition of the wider Christian church. Jürgen Moltmann flags another reason why conversation has been difficult: "Many scientists, and a good many theologians too, lack the knowledge of philosophy which would provide a mediating level."[6] Turning Moltmann's observation on its head, Freeman Dyson respects Paul Dirac's legacy in science as someone who refused to be drawn into the philosophical arguments about the interpretation of quantum mechanics. Regarding these debates as meaningless, Dirac believed that since mathematics is the language nature speaks, confusion arises from misguided attempts to translate the laws of mathematics into human language. Freeman's judgment is like-minded, regarding human language as suitable for describing everyday life, and therefore "we should stop arguing about words, stay with mathematics, and allow the philosophical fog to blow away."[7]

To be sure, there is both a popularized form of dialogue (Dawkins, Dennett, Harris, Eagleton, Michael Ruse, etc.) and a more disciplined approach; the latter being dedicated to the long tradition of critical appraisal between the disciplines of theology and science. In books and the press, the overwhelming impression is an academia content with caricatures typical of a milieu when supernaturalism and dualism ruled the day. The preference to pair science with religion, rather than with theology, also points to the difficulty that occurs when scientists, along with the public, think they have something to say about religion, but demonstrate that

---

6. Moltmann, *Science and Wisdom*, 24. A change is taking place notably in the evolutionary sciences, where philosophy is a common component of arguments being made. Maxine Sheets-Johnston, for example, thinks of herself as doing philosophical anthropology and her ground breaking interdisciplinary trilogy published by Pennsylvania State University Press (University Park, PA) is an excellent example: *The Roots of Thinking* (1990), *The Roots of Power* (1994), and *The Roots of Morality* (2008).

7. Dyson's review of Graham Farmelo's book *The Strangest Man: The Hidden Life of Paul Dirac*, *The New York Review of Books*, February 25, 2010, 23.

they do not know how to think theologically. When religion is the subject it is usually treated as a human phenomena to be explained along biological and evolutionary lines; this leaves little space for any kind of meaningful theological exploration.

Attempts to convene scientists and theologians for the purpose of meaningful dialogue have met with mixed results. As Senior Scholar for Research at the Center of Theological Inquiry at Princeton, Robert Jenson reported in conversation that an interdisciplinary research program in theological anthropology planned by the center was aborted "in part because of the sheer non-cooperation of the scientists involved." Assessing a four-year consultation organized by the Center of Theological Inquiry in Princeton (1993–97), theologian Michael Welker reports on a different experience: "The Princeton discourse was different: there was an eagerness on the part of many scientists to engage in some theological complexity."[8] Welker, though, adds the qualification that many, but not all, of the participating scientists showed a limited interest in theological complexity. This hints at either a lack of expertise or a lack of sustained motivation. Hans Küng observes that in comparison with Europe, the Anglo-Saxon sphere has been the scene of theologians and physicists deeply involved with "important mediating work."[9] But whether in Europe or the United States, Moltmann cites an obvious reason why attempts to bring science and theology into direct dialogue has been an exercise in frustration: "For one thing, scientists do not expect this dialogue to bring them any increase of knowledge in their own field."[10]

Theologians also have their reasons for steering clear of science. The distinguished codiscoverer of DNA, Francis Crick, exhibits both hubris and a kind of reductionism that shuts the door to dialogue and assumes that theology is irrelevant to anything important. In his exploration of human consciousness, Crick reduces our sense of personal identity, our free will, our sorrows, memories, and ambitions to the behavior of a vast assembly of nerve cells and their associated molecules. And in a book with the subtitle *The Scientific Search for the Soul*, no attempt is made to understand how theologians go about building consonance between contemporary science and Christian faith by rejecting the thesis of the soul as an entity separable from the human body.[11] Since Crick believes

8. Polkinghorne and Welker, *Faith in the Living God*, 115.
9. Küng, *The Beginning of All Things*, 38.
10. Moltmann, *Science and Wisdom*, 24.
11. See Crick, *The Astonishing Hypothesis: The Scientific Search for the Soul* (New

the soul is an unnecessary hypothesis because it requires "the idea that man has a disembodied soul," there would be no reason to consult the authors of *Whatever Happened to the Soul?*, who build on a Christian understanding of the soul "as that which enables us to relate to God" and is therefore embodied in all that we are.[12] Thus a case in point of "closing the door" by presuming a naturalistic view of human life is alien and forbidden to Christian theology.

What is the point of conversation if science is only interested in explaining human life as a natural phenomenon and nothing more? The hegemony of science is such that theologians are made to feel inadequate if they ignore the relevant findings of science, but never is the reverse operative. Sooner or later, we reach the same predictable sticking point. Science wants to explain religion as a natural phenomenon, and even to use science against religion as made evident by such books as *God: The Failed Hypothesis: How Science Shows that God Does Not Exist*, by Victor Stenger and Christopher Hitchens.

A level of frustration exists on both "sides" of the divide. Scientists are quick to point out that empirical and religious explanations do not mix very well. Scientists have little tolerance for any kind of supernatural explanation, whether folkish or sophisticated. From where they stand, the chief offenders come from the intelligent design camp because it rejects well-established scientific premises while insisting on the soundness of its scientific arguments. Theologians are frustrated by a scientific naturalism that refuses to make space for a more holistic approach, or in the language of John Polkinghorne and others, for thicker explanations.

A fair "fight" would be refreshing, but it cannot happen until we are finished with tired caricatures of religion and God drawn from a juvenile understanding of the Bible coupled with an arrested understanding of Christianity (see the discussion of E. O. Wilson below). Neo-atheists write and speak as if they have never met, and will never meet, a self-critical Christian, much less converse with a self-critical tradition that has subjected every biblical text and every theological assertion to searing analysis. When, it should be asked, are the self-described hardheaded rationalists who do not consider theology to be a valid or valuable way of knowing going to engage Christians who have nothing to fear from

---

York: Scribner's Sons, 1994) and Warren S. Brown, N. Murphy, and H. Malony, eds., *Whatever Happened to the Soul?* (Minneapolis: Fortress, 1998).

12. Warren S. Brown, et al., *Whatever Happened to the Soul?*, 27.

an evolutionary perspective, and who are undisturbed by the notion that religion is a natural phenomenon?

Dennett is not alone in his opinion that to be a religious believer is tantamount to being irrational, yet no one in the scientific community thinks of Francis S. Collins as being intellectually challenged. Collins, former administrative head of the American branch of the Human Genome Project and the recently appointed Director of the National Institutes of Health, is a professing Christian and author of *The Language of God: A Scientist Presents Evidence for Belief.* The book is nothing less than a passionate demonstration of faith and reason working together to understand the universe and our place in it. Adamantly rejecting the accusation that faith is irrational, Collins depicts himself as a hard-nosed scientist who believes in a redeeming God revealed in Scripture. While his book is not going to displace any number of first-rate systematic theologies, it does encapsulate a tradition many centuries old, encompassing the diversity of Augustine, C. S. Lewis, Paul Tillich, and John Polkinghorne.

Those who like to challenge Christianity often start with religion. I can understand the fascination with primitive religion from an evolutionary perspective. James Frazer's *The Golden Bough* (1890–1915, twelve volumes) laid the groundwork for an anthropological-sociological approach to the study of religion. But science moves on, and a method of comparative religion is displaced by methods utilizing sophisticated tools of evolutionary psychology, evolutionary biology, cognitive psychology, neuroimaging, and genetic markers.[13] Today's science is eminently biological and will not rest until it has laid bare the fundamental reasons why humans believe in the supernatural. The target is not organized religion but believing itself; thus the title of Pascal Boyer's influential *Religion Explained* (2001). This is reductionism at full tilt, or what David Fergusson identifies as the type of explanation offered by evolutionary accounts of religion that tend to work downwards in a reductive direction.[14] Those attempting to fashion a scientific account of religion are suggesting a variety of explanations: some rely on cognitive theories, others on genetic

---

13. For two examples of how faith is hardwired into our genes, see Dean Hamer, *The God Gene* (New York: Anchor/Random House, 2004) and Nicholas Wade, *The Faith Instinct: How Religion Evolved and Why It Endures* (New York: Penguin, 2009). A more robust account is Justin L. Barrett, *Born Believers: The Science of Children's Religious Belief* (New York: Free Press, 2012).

14. Fergusson, *Faith and Its Critics: A Conversation*, 85. Fergusson is to be commended for his effort to engage the new atheists in a fair and open conversation. The book comprises the Gifford Lectures he delivered in April of 2008.

factors; some argue that religion is an adaptive response akin to altruism, others that religion is a by-product of biological adaptations gone awry.

One of the more interesting suggestions is the evolutionary development of a facility that infers the presence of another agent that might do harm or might bestow benefits. "Agent detection," as the facility is named, would have been very adaptive in giving advance warning to pending danger. A caveman on the savannah is better off presuming that the motion in the brush is an agent and something to run from, even if he is wrong. Agent detection becomes nonadaptive when extended to the belief in invisible agents, gods or God, who provide goods and services such as immortality or reproductive advantage when appeased or properly petitioned. Other proposals for the evolution of religion include causal reasoning or the capacity to impose a narrative on seemingly random events, and the cognitive ability to separate the visible (the body) from the invisible (the mind). The propensity to posit the existence of minds, our own and the omniscient, becomes the basis for belief in immaterial souls and a transcendent God, so argues Paul Bloom in his 2004 *Descartes' Baby*. The bottom line of all by-product explanations—religious belief as adaptive or nonadaptive responses—is the conclusion that we have matured (or should mature) beyond the primitive responses of our distant past.

Of course, scientists are interested in the origins and development of religious belief, but then let that interest include a richer understanding of religion's origins. Elizabeth Johnson, associate professor of theology at Fordham University, comes right to the point: "At the root of all religious imagery and its doctrinal elaboration lies an experience of the mystery of God."[15] Absent from various explanations of religion as a natural phenomenon are the fundamental and seminal works of Rudolf Otto (*mysterium tremendum*, the "wholly other"), Marcia Eliade (hierophanies, sacred time, symbols, myths, and rituals), Paul Ricoeur (metaphor, narrative, memory and history), Carl Jung (archetypes, symbols, shadow self), and Joseph Campbell (spirituality, stories, universal truths). Otto paved the way with his notion of the numinous, which he identified as the ineffable core of religious experience, an experience that cannot be described in terms of other experiences. Even from a purely sociological and anthropological perspective, religion is wrapped in mystery because it begins with the experience of something we use the word *holy* to de-

---

15. Elizabeth Johnson, *She Who Is* (New York: Crossroad, 1992), 124.

scribe. Martin Marty explains why "the holy" is not same as sacred: "*Holy* clearly refers to some sort of intrusion into our mucky world on the part of a separated or transcendent reality—an intrusion which can be both devastating and ennobling."[16]

There is something abortive in a methodological decision to explicate religion by eliminating the supernatural when the something beyond (more than what is regarded as natural) is what we are trying to understand. An experience of transcendence and a search for ultimate meaning have always been part of the human experience, and to dismiss this phenomenon is tantamount to diminishing what it is to be human.

In the end, it does not matter to theologians whether anthropologists or evolutionary psychologists explain religion as an adaptive or maladaptive response to various survival situations. And while Boyer is careful not to say humans created religion, it is evident that he wants to exclude any impression that a Creator formed us in such a way that we have the capacity for belief, or *given* in the sense that God's mysterious presence is something more than what we imagine. This exclusion of the transcendent is acceptable and understandable from a scientific perspective since the supernatural cannot be studied empirically. What does not constitute a level playing field, however, is the position that theology offers nothing in the way of an explanation. The issue is not the naturalness of religion, or its evolutionary rootedness, but the premise that evolutionary or cognitive psychology offers a complete account of religion.

And isn't the field tilted just because scientists decide to study religion, and primitive religion at that? Isn't it convenient that by placing primitive religion up against contemporary science one can maintain that science has better explanations for everything? The novelist, and theologian in her own right, Marilynne Robinson makes essentially the same argument in her review of Dawkins's *The God Delusion*.[17] When primitive religion is put up against modern science as a model of explanation, we know we have a straw man type of argument. Patently, religion

---

16. See Martin Marty, "H is for holy," *The Christian Century*, July 28, 2009, 13.

17. Marilynne Robinson, "Hallowed Be Your Name," *Harper's*, November 2006, 84. Her most theological excursion is *The Death of Adam* (New York: Houghton Mifflin, 1998). Directing his critique at Pascal Boyer's *Religion Explained*, Niels Henrik Gregersen complains that Boyer's explanatory model is overly dependent on examples from so-called primitive societies and neglects "the vastly important shifts in religious perception within cultural evolution. See Gregersen, "What Theology Might Learn (and Not Learn) from Evolutionary Psychology," in F. LeRon Shults, ed., *The Evolution of Rationality* (Grand Rapids: Eerdmans, 2006), 321.

has matured, or rather our understanding of God has matured as we have evolved. The "work" of theology is to continually develop an understanding of God that meets the intellectual rigors of one's time and place. What can trip up the "outsider" is the juxtaposition of "a timeless truth for a timely occasion."

The sociobiologist E. O. Wilson, most pointedly in his book *Consilience*, brings some wrongheaded expectations to the conversation (not the least being the opinion that all legitimate disciplines should be a subset of science). For example, he argues that if the biblical accounts are a revelation of truth, we should expect their writers to make some provision for evolution. For Wilson, the inclusion of revelation means the biblical writers would be acquainted with a world view that is consistent with science. Ironically, "creation scientists" try to measure up to this standard, but Wilson deems their effort to be an inferior kind of science. But the Jewish and Christian Scriptures are not revelatory because they are a reliable account, scientifically speaking. It makes no sense to place Darwinian science in competition with the biblical stories of creation. The biblical writers were simply not interested in our contemporary notions of causal explanations. What they did accomplish, though, was to theologize everything, and that included everything from history (Kings and Chronicles) to eschatology (Daniel and Revelation), from poetry (the Psalms) to biography (the four Gospels). Wilson misconstrues revelation because he is expecting truths that transcend their own time and place. That is not an unwarranted assumption except when the expectation is for a timeless word in a timeless way (unconditioned by time). Whether for the sake of convenience or out of ignorance, Wilson ignores theology's own wrestling with a slew of hermeneutical questions.[18]

Perhaps scientists prefer not to go anywhere near revelation and biblical authority, and who can blame them if visions of God speaking literal words in the ears of believers is the extent of their understanding? Whatever theologians' claim for revelation, they start with faith in an ineffable God. A great number of silly inferences concerning revelation fall to the side once we take into account the obdurate fact that Christian theology, both before and after the Enlightenment, has struggled arduously with what it means for a God of incomprehensible otherness to communicate with human beings who are bounded by space and time.

---

18. So many suggestions come to mind but two stand out: Wolterstorff, *Divine Discourse* and Thiemann, *Revelation and Theology*.

If scientists, and philosophers of science, are sincerely interested in a meaningful conversation, and want to spar with a worthy adversary, they should look to theology in its mature and conciliar (ecumenical) form. Forget the literalists and fundamentalists for that is a dead end. Instead, they should lock horns with a liberal tradition shaped by its own effort to accommodate critical thinking.[19] One wonders how such a rich, broad, and deep reading of Scripture and tradition is so consistently ignored and dismissed by those who are obviously intellectually gifted. Even if most of what they say is true about religion, especially in regard to its evolutionary origins, they have conveniently failed to incite a meaningful theological debate about the particularities of a particular religious tradition. By pursuing a single course of argument—showing religion to be a natural phenomenon and nothing more—they have promulgated the idea that by unearthing its origins, and nothing more, they have explained religion. A distinguished Scottish theologian David Fergusson comes to the same conclusion. While affirming that cognitive science has something useful to offer in describing why human beings are disposed to believe in the supernatural, he complains that "in dealing with the emergence of relatively long and self-reflective religious traditions a broader set of descriptive tools and evaluative concepts will be required."[20]

Taking a page out of history, when the Spanish Inquisition poisoned the air by condemning outright another person's error, St. Ignatius Loyola urged a different possibility. "It is necessary," he wrote, "to suppose that every good Christian is more ready to save the proposition of another than to condemn it as false." If your only intent is to prove someone wrong, you cannot listen as you should since your are only interested in separating truth from error rather than trying to save another's proposition. Instead, if you begin with the motivation that the other person does not understand fully what you are saying, then your attention is turned toward hearing everything that is true about what is being said. Hearing in order to save is far better than not hearing in order to condemn. And in a world where the former is in short supply and the latter is rampant, could we not begin by turning down the rhetoric and finding matters of substance to dispute?

---

19. See Gary Dorrien's *The Making of American Liberal Theology*, published in three volumes (Louisville: Westminster John Knox, 2001–2006).

20. Fergusson, *Faith and Its Critics*, 83.

The Shortfall of Separate but Equal Domains

Given their recent history of amicable separation and the arguments advanced here for their respective distinctive core identities, why not let science and theology go their separate ways? It is difficult to resist its pull because this approach makes such good common sense. Two incompatible methodologies are separated, deemed legitimate, and allowed to pursue their own truth in their own way. I find myself sympathetic for many reasons, hoping that each discipline remains faithful to its core identity. Nevertheless, in spite of everything argued heretofore, I wish to register my strong discontent with the model of separate but equal domains. Like separate but equal schools—it all seems so natural, but in the end is such a bad idea.

Stephen Gould's nonoverlapping domains and Willem B. Drees's practical functionalism represent the best that can be said for the position that good fences make for good neighbors. Their logic is clear, consistent, and sorely tempting. The basic argument is that religion and science function best within their own domains. Drees is leery of attempts of joining science and theology at the level of explanation or ontological claims of a universal scope. His book, *Religion, Science and Naturalism*, is a deconstruction of such attempts. Gould is more emphatic when he writes: "This book rests on a basic, uncomplicated premise . . . NOMA [non-overlapping magisteria] is a simple, humane, rational, and altogether conventional argument for mutual respect, based on non-overlapping subject matter, between two components of wisdom in a full human life: our drive to understand the factual character of nature (the magisterium of science), and our need to define meaning in our lives and a moral basis for our actions (the magisterium of religion)."[21]

Stephen Gould (1941–2002) had a most distinguished career at Harvard University both as a popular interpreter of science and a recognized authority in the field of invertebrate paleontology. Though he periodically expressed an interest in a "loving concordat between science and religion," it was difficult to know how the professor truly felt. With the publication of *Rocks of Ages: Science and Religion in the Fullness of Life* near the end of his career in 1999, Gould declared himself. *Rocks of Ages* is meant to be a common sense book espousing what many of us feel; the rightness of the old cliché that science studies how the heavens

---

21. Gould, *Rocks of Ages*, 175.

go while religion shows us how to get to heaven (Gould himself employs the cliché).

Separate domains have recognizable boundaries, and Gould certainly chooses the terminology of "non-overlapping magisteria" because he feels uneasy with the prospect of conflation or integration. By using the strong language of magisterium—"a domain where one form of teaching holds the appropriate tool for meaningful discourse and resolution" — Gould underscores a long-standing position among scientists that religion and science represent two kinds of truth. Believing history is on his side of the argument, Gould provides two historical examples to illuminate what happens when boundaries are not respected, namely, Galileo's trial and the Scopes trial.[22] Never far from his mind is "modern creationism" as chief exemplar of "when a small group allied to magisterium tries to impose its irrelevant and illegitimate will upon the other's domain."[23] In an example of a different kind, Gould points out that Newton "spent far more time working on his exegesis of the prophecies of Daniel and John, and on his attempt to integrate biblical chronology with the histories of other ancient peoples, than he ever devoted to physics."[24] The professor counts this as an awful waste of time and talent. Newton represents the inevitable distraction when science and religion are mixed.

Gould's reading of history is truncated and selective. Surely not "all apparent struggles between science and religion arise from violations of NOMA."[25] A more careful reading of history, as demonstrated by a case history approach exemplified in Lindberg and Numbers's *When Science and Christianity Meet,* reveals complex issues requiring an interdisciplinary inquiry. Not everything meaningful and interesting falls into logically distinct categories of religious and scientific. Quite the opposite is true.

There are two primary assumptions behind NOMA. First, the domains of science and religion are equally worthwhile in explaining the totality of human life. Second, they should remain logically distinct and fully separate in their style of inquiry.[26] Gould would like to see insights from both styles of inquiry integrated in order "to build the rich and full view of life traditionally designated as wisdom."[27] The philosophy behind

22. Ibid., 125–70.
23. Ibid., 125–26.
24. Ibid., 84.
25. Ibid., 125.
26. Ibid., 58–59.
27. Ibid., 59.

two magisteria leaves us wondering how is it possible to integrate truths that are logically distinct and functionally so different. What banishment to separate domains does accomplish is barring the door to interdisciplinary inquires when overlaps arise naturally and exploring them is intriguing.

Gould would have us believe that we can practice a value-free science and isolate it from the messy nature of religion (and the speculative nature of theology). If there is one place where Gould's core argument is unsupportable, it would be his belief that separate but equal domains will protect their purity and equality. Gould fails to recognize the way the truth of one discipline is always an interpreted or contextualized truth.[28] He seems to ignore the facile way the Newtonian science of principles and equations engendered a hard mechanistic, materialistic world view,[29] or how Darwin's meticulous observations morphed into various forms of neo-Darwinism feeding the human psyche for domination and a superior race.[30] Scientists, who wish to build a wall between personal values and empirical observation in order to keep their science "pure," are no less likely to include "various assumptions about human nature into their theories."[31] At very subtle levels Holmes Rolston III exposes the hidden mix of assumptions in E. O. Wilson's "selfish gene" paradigm and Dawkins's "gene law of universal ruthless selfishness." Rolston argues that words such as "altruism" and "selfishness" are borrowed from culture and forced to fit a biological world that is amoral.[32]

Gould's usual insights into history fail him at another point, because separate does no necessarily foster or insure equality. The exact phrases Gould uses are "equal worth" and "equal status."[33] The history of religion and science interacting shows us a period when theology

---

28. For a specific example see Carolyn Merchant, *The Death of Nature: Women, Ecology, and the Scientific Revolution* (San Francisco: Harper & Row, 1983). And for a more generalized approach see Labinger and Collins, eds., *The One Culture?* (Chicago: University of Chicago Press, 2001).

29. See Dobbs and Jacob, *Newton and the Culture of Newtonianism*, ch. 2

30. See William Leis, *The Domination of Nature* (Boston: Beacon, 1972).

31. So Francis Fukuyama argues in *Our Posthuman Future*, 120.

32. See Holmes Rolston III, *Genes, Genesis and God* (Cambridge: Cambridge University Press, 1999), 47ff., 83ff., 277. Mary Midgley levels the same critique at Wilson and Dawkins and refers to "a species of general thinking that uses scientific imagery to give force to its ideas." See Mary Midgley, *The Solitary Self: Darwin and the Selfish Gene* (Durham, England: Acumen, 2010), 7.

33. Gould, *Rocks of Ages*, 58–59.

"ruled" as queen, and a more recent period when science asserted itself as a separate but superior discipline. As rival paradigms emerged[34] and methodological questions were raised and decided, the "dialogue" fluctuated from amicable to contentious, but "separate and equal" is not an especially accurate depiction. If my historical analysis is valid (chapter 2), science and theology (as distinct from religion) are sibling rivals who share a history of contending over the same intellectual territory, that is, until it was divided up.

On one level we should have considerable sympathy for Gould's proposal, especially in regard to *religion* and science. As he argues, NOMA attempts to avoid "false fusions" by insisting that two distinct sides stay on their own turf in order to enjoy the value of reciprocal enlightenment.[35] Nevertheless, the possibility of fruitful dialogue regarding questions of human existence is certainly lifeless without the engagement of religion or theology and science. Gould further spoils this scenario by adding the qualifying phrase, "each covering a central facet of human existence."[36] If only human existence were so tidy, but since it is not, who wants to pass on a good clean fight (apologetics and not polemics) when there is much to be learned? There is, though, one other enticing possibility: a marriage of complements (next section).

Willem Drees's *Religion, Science and Naturalism* is the most thoughtful and complex book to argue the case for a practical functionalism, which is his language for separating science and religion by function.[37] Drees, who has advanced degrees in philosophy, theology, and theoretical physics, is especially insightful in his assessment of critical realism as the linchpin between science and religion.[38] The critical realism of science is not the critical realism of theology because the former is a realism that

---

34. Regarding rival paradigms see Coleman, *Competing Truths*, 42–55.

35. Gould, *Rocks of Ages*, 210–11.

36. Ibid., 5.

37. Willem Drees, *Religion, Science and Naturalism* (Cambridge: Cambridge University Press, 1996). Also to be considered is Francisco Ayala, biologist and former Dominican priest, who argues forcibly for nonoverlapping domains because science is concerned with "what is" and religion with "what ought to be," and on this basis science and religion "cannot be in contradiction because they concern themselves with different matters." See Francisco Ayala, *Darwin's Gift to Science and Religion* (Washington, DC: Joseph Henry, 2007). Ayala declared the very same position when accepting the Templeton Prize in his March 25, 2010 news conference. Drees restates his argument in his *Religion and Science in Context: A Guide to the Debates* (London: Routledge, 2010). In 2009 Drees assumed the editorship of *Zygon* upon the retirement of Philip Hefner.

38. Drees, *Religion, Science and Naturalism*, 130–61.

is testable and confirmable. Religion is nothing like this, Drees insists. Religion is more a way of life than a theory about the way things are. And even though theology is the exploration of both God and creation, the contrast between a realism dedicated to causal explanations and a realism dependent on semantic explanations is genuine and valid for both religion and theology. Semantic explanations do not lead to empirically testable, predictive theories. Theological statements are not constructed to be experimentally confirmable. Instead, they proffer a coherent picture about how things relate to one another.[39]

No one argues with the premise that religion is a way of life driven by ultimate questions and ultimate ideals such as kingdom, paradise, nirvana, immortality, and unconditional love. A religious way of life is rooted in certain claims about historical events, inspired words, and revealed commandments. Worship and other forms of ritualistic behavior express and nourish the individual as part of a larger spiritual community. Theology, then, becomes the discipline that elaborates and brings order to these practices and ideals. Since Drees is not a critical realist at heart, he takes issue with Philip Hefner and Gerd Theissen for thinking religion answers questions about the way things really are or the way reality ultimately is. He writes, for instance, "This seems to me to be a claim that goes—when understood in a realistic way—too far beyond, if not counter to, experience. And if the religious ideals are claimed to correspond to the way reality really is, the crucial function of tradition, namely, in providing a guiding vision that shapes our way of life by envisaging a reality different from the way things are, is undermined."[40]

The argument Drees advances is definitely muddied by not always making a clear distinction between the function of religion and theology. It is not clear how it would change if science were set against theology. Nevertheless, he writes, "I appreciate the engagement of theological realists with scientific insights, but I do not believe that attempts to formulate theological views in continuity with scientific insights will succeed"[41] He continues by saying that such a success, if possible, runs the risk of dampening the prophetic role of theology.

A slight detour is in order here—though one that is alluded to throughout this book—because Drees is sounding very much like George

39. Cf. Niekerk, "A Critical Realist Perspective," 73-78.
40. See Willem Drees, "Postmodernism and the Dialogue between Religion and Science," *Zygon* 32 (December 1997), 539.
41. Drees, *Religion, Science and Naturalism*, 149.

Lindbeck and Walter Brueggemann, and this brings us to the strength of functionalism. While scientists have fought a long battle to remove unwarranted theological presumptions from the domain of science, Lindbeck just as emphatically insists that in order to keep the Christian vision free of distortion it must resist the temptation to provide answers to questions posed by some aspect of contemporary culture. Lindbeck does not want to see the truth of Christianity become dependent on a model of correspondence—language fitted to the way the world is—except when that correspondence is the lived life. Since science is not about formulating ethical ideals or a way of being in the world rooted in beliefs and convictions, theological conceptual assertions function very differently.

Writing from a deep immersion in Scripture, Brueggemann urges Christian proclamation to reclaim those forms of daring speech that shatter settled reality, evoke new possibilities, and construct an alternative reality. Christians look to Scripture because here are stories that disclose a God who invites us into a counterstory about world, neighbor, and self. This calling and sending from a God with powerful intentions is a word that is "in profound contrast to the dominant account of reality into which we are all summarily inducted."[42] Lindbeck, in a conceptual way, and Brueggemann, in a practical way, buttress Drees's functionalism because religious faith, and Christian theology, are understood in such a way that science has little to contribute that is essential for theology.

For anyone willing to advocate separate domains the foremost question is whether such a strategy is a disguised form of the Two Truths philosophy. Pascal's famous aphorism, "The heart has its reasons the mind knows not of," expresses an ancient separation of knowledge of the heart from knowledge of the mind, each located in a different human organ, with the soul being a third seat of knowing, a pietistic kind. Descartes's clear and distinct ideas of the mind, and the dualism he fashioned between mind (*res cogitnas*) and body (*res extensa*), left an indelible mark on Western thinking. Throughout Western civilization, philosophers and theologians have fine-tuned their arguments for various ways of coming-to-know; but in the end, and as a consequence of the rise of secular knowledge, we in the West have settled for just two kinds of truths. There are truths that are evident to an empirical style of reasoning, and there are truths made evident by revelation through faith. Charles Taylor

---

42. Reference to daring speech is from Walter Brueggemann's *Finally Comes the Poet: Daring Speech for Proclamation* (Minneapolis: Fortress, 1989), and the quote is from his *The Word that Redescribes the World*, 95.

proposes a more dynamic understanding of how Western epistemology *developed:* disengaging from supernatural agent as causation, mapping a disenchanted world, breaking down into the most elemental parts and building up into universal solutions, renouncing authority and tradition for the sake of objectivity, and valuing personal authority through the claim of verification.[43]

Some will despair and others will rejoice in a modern context where knowledge born of faith and revelation, honed by theology, and lived by believers is suspect. But surely we know that separate realms seal the deal, and the consequence is to sink deeper into a two-culture mentality. Not only is the two-domain scenario a *stagnant* proposal to minimize conflict, it comes at a time when theology and the natural sciences need to dispute with each other because the "what is" of human nature requires an interdisciplinary approach.[44]

Separating religion and science into two noninteracting spheres looks like a ploy to avoid honesty and the dissonance that follows. Gould and Drees argue that a policy respectful of the inherent function and strength of science and religion is necessary in order to safeguard against pernicious intrusions and unnecessary conflict.[45] And they may be right but safe distance is created at the cost of losing a critical one, and that is unacceptable because self-criticism is limited and often fallacious. Polkinghorne's critique of NOMA is also unarguable. Gould's approach, he surmises, appeals to highly dubious dichotomies, encourages false alternatives, and sets up straw man-type arguments of little intellectual worth.[46] I would not say "of little worth" because there has certainly been a history of false conflict, misguided motivations, and superficial conflation. But without engagement, science and theology lose the opportunity to explore the kind of truths that each alone is incapable of reaching. This

---

43. Charles Taylor, "A Philosopher's Postscript: Engaging the Citadel of Secular Reason," in Paul J. Griffiths and Reinhard Hütter, eds., *Reason and the Reasons of Faith* (New York: T & T Clark, 2005), 345.

44. The discussion may have begun with C. P. Snow's *The Two Cultures and the Scientific Revolution* (originally a lecture given in 1959 by the British scientist and novelist) but it continues in new way as demonstrated by James Davison Hunter, *Culture Wars* (New York: Basic, 1991).

45. Francisco Ayala comes to mind as someone who is convinced that science and religion can avoid unnecessary conflict if they just respect how each functions. Besides *Darwin's Gift to Science and Religion*, see Francisco Ayala, "Evolution Beyond Biology: Comments and Response, *Theology and Science* 7/4 (2009) 379–90.

46. Polkinghorne, "The Continuing Interaction of Science and Religion, *Zygon* 40 (March 2005), 45.

implies, of course, that even though empirical truths and revealed truths function first and foremost in a domain of their own, there is nevertheless a "realm" where heart and mind and soul meet.

Science and Theology Complement Each Other

If separate domains is a flawed scenario, why not pursue a model of complementarity since that dignifies the integrity of each discipline while looking toward a broader and deeper understanding? In the best of all possible scenarios, two independent contributions brought together to form a holistic world view is a promising model. The NR represents a considerable consensus that science and theology are sufficiently commensurate to form such a whole.

Who wants to disagree with the proposition that together, and only together, can science and theology provide an understanding of the universe that is richer and more satisfying than what either discipline in itself can provide? Perhaps an integrated world view implies too much, but if we reduce our expectations and look for limited complements—limited in scope and focused toward particular conjunctions of science and theology—then we entertain a more promising and feasible prospect. Let us see how this works out in practice.

First, let's consider a few generalities. John Polkinghorne offers up an enticing pictorial representation. If we accept the premise that reality is such that no one perspective is adequate to understand it in all its dimensions and facets, and if we believe in the unity of truth based on the unity of reality, then various windows will give us access to the truth about reality, but not the whole truth. "It is by combining the different perspectives afforded by these many windows that we shall gain the most adequate understanding of who we are, what we can believe and what we can hope for."[47] While the premise may be true enough, it begs the question: How can we be certain that the views afforded by each window (read each discipline) will complement each other? What guarantees that one window will not be distorted and another askew? And who will do

---

47. Polkinghorne and Welker, *Faith in the Living God,* 101. Karl E. Peters suggests a similar proposal to envision how science and theology complement each other. Two kinds of maps are required to adequately describe a city. While quite different in function, a street map and a subway map complement each other in way not unlike how science and theology come together to understand the universe. See his *Dancing with the Sacred: Evolution, Ecology, and God* (Harrisburg, PA: Trinity International, 2002).

the integrating? You might argue that it will be a collaborative effort, but we know from experience that is an unfounded optimism. Truer to our actual experience is the likelihood of complements with ugly remainders and claims of superiority.

For the most part interdisciplinary conversation takes place at the level of abstraction. Van Huyssteen rightly cautions against "esoteric and baroquely abstract" conversations and offers a model of a more limited identifiable problem such as human uniqueness.[48] In van Huyssteen's reconceptualization of the theological notion of the *imago Dei,* the biblical concept is powerfully revisioned as "having emerged from nature by natural evolutionary processes."[49] Furthermore, "the image of God is not found in some intellectual or spiritual capacity, but in the whole embodied human being, 'body and soul.'"[50] I have no quarrel with van Huyssteen's biblical explication of the *imago Dei,* and the scientific contribution is indeed a powerful revision of how we normally and traditionally understand "made in the image of God." But is it justified to say that together both views, theological and scientific, complement each other in that together they yield a more robust understanding of human uniqueness? I think "yes" in this instance, and such is the contribution of the NR. But we should not fool ourselves that this is an example of complements coming together. Rather, theology is making space to accommodate another perspective (an evolutionary one).

In order to bring theology and science into the same discussion, van Huyssteen minimizes points of contention and maximizes points of possible consensus, and little is said about any residue issues such as original sin and the central thrust of the *imago Dei* that human beings are a species set apart to be in communion with God and to oversee creation. And if original sin is a nonnegotiable Christian tenet, does it require empirical substantiation to be credible? In this instance, the theological and scientific perspectives on human nature do not complement each other because science is not making space for a theological understanding of being human. Undoubtedly van Huyssteen is aware of the difficulty any notion of transcendence or spirituality causes for science, and he suggests as much at the end of his book when he writes of the challenge of lifting up the sensitive issue of the inclusion of "broader, nonempirical

---

48. Van Huyssteen, *Alone in the World?,* 219.
49. Ibid., 322.
50. Ibid., 320.

or philosophical dimensions of theological discourse."[51] To be even more specific, how does interdisciplinary dialogue included the disruptive remark by Lutheran theologian Robert Jenson: "it is a nonnegotiable item of Christian understanding: no creature has in itself any spark of divinity; the only divinity is the Creator God, while creatures are creatures all the way down"?[52]

In a model of complements how does one deal with the standard proposition that science is not in a position to address the deeper questions of life and universe? Individual scientists do not always accept this proposition, but those who do point to a methodology that is self-limiting to what is empirical, and their lack of interest and training in philosophy and theology. Theologians are quite willing to invite scientists to ask metaphysical questions, but quite honestly do not expect much in the way of a sustained discussion because each dialogical partner begins with a body of self-enclosed knowledge. In a short piece entitled "Religion and Science—Two-Way Traffic?," Philip Hefner, as editor of *Zygon*, describes religion's contribution as "to probe the MORE and the BEYOND of nature that science describes and explains."[53] Hefner also picks up an argument of the NR that science itself points to the MORE and the BEYOND of reality, that is, those aspects of reality that beg to be interpreted theologically (or at least metaphysically). For example, Hefner continues by highlighting the way science on its own deepens our religious understanding of altruism, morality, human dignity, and spirituality. So then, what exactly is the "MORE" that religion or theology adds to a scientific perspective? If this MORE can only be languaged theologically, accessible only through word truth, just as there may be a "more" that is only accessible mathematically, then theology and science bring to the table complements that are difficult to synthesize (at least more difficult than the NR is willing to acknowledge). Whatever the MORE is, it is central to what theology contributes to the dialogue and remains an awkward reminder that what one discipline delights in and embraces, another discipline shuns and hesitates against.

In his well-regarded *The Language of God*, Francis Collins weaves together the factual world of science and the Christian preserve of belief. All of this is possible when the book is a personal testimony. Owen

51. Ibid., 325.
52. Jenson, *On Thinking the Human*, 25.
53. Philip Hefner, "Religion and Science—Two-way Traffic?" *Zygon* 41 (March 2006), 305.

Gingerich is more guarded than Collins to integrating elements of science and theology in order to produce a coherent and consistent world view. Gingerich is willing to grant that the notion of design helps us understand why the universe is the way it is, but the move from design to Designer "takes the eyes of faith."[54] His position, and it may be that of Collins as well, is to acknowledge a particular but circumscribed role of faith. Neither Collins nor Gingerich sees faith to be at odds with reason, thus giving credence to Richard Rubenstein's conclusion that "in the modern period, faith and reason would enter upon a new relationship—no longer a turbulent marriage, but a fractious divorce in which the alienated parties, greatly changed by their separation, meet periodically to argue about the terms of their separation, and, on rare occasions, to take inspiration from each other."[55]

Writing as full-fledged members of the scientific community, Collins and Gingerich may well be exceptions, for each in his own way draws inspiration from both science and theology. But that hardly qualifies as the substance of a new tradition where two separate disciplines, each now with a separate history, complement each other. Do we think that by mixing ingredients (complements) taken from science and theology in order to bake a cake, we have reached the goal of integrating parts to make a whole? It is an interesting question when applied to Polkinghorne's "thicker explanation" or Haught's metaphor of "layered explanation."[56] A layered explanation, though, is a long way from a coherent and consistent picture of a universe mutually acceptable to science and theology.

The faith-reason conundrum is not a major obstacle until theology claims a higher truth because of revelation and faith. Faith and reason become a pernicious mix when theologians make truth-claims beyond, or in spite of, the evidence. To use familiar language, does reason plus faith translate into a superior faculty to know truths that are often associated with the word *supernatural*? Theologians of the NR make a conscious effort not to draw conclusions that exceed the evidence at hand. But when theologians join a theological interpretation with an empirical interpretation in order to fashion a thicker or deeper understanding, faith can supply both a distinctive motivation that employs a distinctive style of reasoning; the kind of theological logic evident in every type of theological thinking from apologetics to dogmatics. Not in spite of, but

54. Gingerich, *God's Universe*, 77.
55. Rubenstein, *Aristotle's Children*, 280.
56. Haught, *Is Nature Enough?*

because theology is a discipline practiced by those holding a personal faith in a sovereign Creator, faith causes theologians to think outside the naturalistic box, to go where others fear to tread. Daniel Miglorie appropriately quotes the eminent Catholic theologian, Edward Schillebeeckx: "Christian faith 'causes us to think.'"[57]

Scientists have their reasons to distrust faith and theologians have their reasons to distrust reason, and this rehearsal of age-old animosities disturbs the idealism of creating a coherent whole of thicker parts. The very fact that theology finds it necessary to reassure the empirically minded that faith is not an excuse to lapse into speculation speaks to the suspicion harbored by scientists. On the other side, theology's long-standing suspicion about reason is rooted in the Reformation and even earlier. The theological lineage includes St. Paul, Augustine, Aquinas, Luther, and Calvin, and continues in the tradition of Reinhold Niebuhr, Karl Barth, G. C. Berkouwer, and David Bentley Hart, to name just a few. The standard argument goes something like this: Reason cannot be trusted because it so easily falls into the clutches of sin. Calvin's most effective image to interpret sin's disruption of reason is the comparison of the sinner to an old man whose eyesight has been dimmed by age, and because of his age he can only read a book if he is given spectacles. So, too, fallen humans cannot read the Book of Nature and learn the full truth about God without the assistance of the spectacles of faith and revelation. But here Calvin is not considering a generalized knowledge of the world and leaves us asking whether the human faculty of knowing is impaired, or if that impairment only pertains to matters divine and for our salvation? I am waiting to be convinced that a saved-from-sin Christian is able to reason better than a not-saved atheist, and the converse. On the other hand, there is something to be learned from Luther's warning not to trust reason ("the whore that reason is") because of reason's vulnerability to corruption and idolatry. Perhaps it is only our will that is corrupted while our conceptual abilities remain intact. Perhaps not. In either case, the language of "fall" and sin point to a reality not to be taken lightly. Like Adam and Eve, who lost faith in God and trusted the incitement of the snake "to know all things," we who live in an age where knowledge is power find that the desire to know all things may well be our gravest temptation.[58]

---

57. Migliore, *Faith Seeking Understanding*, 3.

58. See Coleman, *Eden's Garden*, ch. 4, for a fresh exegesis of Genesis 2 along the trajectory that sin is rooted in our desire to know all things.

By its very disposition, a model of complements is difficult because it presumes that we are constructing a whole truth from two parts that are inadequate in the first place. Since when does either science or theology think of itself as having exhausted its own frame of reference and therefore being sorely in need of correction because of its inadequacies? Theology and science are very comfortable with their own methodologies, and a firmer hope rests with those individuals who sense the incompleteness of their own tradition. The importance of philosophy is demonstrated once again when Alasdair MacIntyre points out that rationality is not something that exists independently of a discipline's conceptual framework and practices.[59] While there may be laws of logic and universal standards for what passes for a rational argument, traditions of knowing have their own norms of justification. What counts as a reason to draw a conclusion in one tradition might not count as a reason in another tradition. It is more than possible, it is probable for there to be equally coherent but mutually exclusive sets of beliefs for interpreting the universe. Assuming that knowing requires a particular perspective and that there is a scientific perspective as well as a theological perspective arising from distinctive methodological practices, governing interests, professional training, language-in-use, core identities, and the history of one's tradition, science and theology necessarily begin conversing with miles to go and much to learn. And yet for all the ballyhoo that presumes a posture of critical dissonance must be avoided at all cost, a fruitful dialogue also includes an exploration of places where respective truth-claims do not complement each other (at least not yet).[60]

If it is true that theology has lost its way by emulating an empirical methodology, then its first internal task is to reaffirm what makes it a distinctive discipline with its own unique methodology. To the extent that interdisciplinary dialogue fails to address the significant differences in methodological styles and assumptions, it only postpones the inevitable. The normative process is for theologian A or scientist B to set forth his or her arguments hoping to find common ground. Consequently, the normative outcome is less than satisfying because both participants experience the difficulty of integrating two *kinds* of arguments. Such was the experience of research fellows gathered at the Center of Theological

59. MacIntyre, *Whose Justice?*, 9.
60. See James M. Gustafson, who is both uncommonly insightful and brave to raise the issue of "conceptual dissonance" and "strategies to avoid the issues" (*An Examined Faith*, 9, 13ff.).

Inquiry in Princeton, New Jersey, to discuss human nature and evolution. After recognizing that even though they shared a common commitment to truth, the research fellows from a diversity of disciplines were confronted by how "vastly different" their methodologies and starting points were, and concluded that "until these methodological distinctions are recognized, it is hard to make progress in conversation."[61] A different course, then, would be that if from the beginning the focus is on the kind of argument each brings to the table, leading to the expectation that the juxtaposition of perspectives would point to a truth that eludes both science and theology.

Standing between science and theology is the simple fact that science and theology function with methodologies that are not only distinct but also incompatible. The practice of two methodologies—one empirical and one theological—means acknowledging a major obstacle in putting together complementary truths to compose an integrated view of the universe. To date, the NR represents an approach to find a middle ground based on postfoundationalist notions of rationality.[62] The effort is certainly commendable as long as it is recognized that in a postmodern context empiricism dominates in a way that makes it resistant to more comprehensive and holistic approaches to truth.

A Place at the Table

The table is where disciplines gather to discuss what matters most for the common good. It is public in the sense that these are matters of public concern, and because the invitation requires participants to be transparent and reasonable. And while many disciplines will accept the invitation, my concern is with how theology and science interact as distinct disciplines in the public sphere.

In an essay about "Public Truth in Religion," Arthur Peacocke voices sentiments commonly heard among advocates for rapprochement.

---

61. Celia Deane-Drummond, Dominic Johnson, Agustin Fuentes and Robin Lovin, "Highly Evolved Questions," *The Christian Century*, August 7, 2013, 30–33. For a real-time account of the engagement, and ultimately, failure, of the collaboration between the new science of synthetic biology and the discipline of anthropology (the role humans play in biological research), see Paul Rabinow and Gaymon Bennett, *Designing Human Practices: An Experiment with Synthetic Biology* (Berkeley: University of Chicago Press, 2012).

62. Van Huyssteen, *Alone in the World?*, 12–23.

Peacocke begins with an important observation: "Now, early in this third millennium, science is providing across all the global village we now inhabit, a common public truth which shapes human horizons."[63] The same cannot be said for theology. Theology shoulders the opposite perception of being anything but a public discussion of universally held precepts, finding itself saddled with a public opinion of being sectarian and divisive across the global world. Peacocke, then, lays down this challenge: "Only a theology that can be *public* truth . . . is likely to be respected in the intellectual world of the modern university."[64] As the intellectual articulation and justification of Christian beliefs, theology (not religion) is thereby obligated to employ the criteria of reasonableness that characterizes the rest of human inquiries, and in particular, science, or "its demise and diminishing influence in the serious thinking of Western society will continue and it will never recover from the present parlous state of its intellectual reputation."[65] Peacocke's language is justifiably strong. Nevertheless, I wish to challenge the assumption that equates reasonableness (even rationality) with empiricism and concludes that theology's intellectual honesty and integrity are dependent on following this course.

Without a doubt, theology is situated between a rock and a hard place. According to Peacocke, theology will continue to suffer exclusion from matters most important if it does not meet the standards of public debate, and those norms for the most part follow the gold standard of empiricism. While I do not question the necessity for theology to enter the public square more openly and more willingly to accept the responsibility such exposure requires, I also believe theology does not have to behave like the sciences. The first question becomes what does theology bring to the table that is unique or particular to its discipline? As we examine this question it becomes clear why it cannot be assumed that theologians should understand themselves as offering another informed perspective among others. Eastern Orthodox theologian David Hart demurs by warning that as soon as theology "consents to become a perspective among the human sciences, rather than the contemplation of the final cause and consummation of all paths of knowledge, it has ceased to be theology and has become precisely what its detractors have long suspected it of being: willful opinion, emotion, and can't."[66] Taking part

63. Peacocke, *Evolution: The Disguised Friend of Faith?*, 192.
64. Ibid., 187.
65. Ibid., 193.
66. Hart, "Theology as Knowledge," *First Things,* May 2006, 27.

in the same symposium on "Theology as Knowledge" in *First Things*, Paul J. Griffiths resists the premise that theology is a public discipline because it is foremost a work of the church, "a work of the faithful, an elucidation of what God as revealed and the Church does its best to understand and teach (speaking now of its Catholic variety)."[67]

According to Peacocke, if theology hopes to be regarded as worthy to sit at the table, then it must meet the minimal intellectual standards of our times. And these include: "comprehensiveness, fruitfulness, general cogency and plausibility, internal coherence and consistency, and the avoidance of undue complexity (if possible)."[68] Accordingly, theology is required to compete with other truth-claims at the level of the best argument. This makes good sense to the extent that theology and science put forth explanations and accounts concerning physical realities. But what happens, and do the same rules of public truthfulness apply, when theologians propose accounts that are uniquely theological, such as the incarnation or Trinity? Peacocke is nothing less than thoroughly consistent when he dismisses the requirement to honor "an authoritative book or authorizing community or supposed self-evident a priori truths," for these he judges to be "circular and cannot meet the demands for validation from any external universally accepted stance and so cannot qualify as *public* truth."[69] Polkinghorne is less willing to discard the authorizing communities that "house" theology, and he would not assume authoritative claims to be necessarily circular. It seems to me that Polkinghorne is correct to claim for theology a distinctive contribution precisely because it is shaped by its understanding of authority, which in turn has everything to do with faith, revelation, and a commitment to the church of Jesus Christ.

So much has been made about the question of whether theological arguments are rational by public standards that the same public conveniently overlooks the possibility of a rationality uniquely suited to its subject matter. The issue is not whether theological statements should be placed beyond the reach of appropriate evidence or critical examination, but is rather what evidence is appropriate to a discipline dedicated to explicating knowledge of God. Theology can be fully reasonable while not being empirical. Surely theologians can practice critical reasoning and be realistic in their own particular way apart from mimicking science,

---

67. Griffiths, "Theology as Knowledge," *First Things*, May 2006, 25.
68. Peacocke, *Evolution: The Disguised Friend of Faith?*, 190.
69. Ibid., 194.

since rationality and empiricism are not identical. Only empiricism, and not rationality, requires evidence to be falsifiable or confirmable using empirical (measurable and confirmable) standards. Theological statements are supported by evidence or they become unreasonable, but the evidence is historical, biographical, autobiographical, textual eyewitness reports.[70] Nevertheless, to ask whether theology is obligated in any way to meet scientific standards of evidence and rationality is not to ask a rhetorical question looking for an emphatic "no," because the question deserves a nuanced response.

A place at the table is complicated by the presence of Creationists and advocates for intelligent design (ID), for they represent how *not* to enter the public discussion. When the Kansas school board held hearings during the summer of 2005, scientists opposing changes to the state standards for public education boycotted the hearings saying their presence would lend credence to the ID theory of evolution and would introduce metaquestions concerning the origin and purpose of life into a science curriculum. Advocates of ID, on the other hand, argued that fantastically complex features, such as eyes, beaks, and minds, could not emerge without the intervention of a designing mind, which placed them squarely at odds with Darwin, who argued for just the opposite. The troublesome aspect of ID for a mature theology-science dialogue is not its critical stance toward science per se. Science must always be open to alternative understandings. The pivotal issue is once again methodological. Scientists are quick to ask if the hypotheses of ID, which at times can be very sophisticated, constitute a viable research program. What nontrivial experiments and what fruitful lines of research has ID inspired? Methodologically speaking, all meaningful lines of research are obstructed when a Designing Mind is used to answer an empirical question. If intelligent design is to be included in a school curriculum, its proper and useful place is with the discussion of metaquestions, such as religious questions pertaining to the purpose and value of life. If it is included in the science curriculum, then it must first demonstrate to the community of scientists that its theory of evolution is methodologically sound and supports new lines of research. And yet, scientists can be hypersensitive

70. See Richard Bauckham for a well-developed argument for the validity of testimony given by eyewitnesses. For instance, he writes that "trusting testimony is not an irrational act of faith that leaves critical rationality aside; it is, on the contrary, the rationally appropriate way of responding to authentic testimony. Gospels understood as testimony are the entirely appropriate means of access to the historical reality of Jesus." Bauckham, *Jesus and the Eyewitnesses* (Grand Rapids: Eerdmans, 2006), 5.

when they are unwilling to entertain and examine boundary questions that arise naturally from theories that are themselves theologically provocative (e.g., is evolution directional, and if so, what are the implications for understanding the meaning of life?). The biological sciences present another kind of dilemma because they invariably raise significant ethical questions, which deserve a place at the table, even the table set within public schools.

For theology, entering into the public discourse is nothing less than an obstacle course. The first task is to convince others that theological knowledge is crucial for the public discourse of what matters most, and to do so apart from the customary argument that religion is a social good. Rather, theology should be valued because it brings to the table a theological perspective. And while that perspective includes wisdom and moral insight, which are also present in various philosophies and religious traditions, theology is the *critical* reflection on the experience of living in the face of God. Unfortunately, authentic knowledge has become synonymous with knowledge that has market value; and that would be a value equated with producing a monetary return. Theologians can be thankful that they are not caught in the vortex that pulls learning and education into the muddy waters of profit, patent law, and secrecy.[71]

The theological perspective so badly missing in the university and on Capitol Hill is not so much the systematics of John Calvin or the dogmatics of Karl Barth, though they would be more than refreshing, but the down-to-earth realism of Reinhold Niebuhr, which is itself a running critique of secularization and idolatry. What critics of Christianity fail to see is how Christian theology is the ultimate critic. Insofar as Christians refuse to ally themselves with kings and princes, speak truth to power, and proclaim good news to the poor, nothing in the public square is secure.

In what manner is theology to be judged like other disciplines? All the rules of a good argument apply but become peripheral when rising to the surface is theology's oddity. Stanley Hauerwas, in concert with Gavin D'Costa, underscores how theology stands apart "because theology cannot be done with intellectual rigor outside the context of a love affair

---

71. See Corynne McSherry, *Who Owns Academic Work?* (Cambridge, MA: Harvard University Press, 2001); Sheldon Krimsky, *Science in the Private Interest* (Lanham, MD: Rowman & Littlefield, 2003); and Karen Lebacqz, "Fair Shares: Is the Genome Project Just?" in Ted Peters, ed., *Genetics: Issues of Social Justice* (Cleveland: Pilgrim, 1998), 82–107.

with God and God's community." Hauerwas continues, "The formal object of theology is God, and, like other disciplines that require practices and virtues constitutive for knowing the object of investigation, theology requires prayer."[72]

Sometimes, and often in the context of rapprochement, the argument is made that theology should play the role of the great integrator. Since there is a consensus among theologians that their unique contribution falls along the line of holistic arguments and integrating otherwise unconnected insights from various disciplines, this seems a prudent and laudable role of theology. Stanley Hauerwas, who has had a lifetime of interaction with academia, cautions that theology should put aside any impression of epistemological superiority and position itself as learning from other disciplines. Over the centuries, and whenever theology remembers that humility undergirds its work, it has shown a particular facility for listening and learning. Hauerwas gives good reasons to concur with Cardinal Newman's assessment that the philosopher's role is "to raise if not force questions concerning limits, possibilities, and connections between disciplines."[73] And in this vein, the role of theology in the public square is to force theological questions concerning everything. If this counts as adding another perspective, then at least it is a perspective that presses theological questions, which, because theology is grounded in an uncommon authority, will be unlike any other kind of perspective.[74]

Once again we ask: What does theology bring to the table that matters? Consider the possibility of more holistic descriptions of reality that resist the thinning of truth in its secularized forms. One hopes the public would welcome the intrusion of theological truth-claims because their inclusion means the hegemony of rational control will have a critic. The list of things theologians might be against, or caution against, is what some have come to expect of religious leaders. But I have no such list

---

72. Hauerwas, "A Symposium," *First Things,* May 2006, 23; and in particular Gavin D'Costa's *Theology in the Public Square: Church, Academy, and Nation* (Malden, MA: Blackwell, 2005), notably a chapter entitled "Why Theologians Must Pray for Release from Exile." Prayer certainly does constitute an "oddity" in the public square.

73. Hauerwas, *The State of the University,* 29.

74. Hauerwas is sympathetic with the notion that secular science should be allowed to be secular, but he also realizes that Christians may very well think differently about economics, biology, and physics and how these subjects are now structured in the university. Christian theologians have a particular reason to speak out because of "the intellectual paradigms that dominate fields like economics and political science" (*The State of University,* 31-32).

in mind because a theological word is not necessarily a stop sign in the face of progress.[75] And yet, when theologians speak, they speak from a Word that is disruptive by nature; thus the reason theologians seem to be against so much. Since theologians have something to say about so many matters of importance, it is an indication they are not content with most of what is being said, because most of what is being said claims to be true merely on the basis that it has been objectified and detached from who we are. And that is a disastrous course to pursue because the twenty-first century will be about knowledge intended to remake ourselves.

Moving forward, let's keep in mind that the modern quest for knowledge is based on the premise that clear and distinct knowledge in universal forms is the fruit of disengaged reason. Individuals who are able to practice disengaged reason are those who have freed themselves from all forms of external authority and who place their trust in rationality. Objective knowledge—the same truth for everyone—is a particular kind of truth, namely, a rationality defined procedurally according to a set of established standards. Descartes and Bacon were not shy about touting a way of knowing that "renders ourselves the masters and possessors of nature" (Descartes). Bacon's utilitarian knowledge for the good of humanity through the technical mastery of the physical world was meant to turn us into masters rather than victims of fate. Technological knowledge, the epitome of rational control, shows us how to engineer matter for a better tomorrow. If only history told the story of how more knowledge leads to the end of cruelty, ideological conflict, war, and the end of history.[76]

Alongside a tradition of disengaged reason runs a tradition of introspection. Charles Taylor points out that Descartes was "in many ways profoundly Augustinian by espousing a radical reflexivity."[77] From Descartes runs a river of ideas that embolden the individual to be more

---

75. Ted Peters, Karen Lebacqz, and Gaymon Bennett chafe against the notion that Christian theologians, ethicists more precisely, should be placed in the role of "no" sayers, erecting "no trespassing" signs everywhere. See their *Sacred Cells?*, viii. Speaking of their own constructive role, the three coauthors write: "The job of the ethicist is to display with as much rigor as possible the important ethical issues at stake and to work with people in making ethical decisions" (viii).

76. The last reference to the "end of history" has in mind Francis Fukuyama's fine book, *The End of History and the Last Man* (New York: Free Press, 1992). This is a book that is both optimistic (history culminating in liberal democracy) and pessimistic (can we ever progress beyond instinctual human desires?) and seems to ask some of the right questions (see below).

77. Taylor, *Sources of the Self*, 143.

responsible, more self-sufficient, more generous, and more self-assured.[78] This is a thoroughly modern reflexivity that fits the modern task of self-making and world-reshaping. It all fits together so well that we wonder if it was not contrived in order to feed an insatiable human ego. Augustine's radical theism takes him in a very different direction. When the self turns to God, the imperfect self is thrown on the mercy of God. The thinker comes to question (the "moment" of conversion) more and more his capacity to save himself, or anything else, because he sees the self as the source of endless self-deceit. For Descartes, by way of sharp contrast, Taylor writes, "the whole point of the reflexive turn is to achieve a quite self-sufficiency certainty."[79]

There is no modern myth more monumental, says theology, than the conviction that we are the masters of our fate. In her very perceptive book, *Evil in Modern Thought*, Susan Neiman writes: "It's on the problem of evil that reason truly stumbles."[80] According to her reading of history, the Holocaust ushers us into an era of unimagined *meaningless* violence, and Auschwitz stands as one of those stubborn facts that reminds us of "a possibility in human nature that we hoped not to see."[81] Her analysis is compelling that after Auschwitz our conceptual resources (read Enlightenment) are exhausted. But are they, really? Have we not found new ways—especially through the promises of technology—to reinvent ourselves and convince ourselves, once again, that reason will prevail? Say what you like about the tenacity of theology's hold on original sin, it goes a long way toward elucidating why we continually do evil we do not intend, and see our good intentions turn into disaster. A theological word is so disruptive because it knows better than any other word that to know is not the same as to act on that knowing, for we never lack for ideals and yet idealism has led to more deaths than anything else. (As Solzhenitsyn caustically pointed out, to kill by the millions you need an ideology.)[82]

What price is theology willing to pay in order to be respected and accepted as speaking "a public truth which is accessible to, and worthy of consideration by all"?[83] Once theology commits to being a player in

78. Ibid., 153.
79. Ibid., 156.
80. Neiman, *Evil in Modern Thought*, 168.
81. Ibid., 254.
82. Pinker's analysis of "the trajectory of genocide" is superb. See his *Better Angels*, 320–61.
83. Peacocke, *Evolution: The Disguised Friend of Faith?*, 187.

the secular arena of truths that matter most, the unavoidable question becomes one of price. The counsel of philosopher Jeffrey Stout is as good now as it was in 1981. "Theologians determine their relationship to the culture, now as in Tertullian's day, largely by saying what they say about paradox. Kierkegaard was right in thinking that the recovery of paradox moves genuinely Christian thought and experience to the periphery of the culture." So, on the one hand, Stout provides an explanation for why serious talk about God happens on the periphery of the public square. But Stout, in agreement with MacIntyre, whom he quotes, challenges theology to enter the fray on its own terms: "the lack of confrontation is due not only to the direction in which secular knowledge is advancing but to the direction in which theism is retreating."[84] My counsel then is this: We who seek truth do not gather in the public square in order to reconcile our differences but to explore them; not to use those differences against one another, but to respect and to learn, even to be humbled by them.

Engagement as Disputants

I have argued throughout that since the purpose of the NR is to accommodate science in a conciliatory manner, it slights long-standing differences that support the core identities of science and theology. While the NR bequeaths to us a level of abstraction that went a long way toward building bridges between science and theology, the benefits of engagement at that level are passé. My definition of engagement includes elements of friction and head butting. But this engagement is without hostility. It is positive and constructive because ultimately there is one truth, and since there is one truth, we are beholden to work towards it without presuming too much about our own particular discipline. Hopefully we can concur that both science and theology are beyond defensive posturing and ready to practice mutual respect. Constructive engagement begins by assuming that science is committed to providing a fully naturalistic account of the universe, while theology is committed to providing a fully theological account of God as Creator of the universe. As such, they could go their separate ways save for the fact that they share important overlapping interests (see below). Any model of engagement must acknowledge some deep-seated contra positioning, but then resist the pull toward a win-lose situation. Theology and science, after all, have persisted in a long

---

84. Stout, *The Flight from Authority*, 147.

sibling relationship and should be able to be competitive without being adversarial.[85]

Missing from Barbour's original fourfold classification of conflict, independence, dialogue, and integration is the possibility of engagement around issues of dispute.[86] One reason why rapprochement has not been truly dialogical is an underlying apprehension that theology and science have unresolved differences of considerable importance, and that at a fundamental level those disagreements may be irresolvable. In his evaluation of Barbour's way of relating science and theology, Christian Berg suggests Barbour operates with a rather narrow interpretation of dialogue.[87] Similarly, Hans Küng seems locked into a constricted view of dialogue when he writes that a confrontational theology is out of date, whether put forward by fundamentalists believers or by rationalistic scientists.[88] The image that plagues us is of fundamentalists and narrow-minded rationalists fighting intellectual battles that lead nowhere. Lingering in the minds of many is an apprehension that to challenge science is to make combatants of all of us. The NR has spent its energy in just one form of dialogue where dissonance is kept to a minimum. David Hollinger, a historian overlooking the contemporary scene, laments the lack of critical engagement as well as the absence of even the respect of engaged opposition.[89]

Neither theologians nor scientists are immune from thinking of their discipline as superior, and this at times makes engagement a sensitive matter. For many centuries theology was afforded the unofficial of title of queen of the sciences because she stood at the top of a hierarchy of lesser disciplines, and do not minimize the way the church exercised control over the universities and centers of learning for as long as she could. Science's rise to dominance was the direct result of its application

---

85. Lisa Stenmark writes of a "disputational friendship" between religion and science. She tracks closely the approach I have taken between theology and science, alerting us to the difficulties that arise when we are invested too heavily in an attempt to find areas of agreement. That is a framework, she argues, that inherently privileges science and actually increases conflict between religion and science in the public square. See Lisa Stenmark, *Religion, Science, and Democracy: A Disputational Friendship* (Lanham, MD: Lexington, 2013).

86. See Barbour, *Religion in an Age of Science*, ch. 1; Polkinghorne, *Science and the Trinity*, ch. 1.

87. Berg, "Barbour's Way(s)," 66.

88. Küng, *The Beginning of All Things*, 41.

89. Hollinger, *After Cloven Tongues*; especially pertinent is chapter 10 ("Religious Ideas: Should They Be Critically Engaged or Given a Pass?").

of a generally recognized superior method of coming-to-know. When theology "ruled" she did so by banning (the Index), marginalizing, and absorbing scientific truth claims. In a very different fashion science "rules" by categorizing theology as irrelevant and requiring that it attend to its own matters.

The art of disputation is practically dead, even though almost everyone knows how to dispute. When the monk Gaunilo challenged Anselm's idea of an absolutely perfect being, Anselm published Gaunilo's blunt criticism as an addendum to his original essay. In doing this, Anselm established a model for disputation in the new schools springing up all over Europe. It did not matter that Gaunilo was a person of lesser reputation, and it was not sufficient to make a reasonable argument. What did matter was the quest for truth. Richard Rubenstein summarizes the essentials of disputation in this way: "One must also recognize the opposing arguments, state them strongly, answer them point by point, and then use these answers to restate the original argument more fully and convincingly."[90]

Rabbi Jacob Neusner wrote a book entitled *A Rabbi Talks with Jesus*. After writing the book, Neusner sent it to a Cardinal Ratzinger asking for a cover blurb. The cardinal agreed because he saw something positive in the respectful and frank dispute Neusner was undertaking. The cardinal obviously did not forget *A Rabbi Talks with Jesus* when he was elevated to Pope Benedict XVI, for he devoted a good twenty pages to it in his best-selling *Jesus of Nazareth*. The story continues. In an article for *Forward*, Neusner suggests that their books represent more than an affectionate exchange; they represent a renewal of disputation. Neusner writes: "Disputation went out of style when religions lost their confidence in the power of reason to establish theological truth." Referring to their own exchange as Jew and Christian, Neusner elaborates: "What we have done is to revive the disputation as a medium of dialogue on theological truth. In this era of relativism and creeping secularism, it is an enterprise that, I believe, has the potential to strengthen Judaism and Christianity alike."[91] Rabbi Neusner is surely correct that in an era of relativism, creeping secularism, and political correctness, few are left who care deeply enough about the truth to thoughtfully respond as if the other point of view truly matters.

---

90. Rubenstein, *Aristotle's Children*, 104.

91. Quoted in Meiry Y. Solovechik, "No Friend in Jesus," *First Things*, January 2008, www.firstthings.com/article/2008/01/002-no-friend-in-Jesus.

If theology and science are to engage each other as disputants, we need to ask at what level the engagement will take place. Should it be about empirical evidence, theological insights, philosophical distinctions, ethical implications? When scientists try to be theologically astute and inquire into the nature of God, it usually happens without the benefit of a deep and broad understanding of theology and a particular religion. Why is that? Laziness or lack of interest? The same can be said for theologians who seem content with generalities (usually theoretical and metaphysical) rather than with the particulars of an identified discipline. A lack of competence is always an issue with the consequence of forcing the conversation into the stratosphere of generalities. When scientists or theologians are invited to participate in conversation, it is usually to join a predetermined discussion. The usual course of events is an airing of respective views on a particular subject, or a general airing of views on the subject of religion and science. In the former instance, a topic is chosen because it already has a history of reconciliation or possible reconciliation. Edward O. Wilson, for instance, has written two books advocating cooperation between religion and science to solve the world's environmental problems (*The Future of Life* and *The Creation: An Appeal to Save Life on Earth*). The appeal itself seems sincere, but there is no effort spent to explore the significant theological resources that could serve us as global warming deepens. In addition, one wonders why Wilson makes his appeal to a hypothetical fundamentalist pastor when he knows this is going to bear little fruit.

Speaking from years of experience as one the world's leading ecumenical mediators, Hans Küng advocates for a model of "critical and constructive interaction between science and religion in which the distinctive spheres are preserved, all illegitimate transitions are avoided and all absolutizings are rejected, but in which in mutual questioning and enrichment people attempt to do justice to reality as a whole in all its dimensions."[92] Küng offers this model after rejecting both models of confrontation and integration. But even Küng's attempt to practice what he advocates shows just how easy it is to slide into yet another book that stitches together the latest scientific discoveries with a theological overlay. Rather mildly Küng suggests that since the "sciences demand some hard thinking of theologians," then theologians "may also require a little

---

92. Küng, *The Beginning of All Things*, 41.

thinking from the scientist, when it is about central issues."[93] A stronger expectation would insist that pivotal issues include evidence drawn from history, human experience, and religious texts, and that theology have a say in what those central issues are.

The question is obvious but the answer is sometimes found wanting: Why is engagement necessary?

1. In the first place, engagement is unavoidable, at least for theology. Who will disagree with James Gustafson's assessment that "theologians, pastors, and laypeople inevitably live and think in our scientifically informed culture. It is their daily milieu"?[94] And, as Gustafson continues, contemporary Christians have three alternatives: absorb, reject, or accommodate science. Gustafson mentions a fourth option of critical self-awareness, and that would be a proper starting point.

2. Science and theology will engage each other because there will always be perennial questions scratching at the edges of each discipline; questions that resist being answered by just one discipline. The issues that beset theology and science are perennial because they are so fundamental and not easily resolved.

3. Science and theology are thrown together because both are engaged in a quest for meaning. It has been said in many ways by many individuals, we are an uncommon species that cannot live without meaning. Robert B. Laughlin begins his book, *A Different Universe*, with the observation that there are two conflicting primal impulses of the human mind—"one to simplify a thing to its essentials, the other to see through the essentials to the greater implications."[95] Without making the usual presumption that one impulse drives science while the other motivates theology, human beings continually work at transcending the mundane in order to find and construct something significant. What scientist, in the end, is content with more and more cold, hard facts? What theologian is satisfied with a theological construct that does not eventually prove meaningful?

Although Polkinghorne rightly speaks of "a deeply intelligible universe," I have something different in mind when speaking of meaning or meaningful.[96] To render something meaningful is to render it intel-

93. Ibid., 105.
94. Gustafson, *An Examined Faith*, 76.
95. Laughlin, *A Different Universe*, ix.
96. Polkinghorne, *Science and the Trinity*, 62–64.

ligible, but the universe can be intelligible—"rationally transparent and rationally beautiful in its deep and accessible order"—and nothing more (Polkinghorne). Most certainly, scientists and theologians do what they do because they believe in the intelligibility of the universe. Yet, it is possible that we end up with a universe that is theologically rational and scientifically rational, but still worlds apart. How else are we to understand physicist Steven Weinberg when he declares "the more the universe seems comprehensible, the more it also seems pointless," but then affirms the value of building accelerators and telescopes in order to work out "the meaning of the data they gather"?[97] As Laughlin suggests, we want to know what are the implications, and even though Weinberg is not interested in pursuing what it may ultimately mean, most humans are not content with a pointless life or an absurd universe.

4. Scientists and theologians share a commitment to search for *truth*. Theology and science are bound together historically by their commitment to settle for nothing less than truth. Alister McGrath, a well-known advocate for rapprochement in England, reminds us of the ontological imperative for theological engagement with the natural sciences. "Far from being an *arbitrary* engagement," he writes, "it is a *natural* dialogue, grounded in the fundamental belief that the God about whom Christian theology speaks is the same God who created the world that the natural sciences investigate."[98] In a reference to a conversation he once had with the famed physicist John Archibald Wheeler, Paul Davies, himself a noted physicist, reflects on a similar commitment to truth. "In his beliefs and attitudes, Wheeler represented a large section of the scientific community: committed wholeheartedly to the scientific method of inquiry, but not afraid to tackle deep philosophical questions, not conventionally religious, but inspired by a reverence for nature and a deep sense that human beings are part of a grand scheme that we glimpse only incompletely, bold enough to follow the laws of physics wherever they lead, but not so arrogant as to think that we have all the answers."[99] No matter how divergent their discernible pursuits play out, scientists and theologians will inevitably bump into each because both pursue truth passionately.

---

97. Weinberg, *The First Three Minutes* (New York: Basic, 1977), 154–55.
98. McGrath, *The Science of God*, 21.
99. Paul Davies, *Cosmic Jackpot: Why Our Universe Is Just Right for Life* (Boston: Houghton Mifflin, 2007), xiii.

5. For both scientists and theologians reality really matters, though perhaps for very different reasons. Let us put aside the implications of "for very different reasons" and affirm the importance of a common physical reality consisting of the universe, our planet, and human life on this planet. Whatever the reason for theology's turn toward critical realism, it stands over against a history of looking elsewhere for the reality and truth of God. Whether in the form of scholasticism or simply the inclination to think of truth isolated from an actual physical reality, we can hope theology has learned to guard against its proclivity to indulge itself in word games and meaningless trivialities. Even though not all truth resides in the physical reality of the universe (à la J. Ellul), any reality not of my own making has the potential of disclosing God the Creator.

6. Both theology and science need to heed the cardinal rule that no discipline of inquiry can escape its own epistemological circle, and for that reason alone engagement is necessary. Inevitably, scientists and theologians are ensnared within their own traditions of framing the questions and answering them. Speaking a sentiment that Alasdair MacIntyre brings to the fore, van Huyssteen writes, "As we find ourselves deeply embedded in the very specific research traditions of our disciplines, an interdisciplinary awareness may now help us also to realize that a particular tradition, in this case Christian theology, may also generate questions that cannot be resolved by going back to the resources of that same tradition alone."[100] MacIntyre himself verges on a pessimistic assessment that incommensurability is to be expected since the language-in-use of each tradition is so entrenched as to resist change. On the other hand, MacIntyre refers to a history of "epistemological crisis" occurring when anomalies or questions arise that so challenge the normalized epistemological framework that something has to give.[101] By his understanding of that history, rationality wins out when a new theory or paradigm introduces a new conceptual framework while gathering up what is still valid about the presiding theory.[102] Much attention has been paid to how

---

100. Van Huyssteen, *Alone in the World?*, 162.

101. MacIntyre, *Whose Justice?*, 166ff., 361ff. MacIntyre cites examples of epistemological crises occurring in the history of individuals, such as Augustine and Descartes, among rival traditions of rationality, such as the Aristotelian and the Augustinian, and among different sources of authority, such as the standoff between Galileo and the Catholic Church.

102. In *The Structure of Scientific Revolutions*, Thomas Kuhn uses a different language from MacIntyre (normal science, paradigm shifts, anomalies) but presents

this happens within traditions (intradisciplinary). It becomes much more difficult to cite interdisciplinary examples when one discipline creates an epistemological crisis for a different discipline resulting in a resolution worked out cooperatively. This in itself is not surprising without a common framework of meaning and justification.

MacIntyre points out that when two rival large-scale intellectual traditions confront one another, as they did in the trial of Galileo, "there is no neutral way of characterizing either the subject matter about which they give rival accounts or the standards by which their claims are to be evaluated."[103] By extending this insight, we can speak of a methodological crisis between two rival large-scale intellectual traditions, namely, theology and science. Empiricism clearly introduced a new conceptual framework capable of answering questions that theology could not. The success of empiricism provoked an epistemological crisis within theology. How else do we explain theology's preoccupation with methodological questions? This did not happen, however, in a deliberate way; that is, it did not happen as a direct consequence of an interdisciplinary dialogue between theology and science. The scenario is better described as a crisis precipitated by science's methodological success, compelling theology to reexamine its methodology in order to compete in a secular world. MacIntyre's judgment still holds: Science and theology have great difficulty establishing a neutral or common way of characterizing either the subject matter or the standards by which their claims are to be evaluated. The NR is trying to find common ground where two large-scale traditions can become an integration of complementary truths or a meeting place to exchange ideas of mutual interest. The latter is quite modest in comparison to the former.

The strongest reason for interdisciplinary engagement is the fundamental insight that theology and science are self-limiting by the epistemological-ontological construct that defines them. Van Huyssteen, for instance, writes in his introduction to his *Alone in the World?* that "theology might suggest to science the interdisciplinary relevance of those elusive but distinctly human characteristics that do not fossilize

---

essentially the same process of progressing to a more fruitful theory. While the literature is extensive regarding paradigm change within science, it is scanty when considering the history of theology. There are parallels, though they are not exactly comparable. See Hans Küng and David Tracy, eds., *Paradigm Change: A Symposium for the Future* (New York: Crossroad, 1989).

103. MacIntyre, *Whose Justice?*, 166.

but are crucial for defining the human condition."[104] A reciprocal response would be for theologians to engage science to learn something of God and God's creation that cannot be discovered utilizing a theological methodology. Insofar as both theology and science practice what they preach—never to stop asking questions and never to cease looking for the most coherent and comprehensive explanation—no further justification for engagement is necessary.

7. Scientists and theologians become colleagues when they resist handing nature over to the exploiters. The ecological crisis is the prime example of finding common ground for a common concern. While Christians may have their theological reasons and scientists may have their empirical reasons, the urgency of the situation overrides the need for long-winded theoretical discussions leading to consensus. It must be said, however, that the ecological mess we have made of the Earth has not exactly sparked a reaching out across boundaries in order to form a united cause. What we see instead is a myriad of independent calls for action.

What Lies Ahead

Two concerns have motivated me to write this book. The first has surely been heard. In the push to reconcile theology and science, the NR underplays the critical distance required for theology to regain a distinctive voice of its own. This critical distance is decisive during a time when it is understood "that everything must be justified by facts, and facts are offered in justification of *everything*."[105] The second concern is a lament: a lament for a time when critical engagement and disputation were honorable. I hear those who think the conversation between science and religion is more vital and invigorated than it has been for centuries. The research projects sponsored and funded by the Templeton Foundation and the Center for Theology and the Natural Sciences represent the cutting edge at this moment in time. For the most part, the projects themselves border on the esoteric, and look more like research in need of a grant rather than a natural progression of interdisciplinary dialogue. The projects themselves do not signal a new era but continue a trajectory of accommodation, corroboration, and reconciliation. Perhaps I am think-

---

104. Van Huyssteen, *Alone in the World?*, xv.
105. Berry, *Standing by Words*, 77.

ing of a very different kind of conversation, but I know that it begins with an honest acknowledgement of long-standing and deep-seated differences. This other kind of engagement of disputation is both positive and critical, and understands reconciliation as secondary.

If the NR is to move forward several things must happen: (1) theology must define its own methodology, but not as a reaction to science, or for the sake of credibility and relevancy; (2) both science and theology must acknowledge the one-sided nature of the conversation to date; (3) and each must acknowledge what each does best, what sets them apart and defines their uniqueness, without falling into the complacency of separate domains. As a proponent for a new and vigorous conversation between the two disciplines, Jürgen Moltmann analyzes the situation this way: "Today the dilemma between theology and science is no longer that they present conflicting statements. It is rather the lack of conflict between statements which stand side by side without any relation to one another, and which no longer have anything to say to each other at all."[106] This quote by Moltmann may represent the situation in Europe more than it does in America, for there is nothing vacant or docile about the interaction between religion and science in many public quarters on this side of the Atlantic. Moltmann also seems to speak for an older generation that sees the past only as conflict between "faith and [secular] knowledge of the world," but he is perceptive about the status quo of separate domains that have little to say to each other. Our present situation, then, is one that eschews conflict because it reminds us of a past we do not want to repeat.

What is the nature of the conversation we seek between theologians and scientists? Rapprochement brings to the table a certain set of expectations ranging from integration to consonance. Ted Peters, editor of *Science and Theology: The New Consonance*, answers his own question with a commonsense expectation. "If both science and theology speak about the same reality, is it reasonable to expect that sooner or later shared understandings will develop? Both science and theology pursue truth; and even though the methods differ, each of the two disciplines should eventually be able to recognize some level of truth reported in the other."[107] The presumption behind this laudable goal is that a deeper understanding will be the fruit of overlapping interests and shared understandings. But from the start, the conversation is skewed toward what is reconcilable by as-

---

106. Moltmann, *Science and Wisdom*, 2.
107. Peters, ed., *Science and Theology*, 1.

suming a common reality, rather than exploring what, at the moment, are irritable differences. We long for consonance but shrink from dissonance.

S. Mark Heim and Jonathan Sacks propose a different tack. Both agree that the vitality of religious truth lies not in its universality but in its particularity. The mistake that Heim and Sacks identify when interfaith dialogue is pursued is to believe the first and most important step is to clarify what is held in common. This requires a level of abstraction that conceals what each religion cherishes most. No one doubts the importance of exposing common threads of belief and conviction. The contrary wisdom argues that because all major religions are not in essence the same, engaging in a worthwhile dialogue requires a presentation and critical appraisal of what is most particular. We honor, then, a religious tradition by its particularities. Thus, Rabbi Sacks speaks of the "dignity of difference," and Christian theologian Heim argues for a dialogue that honors each religion because it honors the particularities of each religion.[108]

The following enumeration spells out places where theology sells itself short, where the NR has been wanting, and where the conversation has room to grow.

1. *Critical distance*—Philosopher Frank Farrell makes the astute observation that we of the Western world have entered into a contract with science whereby "we give up trying to understand the world in its possible metaphysical depth in order to gain greater power to alter and control its appearances."[109] Like many social contracts, there is no formal signing, just an implied trade-off of benefits. Jacques Ellul adds another kind of observation concerning the current state of affairs: "We [Christian theologians] quite willingly accept scientific critiques of the Biblical text, but we should not forget the converse: scientific givens are never as certain as we imagine, and they too must be critiqued from a different point of view, from the standpoint of Revelation."[110] Both are inquiring into resources to disclose very deep truths that in the nature of things can never be obvious.[111]

108. Johnathan Sacks, *The Dignity of Difference* (New York: Continuum, 2002) and S. Mark Heim, *Salvations: Truth and Difference in Religion* (Maryknoll, NY: Orbis, 1995).

109. Farrell, *Subjectivity, Realism and Postmodernism*, 156.

110. Ellul, *Perspectives on Our Age* (Toronto: House of Anansi, 1997), 108.

111. Taylor speaks of a need for subtler languages that have unhooked themselves from intentional objects and where the ontic commitments are unclear, such as music,

Where Do We Go from Here? 249

Theology will encounter a stiff headwind from the academic community if it contends, as Ellul does, that revelation offers a necessary critique of science by opening a way to a universe of word truth that stands over against a universe of verifiable and objective truths.[112] The immediate problem of relying on the autonomy and irreducibility of God's self-disclosure is the inherent way a revealed theology undermines the preconditions for genuine debate. The critique, nevertheless, is one theology must undertake. Although revelation is a slippery and elusive thing, we can say for certain that it is preeminently embodied in Jesus Christ, witnessed to by Scripture, and interpreted by tradition. For Ellul, the practical outcome of revelation is the way it calls into question everything, and as such, leads to a life of hope and resistance. The freedom of God to be God—to use a Reformation formula—is another way to speak of God's disclosing and the discomfort it causes. Certainly the Barmen Declaration and Karl Barth's emphatic "*Nein*" to a national church was a historic moment when the theological prerogative to speak a word of judgment against all human ideologies erupted.

Exercising a critical distance presents its own unique issues for theology and science. The NR sacrifices the benefits of a critical distance for the benefits of reconciliation. For science, a critical distance is only important as a way to preserve firm boundaries. Theology has much more at stake because a critical distance is what it does—it creates a critical space, and it depends on a critical distance in order to speak a word like no other. It is more than just a little presumptuous to argue that since theology possesses a word that comes from God it can claim the higher ground. More to the point is theology's love of the word: a double-edged sword that strikes any place at any time. A critical distance that is theologically motivated will always be prophetic. This does not necessarily mean there is no place for theologians to explore the possibilities of a thoroughly consistent, coherent, and empirically sound understanding of the universe. Nevertheless, the foil of Christian scholarship, with little or no parallel in scientific academia, is to participate in the business of the better argument while holding forth the mysteries and paradoxes resistant to every kind of rationalization.

---

poetry, and non-representational painting. See *A Secular Age*, 356–61.

112. See Hinlicky, who attempts to reinvigorate a revealed theology (*Paths Not Taken*), and Stout, who seriously questions, as I do, this approach to engage science, and in particular secular thought (*Flight from Authority*, 145).

Science seems to have a firm grasp of its core identity, while theology resonates with inconsistency and insecurity. Science has the advantage of presenting to the public a unified front, while religion always seems to be a house divided. Theology shoulders the added burden of reinterpreting its core beliefs for a new generation, a new cultural setting, a new historical moment (*kairos*). By necessity and by choice, theologians continuously engage in reinterpretation because proclamation and witness demand it. On the other hand, science rises above what is historically and culturally transient. Even though science moves between paradigm shifts, it needs only to acquaint a younger generation of scientists with previous theories now rendered inadequate by a new theory. A standard model is always in existence. While theology may have its standard models (orthodoxy), it is nevertheless a discipline dependent on traditions that are diverse and complex. Thus, rapprochement will mean something different for theology and science because theologians inevitably find themselves protecting something they hold dear from change, while scientists love everything about the next best thing.

Finally, it needs to be pointed out that theology respects the *one truth premise* that a truth about the physical universe is a truth about God. John Paul II also holds forth "a profound and indissoluble unity between knowledge of reason and the knowledge of faith."[113] Ted Peters states his assumption that "if genuine science provides an accurate picture of human nature, we will find it consonant with the best insights of the Christian tradition."[114] Scientists do not labor under such an expectation, namely the expectation that a truth about God is a truth about the universe. From where they stand the convergence of two orders of truth—knowledge of reason and knowledge of revelation—is neither conducive nor necessary for good science. From their own experience theologians have found that good science only makes their theology better. It becomes their responsibility, nevertheless, to convince scientists that good theology engenders a necessary line of sight to understand fully and deeply the way things are.

2. *Thicker Accounts*—If the NR has shown us anything, it is the importance of thicker accounts of truth. But thicker in what sense? The NR has decidedly rejected accounts thick with supernatural notions of

---

113. John Paul II, *Fides et Ratio*, 29.
114. Ted Peters, et al., eds., *The Evolution of Evil* (Göttingen: Vanderhoeck & Ruprecht, 2005), 22.

divine intervention. Instead, the NR pursues a course of accommodation based on the premise that empirical explanations do not exhaust all the possibilities for fuller accounts. Each discipline wants to contribute its unique perspective and believes it can enrich our understanding of the universe and ourselves. Theology is no different but stumbles out of the gate unsure what it has to offer that is unique. Theology gains little or no traction when it speaks of itself as "the great integrative discipline" (Polkinghorne) or a "constitutional monarch" (Peacocke) or a "systematic synthesis" (Barbour) because by doing so it evokes latent feelings of superiority on the part of science.[115] There may be occasions when theologians, most likely those with training in science, can thicken an empirical explanation, as Polkinghorne attempts in *The Quantum World* and Michael Heller facilitates in *Creative Tension*. Otherwise, the NR seems content with adding a theological interpretation to an empirical explanation, employing a scientific account to bolster a Christian tenet, or building a more comprehensive perspective by including science.

A familiar refrain is that theology begins where science ends. Heller, for instance, writes, "Each time science tries to understand itself, it touches its limits."[116] The NR has shown some sensitivity to avoid relapsing into the all-too-common default position of raising why questions: Why does the world exist? Why is it comprehensible? Instead, the NR prefers to thicken scientific accounts by offering a theological redescription of complex interdisciplinary material. In the end, though, theologians do what scientists prefer not to do by choice, temperament, or training; that is, to ask questions that scientists rarely ask. Whether or not scientists recognize the limits of science, theologians can indeed introduce a creative tension intended to describe a world with theistic implications.

The character of theological reflection propels it toward more inclusive kinds of evidence and broader patterns of meaning. On the contemporary scene, Heller and van Huyssteen show unusual discipline in allowing the integrity of each discipline to speak for itself. With a PhD in cosmology, Heller can discuss the implications of physics and cosmology for theology without leaving the impression of imposing religious beliefs on science. In his own words, he writes about ways to extend our horizon of understanding by allowing theology "to provide a creative environment to think about science, its achievements, its methods, and its

---

115. Polkinghorne, *Scientists as Theologians*, 12; Peacocke, *Imitations*, 13; Barbour, *Religion in an Age of Science*, 28.

116. Heller, *Creative Tension*, 145.

value."[117] The same, of course, could be said of science providing a creative environment for theology to think about its achievements, methods, and value. A theologian by training, van Huyssteen provides us with a case study focused on human uniqueness in science and Christian theology. His method for crossing boundaries is to identify "those interdisciplinary spaces where the relevance of scientific knowledge can be translated into the domain of Christian theology, and vice versa."[118] After doing the best science and the best theology they are capable of, both Heller and van Huyssteen are able to let the chips fall where they may without forcing conciliation or forging a synthesis. Nor do they aim for know-it-all accounts, but rather savor tantalizing loose ends.

When proposed by theologians, thicker accounts have a way of soaring into the metaphysical. In order for theology to keep itself grounded, and to accommodate science, there is common ground to be found in *reliable* knowledge. In his study of how certain societies collapse, Pulitzer Prize winner Jared Diamond reminds us that science is broader than performing replicated controlled experiments in the laboratory. Especially in the historical sciences (like evolutionary biology or astronomy), and in his own investigation, one might employ a rigorous, comprehensive application of identifying universal dimensions of life, statistical analysis, or comparative studies.[119] Since there are many paths to reliable knowledge, science and theology are naturally pulled in new directions with the possibility of asking, and being asked, questions that would lead them to fashion more robust accounts satisfactory to both.

The NR is at its best when it provokes science for settling for minimal truth claims. Again, we ask what kind of robust accounts does theology have in mind? The answer includes arguments that are both more empirically balanced and theologically acute. An example of how theology might go about thickening scientific accounts centers on efforts to rebalance our understanding of human evolution. Sarah Coakley, professor of divinity at the University of Cambridge, and Martin A. Nowak, a Harvard University evolutionary biologist, go beyond the standard fare of how humans evolved. Nowak speaks of counting cooperation as a third evolutionary principle alongside the classic Darwinian duo of mutation and natural selection. Coakley highlights self-sacrificing behaviors

---

117. Ibid., 145.
118. Van Huyssteen, *Alone in the World?*, xv.
119. Diamond, *Collapse*, 17–18.

in order to modify the sanguinary view of nature red in tooth and claw. The upshot is a more holistic understanding of evolutionary processes that includes self-sacrificial and forgiving behaviors that have been long overlooked within scientific circles. The theological impact comes in Coakley's summary statement that these "very remarkable discoveries" are what we would expect of "a Trinitarian God of compassion, providential involvement and sacrificial love."[120] Or to restate what is transpiring here from a different perspective, Alister McGrath asks rhetorically, "What should we expect the natural world to be like if it had indeed been created by such a God?"[121]

A similar type of development is taking place in the rethinking of human nature itself. It seems our human condition is once again a galvanizing topic. Darwin, no less, felt compelled to inquire into what, if anything, differentiates *Homo sapiens*.[122] Contemporary research is coming at the question from many different directions, leading to something of a consensus that our evolutionary history includes behaviors such as empathy, fairness, cooperation, reciprocity, and peacemaking,[123] as well as the hypothesis that we are moral by nature.[124] There is nothing warm and fuzzy going on here, for human beings are still understood as embodying a host of instinctual behaviors associated with the animal kingdom.[125] But added to this picture of man who kills for pleasure is an account of evolution that recognizes the importance of empathy. Here too is a more holistic anthropology, and a case in point where a Christian anthropology may not be satisfied with the best science offers. An interdisciplinary

---

120. Coakley, "Evolution and Sacrifice," *The Christian Century*, October 20, 2009, 10–11; Nowak, "Five Rules for the Evolution of Cooperation," *Science* 314 (December 2006) 1560–63; Nowak and Coakley, eds., *Evolution, Games and God: The Principle of Cooperation* (Cambridge, MA: Harvard University Press, 2013).

121. McGrath, *The Science of God*, 80.

122. Culminating his life's work, Darwin published *The Descent of Man and Selection in Relation to Sex* (1871) and *The Expression of the Emotions in Man and Animals* (1872).

123. For example, from many possible publications, see Arne Robert Boyd, "The Puzzle of Human Sociality," *Science* 314 (2006) 1555–1556; Frans de Waal, *The Age of Empathy: Nature's Lessons for a Kinder Society* (New York: Random House, 2009).

124. For example, from many possible publications, see Maxine Sheets-Johnstone, *The Roots of Morality*; Richard Joyce, *The Evolution of Morality* (Cambridge, MA: MIT Press, 2007).

125. De Waal rightly complains that it is only with regard to noble characteristics that we reference the human species, disregarding that empathy is an evolutionary trait of animals. See his *Age of Empathy*, 209.

theology certainly wishes to participate in discovering what characteristics are species specific to *Homo sapiens*. But Christian theology is also committed to an understanding of human nature that includes the narrative, the historical, and the theological; and whether such a more realistic account is congruent with science is somewhat beside the point. And by that I mean theology will not ignore the scientific evidence, but rather that it will include *dimensions* (experiences of the holy), *interpretations* (human sexuality as sacred and the embodiment of divine love), *moral implications* (the place and meaning of suffering as redemptive), and *biblical/theological warrants* (such as original sin) that may or may not be compatible with a naturalistic methodology.

As a discipline, Christian theology is obligated to pose counter-readings by fashioning accounts of the universe that are notable for their depth and breadth. This is a call to complicate science, just as science has complicated theologizing. Christian theology is constituted, as so many notable theologians have argued, to be a holy irritant. David Bentley Hart, a holy irritant himself, writes these choice words for anyone who holds to a thoroughly reductive account of human nature: "Perhaps more critically," we "ought not to surrender the future to those who know so little of human nature as to imagine that a society 'liberated' from Christ would love justice, or truth, or beauty, or compassion, or even life."[126]

Christian texts arise from the human experience in all its variegated colors. What they give us is much more than a theological overlay, more than just a theological interpretation, but understandings springing from the deepest questions of life and reality. Those very same Judeo-Christian texts become a living voice of individuals and communities who continue to bring to expression a conversation rich with meaning. Thicker accounts are what theology does best, and theology does it best when it speaks from the depths of experiences not circumscribed by preestablished boundaries but open to transcendent contingencies.

3. *More biology, less physics*—The NR was nourished in the environs of physics. It belongs to the twentieth century when physics and astronomy were at the cutting edge science, and when the knowledge that carried the most weight was atomic. Both Barbour and Polkinghorne, and for that matter most of the leading figures of the NR, were trained as physicists. The twenty-first century is a new era. The technological breakthroughs that matter most are biological. While physics in the form of splitting the

---

126. Hart, *Atheist Delusions*, 17.

atom and reconceptualizing the universe was monumental, the biological sciences have the potential of curing disease and changing the very direction of our evolution as a species. By its very nature physics is a discipline of abstractions and so fits very well with theology, which is also a discipline of many abstractions. Boundary or metaphysical types of questions exist along the edge of physics, astrophysics, and cosmology—at the level of the cosmically large and infinitesimally small. We do not, however, find those kinds of metaphysical questions at the core of biological science because biology is eminently personal and particular. Consequently, when theology engages biology it is usually at the level of very personal moral questions. Methodological issues recede into the background and theoretical abstractions give way to specific case deliberations.

Unlike the potential for so much destruction that followed splitting the atom, the gathering at the White House on June 26, 2000 to honor those who had mapped the human genome, James Watson and J. Craig Venter, was met with unfettered expectations.[127] Christian theologians, along with everyone else, found little to challenge. Metaphysical speculations receded and rapprochement was not at stake. The whole world embraced the new biological sciences as the pathway to unlimited benefits. But if Leon Kass is right that "in the realm of bioethics, the evils we face are intertwined with the goods we so keenly seek," then theology will find itself engaging science from a very different perspective.[128]

Among the articles paying tribute to Arthur Peacocke, who died in October of 2006, Ian Barbour reflects on issues they debated: emergent monism or two-aspects process events, pantheism or process theism, creation ex nihilo and/or continuing creation, and voluntary or necessary limitation of God's power.[129] These are questions that have become obsolete, not because they have been settled, but rather because they lack a sense of urgency. For a sign of the times, look to the new program "The Science for Ministry Institute," initiated by Princeton Theological Seminary with a $346,988 grant from the John Templeton Foundation's "Science for Ministry." The program will enable a scientifically curious pastor

---

127. The intriguing story of how these two scientists competed for the ultimate prize is told by James Shreeve, *The Genome War* (New York: Ballantine, 2004).

128. Kass, *Life, Liberty and the Defense of Dignity* (San Francisco: Encounter Books, 2002), 3. Fukuyama comes to the same conclusion: "in contrast to many other scientific advances, biotechnology mixes obvious benefits with subtle harms in one seamless package" (*Our Posthuman Future*, 7).

129. Barbour, "Honoring A. Peacocke," *Zygon* 43 (March 2008) 89–102.

to be paired with a theologically sensitive scientist in order to promote an informed dialogue around issues of theology and science. The core overlapping questions that have been chosen to focus the core curriculum include the question of *origins* (Where did we come from?) and the questions of *human nature* (Who are we?). While these issues have been around since the dawning of our species, they are both timely and urgent; timely because of the explosion of interest from a diversity of scientific disciplines regarding human nature,[130] and urgent because we have the technology to engineer the human genome.

4. *Word truth*—Freeman Dyson's comments on a lecture given by John Polkinghorne on the topic of science and theology is telling. Dyson makes note of Polkinghorne's argument that science and theology are two aspects of a single intellectual adventure, but then says he cannot share Polkinghorne's vision, despite his admiration for it. "To share it," he writes, "you must disregard a crucial difference between science and theology. When all is said and done, science is about things and theology is about words." To press his reasoning further, Dyson points out that quantum mechanics works equally well in all cultures, while theology works in one culture alone. "If you have not grown up in Polkinghorne's culture, where words such as 'incarnation' and 'trinity' have a profound meaning, you cannot share his vision."[131] Dyson knows well enough that scientific concepts, such as quantum mechanics, require their own unique culture of knowing. Dyson, though, is implying that because theology is only or primarily about words, it is inferior to science. What Dyson fails to appreciate is that scientific concepts can only take us so far into reality.

One of the mainstay arguments in Taylor's *A Secular Age* is to describe the way language has been flattened and emptied by the modern preference for "objectification." Consequently, the "revelatory power of language is totally sidelined and ignored, or even denied."[132] Like Ellul, Taylor believes that when words are not tethered to ontological claims they can function to reveal another level of meaning, and this is a difference not of degree but of kind.[133] Wendell Berry reaches a similar

---

130. Steven Pinker, for example, writes in the preface to *The Blank Slate*, "An honest discussion of human nature has never been more timely" (xi).

131. Dyson, *The Scientist as Rebel*, 307.

132. Taylor, *A Secular Age*, 758.

133. For Taylor's discussion of the power of language as found in the new poetics, with Gerard Manley Hopkins as his main example, see his *A Secular Age*, 755–58. For Ellul, see *Humiliation of the Word*, 23.

conclusion that "we have seen, for perhaps a hundred and fifty years, a gradual increase in language that is either meaningless or destructive of meaning."[134] A case can even be made that theology, as well as science, is culpable because of its persistent obsession with literalism and objectivity. But can we not agree, without casting aspersions, that a purely internal or a purely external language does not serve us well? The exclusive focus on word truth, or what Berry refers to as making a world of words, "leads to, and allows, and abets the degradation of the world."[135] On the other hand, a technical language aimed at explaining cause and effect serves to absolve the knowing subject of any responsibility for talking about meaning and consequences. A balanced approach would distance itself from language that has nothing to do with reality (a world of words), and from language that only objectifies reality. The real "trick" is to be able explore a new use of language that is both theologically sensitive and empirically grounded.

Each in his own way—Taylor, Berry, Stout, and Ellul—raises a legitimate question: Has theology lost confidence in the revelatory power of language, and revelation as a legitimate source of truth? As the keeper of theological word truths, theology is obligated to do exactly what science is neither prepared nor obligated to do, namely, to inquire after meaning and purpose that requires a universe of words.

What if theology's role in the public square is not primarily to "explain" the data in competition with science, but to redescribe a world already provisionally described and partially explained by science?[136] Hence, Walter Brueggemann's "word that redescribes the world," and not just any word but a prophetic word.[137] Theology's engagement with science is one where a very peculiar word truth is put into play. New Testament scholar John Dominic Crossan catches the spirit of this kind of word truth when writing about parables: "It is clear that parable is really a *story event* and not just a story. One can tell oneself stories but not parables. One cannot really do so just as one cannot really beat oneself at chess or fool oneself completely with a riddle one has just invented."[138]

134. Berry, *Standing by Words*, 24.

135. Ibid., 9.

136. Here I paraphrase Gregersen, "Critical Realism," 78, 84; and Gregersen, "A Contextual Coherence," 212.

137. In particular, see Walter Brueggemann, *The Word That Redescribes the World* and *Finally Comes the Poet* (Minneapolis: Fortress, 1989).

138. Crossan, *The Dark Interval* (Allen, TX: Argus Communications, 1975), 87.

The *word* that is so important to theologians, whether it comes by revelation or faith, written or spoken, creates something new; something that was not present before—an awareness, a possibility, an imagination, a judgment, and always not just of our own making.

5. *An antidote to amnesia*—If we choose to think of theology as moored in the past while science leads into the future (the next big discovery), then theology will indeed seem passé and irrelevant. When Archbishop Rowan Williams asks in the title of his book *Why Study the Past?*, he speaks of "informed awareness" as a tool for assessing where the fundamentals lie.[139] He also adds an important addendum: The dominant text of any culture is sure to obscure where fundamentals lie. As the dominant text of our time, science is notably susceptible to seeing only what is possible, unencumbered by the past. Motivated by an unbridled optimism characteristic of scientists, Freeman Dyson speaks of the possibility of a new century where technology is guided by ethics, yet knowing that this would be a reversal of our history where technology drives ethics.[140] He does not presume that science itself will provide the ethic, nor does he offer any substantial reason for us to think the twenty-first century will be an overturning of the last century. But Dyson is confident that new technologies will offer us "real opportunities for making the world a happier place."[141] But does Dyson know with equal conviction that such optimism is the gateway to self-delusion, and self-delusion is the pit into which we are most likely to fall when we are hell-bent on remaking ourselves as fast as technology enables us? To view our history to date as merely a learning exercise is to presume that as a rational species par excellence we will learn from our mistakes. The presumption, however, is unfounded though highly beguiling.

How we read history is not incidental to our future behavior. The myths we hold about ourselves, our nation, and our place in the world are what guide us, motivate us, and provide us with a mission.[142] Much has

---

139. Williams, *Why Study the Past?*, 57; and similarly David Hart, "The most important function of historical reflection is to wake us from too complacent a forgetfulness and to recall us to a knowledge of things that should never be lost to memory" (*Atheist Delusions*, xiv).

140. Dyson, *The Sun*, 60–61.

141. Ibid., 61. Such optimism is enthusiastically defended by Matt Ridley, *The Rational Optimist* (New York: Harper Collins, 2010), and subject to the same critique.

142. Besides speaking of "myths," Edward Farley writes of "deep symbols." Deep symbols, he explains, "are the values by which a community understands itself, from

been written about the interconnections between technology and progress, technology and capitalism, and technology and globalization. Books have been written specifically about whether technology drives history.[143] The orientation is always toward the future with little or no space given to the past, because it is assumed that with the help of technology we can overcome the past. If only history were a straight line of learning from our mistakes. Sorely absent is an iconoclast, such as Reinhold Niebuhr, who would once again speak of history as pathos, tragedy, and irony, and of the myths of the chosen and innocent nation.[144] There is no greater myth, Niebuhr would tell us, than the one that believes the passage of time is redemptive and that rationality will displace irrationality. Christian theology has certainly played its part in propagating this myth, but at the same time "houses" a tradition of suspicion and informed awareness. Less clearly defined and understood are the myths transmitted by modern science, but they are immensely powerful, and many of them would fall under Niebuhr's categorization of "children of the light" or Daniel Dennett's more contemporary category of thinkers like himself who are the new Brights.[145] When writing about the new atheism (Dawkins in particular), literary critic James Wood captures the spirit of what drives us forward, as if unfettered in any way by the history we have left behind; we continue to believe in a future "where the sun of science and liberal positivism is shining brassily, casting no shadows."[146]

6. *Limits to rationality*—If our grasp of the world consists of holding inner representations of an outer reality, then a rational correlation of inner and outer things would be sufficient. But in actuality we process, interact with, and explain the world in many different ways, sometimes

---

which it takes its aims, and to which in appeals as canons of cultural criticism. To grow up in a community is to have one's consciousness shaped by these symbols." See Farley, *Deep Symbols* (Valley Forge, PA: Trinity Press International, 1996), 3.

143. See for example the essays in Merritt Roe Smith and Leo Marx, eds., *Does Technology Drive History?* (Cambridge, MA: MIT Press, 1994).

144. See specifically R. Niebuhr, *The Irony of American History* (New York: Scribner's, 1953).

145. What a contrast between Niebuhr's *The Children of Light and the Children of Darkness* (New York: Scribner's, 1946) and Dennett's *Breaking the Spell*, 21. If the contrast has been forgotten, for Niebuhr we are all children of the light and at the same time children of the darkness, while Dennett thinks he can distinguish between nonbeliever Brights and gullible believers. That the two are not speaking the same language may be a distinction easily overlooked.

146. James Wood, "God in the Quad," *The New Yorker*, August 31, 2009, 76.

focused, and sometimes not, on internal processes. Rationality includes a spectrum ranging from rigid rules and procedures to outlandish thought experiments. The same individual can go from writing protocols for an experiment to meditating on a religious text. We are rational beings employing a variety of modes and models of rationality.

The argument has been around for some time that religious fanatics are about as delusional as you can become. That, admittedly, is one kind of delusion, but one that can be parried by what Rowan Williams identifies as the church's way of defining both discipline and doctrine by "a steady process of rethinking and clarifying."[147] It should be enough to point to the enduring Christian tradition of critical examination and reexamination of its own historical, theological, and scriptural claims, to dispel the notion that modernity is defined as an "age of reason" emerging from and overthrowing an "age of faith." That it does not seem sufficiently patent may be attributable to our practice of overlooking how reason led to its own "dark age" of unimagined death and devastation. David Bentley Hart's acerbic comment is that what distinguishes modernity from the age of Christendom "is not that the former is more devoted to rationality than the latter but that its rationality serves different primary commitments (some of which—'blood and soil,' the 'master race,' the 'socialist Utopia'—produce prodigies of evil precisely to the degree that they are 'rationally' pursued)."[148]

On the one hand, we can speak of the limits to rationality by acknowledging the powerful forces that shifted the locus of certainty to the autonomous, disengaged subject at the expense of communal and intuitive ways of knowing. Those same forces are responsible for elevating experience and observation while dampening introspection and contemplation. On the other hand, the limits to rationality can refer to all the rights and privileges granted to reason while denying all notions of the will. Science pays so little attention to, and Christians seem to be ignoring, the tradition emanating from St. Paul of the New Testament, Augustine in his *Confessions*, and culminating with Luther's *The Bondage of the Will* that sets the will as distinct from and "at war" with rationality.[149] To

---

147. Williams, *Why Study the Past?*, 48.

148. Hart, *Atheist Delusions*, 101.

149. In the modern era, rationality usurps will, and almost everything emotive. It is then ironic that Dennett saves human free will from the acid of Darwin's natural selection, because without free will nothing will come of his call to arms to grow up and undertake the Promethean project of doing for ourselves what hitherto we have left to

the extent that theological reflection must always include a "fallen" self, it will be marginalized as unwarranted. But what good is even the best rationality if the knowing self cannot do the good it wills? The reigning wisdom of a rational age is to think of irrationality as something that can be countered by more rationality, or corrected by getting it right the next time.

Both the optimism of a scientific rationality and the very insipid understanding of sin and evil come to the fore when Dyson would have us believe we are well on a way toward a technologically bright future, but for the three devils of disunity, shortage of funds, and fear of a disastrous failure (a failure of nerve).[150] No mention is made of the universal human condition of seeing the good we intend turn into an evil we did not intend. For all who believe rationality enables us to pursue our hearts desire, the President's Council on Bioethics, in its report "Beyond Therapy: Biotechnology and the Pursuit of Happiness," had the uncommon insight to speak of desire and hubris when discussing the golden age of biotechnology.[151]

Theology's oddity ultimately arises from its formal subject matter: God. The nature of God is such that the best we can do as humans is to speak analogically, paradoxically, and obliquely, in metaphors, parables, laments, and adoration. For all the effort expended down through the centuries to render the Christian faith reasonable in order to make it acceptable, the core belief that God is Subject, and as Subject exceeds our efforts of rational comprehension, has only a sporadic history. So often the faith versus reason debate misses the point that faith is not antithetical to reason, but a confession that sometimes truth is a gift. For Christians, and other religions, it is the gift of God's self. Let us keep in mind that faith does nothing to excuse theology from the rigors of rationality; but then again, rationality is neither the first nor the last word when one is seeking to understand something of the mystery of the Creator and "his" creation.

7. *A little humility goes a long way*—Near the end of his *A Secular Age*, Taylor writes that both sides (exclusive humanism and Christian belief) need a good dose of humility. The same, I suggest, is true for both theology and science, and for the same reason that both disciplines harbor

God (*Darwin's Dangerous Idea*, 366, 423).

150. Dyson, *The Scientist as Rebel*, 287–304.

151. The report can be accessed online at bioethics.gov/reports/beyondtherapy.

delusions of grandeur. For theology it is the hubris of knowing the mind of God, while for science it is the arrogance arising from the notion that "science will progressively close the sutures of knowledge until the project of understanding is effectively seamless."[152] Taylor cares less about which side has "the final decisive argument in its armory," but respects "who can respond most profoundly and convincingly to what are ultimately commonly felt dilemmas."[153] And that is a quote worth holding on to.

---

152. Taylor writes: "So that Christians are often induced to claim more than they should, and to begin to offer 'answers'; and in doing so, they fall into the same kind of blindness that reductive humanism suffers from" (*A Secular Age*, 675). Marilynne Robinson offers a similar sentiment in "Credo," *Harvard Divinity Bulletin*, Spring 2008, 20–32.

153. Taylor, *A Secular Age*, 675.

Selected Bibliography

Alder, Ken. *The Measure of All Things*. New York: Free Press, 2002.
Barbour, Ian. "A Personal Odyssey." In *Fifty Years in Science and Religion: Ian G. Barbour and His Legacy*, edited by Robert J. Russell, 17–28. Burlington, VT: Ashgate, 2004.
———. *Issues in Science and Religion*. Hagerstown, NY: Harper & Row, 1996.
———. *Myths, Models and Paradigms*. New York: Harper & Row, 1974.
———. *Religion in an Age of Science*. The Gifford Lectures, vol. 1. New York: Harper & Row, 1990.
Barr, Stephen M. *Modern Physics and Ancient Faith*. Notre Dame, IN: University of Notre Dame Press, 2003.
Berg, Christian. "Barbour's Way(s) of Relating Science and Theology." In *Fifty Years in Science and Religion: Ian G. Barbour and His Legacy*, edited by Robert J. Russell, 61–75. Burlington, VT: Ashgate, 2004.
Berry, Wendell. *Standing by Words*. Washington, DC: Shoemaker & Hoard, 1983.
Blackwell, Richard J. *Behind the Scenes at Galileo's Trial*. Notre Dame, IN: University of Notre Dame Press, 2006.
Bloom, Paul. *Descartes' Baby*. New York: Basic, 2004.
———. "Is God an Accident?" *Atlantic Monthly*, December 2005, 105-12.
Brooke, John. *Science and Religion: Some Historical Perspectives*. Cambridge: Cambridge University Press, 1991.
Brooke, John and Geoffrey Cantor. *Reconstructing Nature: The Engagement of Science and Religion*. New York: Oxford University Press, 2000.
Brown, Frank B. *The Evolution of Darwin's Religious Views*. Macon, GA: Mercer University Press, 1986.
Brueggemann, Walter. *The Word that Redescribes the World*. Minneapolis: Fortress, 2006.
Cathcart, Brian. *The Fly in the Cathedral*. New York: Farrar, Straus and Giroux, 2005.
Clapp, Rodney. "How Firm a Foundation: Can Evangelicals be Nonfoundationalists?" In *The Nature of Confession: Evangelicals and Postliberals in Conversation*, edited by Timothy R. Phillips and Dennis L. Okholm, 81–92. Downers Grove, IL: InterVarsity, 1996.
Coleman, Richard J. *Competing Truths: Theology and Science as Sibling Rivals*. Harrisburg, PA: Trinity Press International, 2001.
———. *Eden's Garden: Rethinking Sin and Evil in an Era of Scientific Promise*. Lanham, MD: Rowman & Littlefield, 2007.
Collins, Francis S. *The Language of God: A Scientist Presents Evidence for Belief*. Waterville, ME: Wheeler, 2007.

Crews, Frederick. "Saving Us from Darwin." *New York Times Review of Books*, October 4, 2001. www.nybooks.com/articles/archives/2001/oct/04/saving-us-from-darwin.

Crick, Francis. *What Mad Pursuit: A Personal View of Scientific Discovery*. New York: Basic, 1988.

Darwin, Charles. *The Autobiography of Charles Darwin, 1809-1882*. Edited by Nora Barlow. New York: W. W. Norton, 1958.

De Chardin, Teilhard. "My Universe." In *Process Theology*, edited by Ewert H. Cousins, 249–55. New York: Newman, 1971.

Dennett, Daniel C. *Darwin's Dangerous Idea*. New York: Simon & Schuster, 1995.

Deutsch, David. *The Fabric of Reality*. New York: Allen Lane/Penguin, 1997.

Dewart, Leslie. *The Foundations of Belief*. New York: Herder and Herder, 1969.

Diamond, Jared. *Collapse: How Societies Choose to Fail or Succeed*. New York: Penguin Books, 2011.

Dobbs, Jo Teeter, and Margaret C. Jacob. *Newton and the Culture of Newtonianism*. Highlands, NJ: Humanities Press International, 1995.

Dupré, Louis. *Religious Mystery and Rational Reflection*. Grand Rapids: Eerdmans, 1998.

Dyson, Freeman. *The Scientist as Rebel*. New York: New York Review of Books, 2006.

———. *The Sun, the Genome, and the Internet*. New York: Oxford University Press, 1999.

Eagleton, Terry. *Reason, Faith, and Revolution*. New Haven, CT: Yale University Press, 2009.

Ebeling, Gerhard. "The Significance of the Critical Historical Method for Church and Theology in Protestantism." In *Word and Faith*, 31–36. Philadelphia: Fortress, 1963.

Ellul, Jacques. *The Humiliation of the Word*. Grand Rapids: Eerdmans, 1985.

———. *Living Faith: Belief and Doubt in a Perilous World*. San Francisco: Harper & Row, 1983.

———. *The Technological Bluff*. Grand Rapids: Eerdmans, 1900.

Fanning, Philip A. *Isaac Newton and the Transmutation of Alchemy*. Berkeley, CA: North Atlantic, 2009.

Farrell, Frank B. *Subjectivity, Realism and Postmodernism*. Paperback edition, 1996. Cambridge: Cambridge University Press, 1994.

Fergusson, David. *Faith and Its Critics: A Conversation*. New York: Oxford University Press, 2009.

Freeman, Charles. *The Closing of the Western Mind: The Rise of Faith and the Fall of Reason*. New York: Random House, 2005.

Fukuyama, Francis. *Our Posthuman Future*. New York: Farrar, Straus and Giroux, 2002.

Galison, Peter. *Image and Logic: A Material Culture of Microphysics*. Chicago: University of Chicago Press, 1997.

Geertz, Clifford. *Available Light*. Princeton, NJ: Princeton University Press, 2000.

Giberson, Karl W., and Francis S. Collins. *The Language of Science and Faith*. Downers Grove, IL: InterVarsity, 2011.

Gingerich, Owen. *God's Universe*. Cambridge: Harvard University Press, 2006.

Gould, Stephen Jay. *Rocks of Ages: Science and Religion in the Fullness of Life*. New York: Ballantine, 1999.

———. *Time's Arrow, Time's Cycle: Myth and Metaphor in the Discovery of Geological Time*. Cambridge, MA: Harvard University Press, 1987.

Selected Bibliography 265

Greene, Mott T. "Genesis and Geology Revisited: The Order of Nature and the Nature of Order in Nineteenth-Century Britain." In *When Science and Christianity Meet*, edited by David Lindberg and Ronald L. Numbers, 139-59. Chicago: University of Chicago Press, 2003.

Gregersen, Niels Henrik. "A Contextual Coherence Theory for the Science-Theology Dialogue." In *Rethinking Theology and Science*, edited by Niels Henrik Gregersen and J. Wentzel van Huyssteen, 181-229. Grand Rapids: Eerdmans, 1998.

———. "Critical Realism and Other Realisms." In *Fifty Years in Science and Religion: Ian G. Barbour and His Legacy*, edited by Robert J. Russell, 77-95. Burlington, VT: Ashgate, 2004.

Gregersen, Niels Henrik, and J. Wentzel van Huyssteen, eds. *Rethinking Theology and Science: Six Models for the Current Dialogue*. Grand Rapids: Eerdmans, 1998.

Gustafson, James M. *An Examined Faith: The Grace of Self-Doubt*. Minneapolis: Fortress, 2004.

Hacking, Ian. *Representing and Intervening*. Cambridge: Cambridge University Press, 1983.

Hart, David Bentley. *Atheist Delusions: The Christian Revolution and Its Fashionable Enemies*. New Haven: Yale University Press, 2009.

———. *The Beauty of the Infinite: The Aesthetics of Christian Truth*. Grand Rapids: Eerdmans, 2003.

———. *The Doors of the Sea: Where Was God in the Tsunami?* Grand Rapids: Eerdmans, 2005.

Hauerwas, Stanley. *With the Grain of the Universe*. The Gifford Lectures (2001). Grand Rapids: Brazos, 2001.

———. *The State of the University: Academic Knowledges and the Knowledge of God*. Malden, MA: Blackwell, 2007.

Haught, John F. *God After Darwin: A Theology of Evolution*. Boulder CO: Westview, 2000.

———. *Is Nature Enough?* Cambridge: Cambridge University Press, 2006.

Heller, Michael. *Creative Tension: Essays on Science and Religion*. West Conshohocken, PA: Templeton Foundation, 2003.

Hinlicky, Paul R. *Paths Not Taken: Fates of Theology from Luther through Leibniz*. Grand Rapids: Eerdmans, 2009.

Holder, Rodney. "Thomas Torrance: 'Retreat to Commitment' or a New Place for Natural Theology." *Journal of Theology and Science* 7 (2009) 275-91.

Hollinger, David A. *After Cloven Tongues of Fire: Protestant Liberalism in Modern American History*. Princeton, NJ: Princeton University Press, 2013.

Holmes, Richard. *The Age of Wonder*. New York: Pantheon, 2008.

Holton, Gerald. *Einstein, History, and Other Passions: The Rebellion against Science at the End of the Twentieth Century*. Reading, MA: Addison-Wesley, 1996.

Hull, David L. *Darwin and His Critics: The Reception of Darwin's Theory of Evolution by the Scientific Community*. Chicago: University of Chicago Press, 1973.

Hunsinger, George. *Disruptive Grace: Studies in the Theology of Karl Barth*. Grand Rapids: Eerdmans, 2000.

Isaacson, Walter. *Einstein: His Life and His Universe*. New York: Simon & Schuster, 2007.

Jenson, Robert W. *On Thinking the Human*. Grand Rapids: Eerdmans, 2003.

John Paul II. *Fides et Ratio*. Boston: Pauline Books and Media, 1998.

Kandel, Eric R. *In Search of Memory: The Emergence of a New Science of Mind.* New York: W. W. Norton, 2006.

Kehlmann, Daniel. *Measuring the World.* Translated by Carol Janeway. New York: Pantheon, 2006.

Koyré, Alexandre. *From Closed World to the Infinite Universe.* Baltimore: Johns Hopkins University Press, 1957.

Kuhn, Thomas S. *The Structure of Scientific Revolutions.* Chicago: University of Chicago Press, 1970.

Küng, Hans. *The Beginning of All Things: Science and Religion.* Translated by John Bowden. Grand Rapids: Eerdmans, 2007.

Laughlin, Robert B. *A Different Universe.* New York: Basic, 2005.

Lightman, Alan. *A Sense of the Mysterious: Science and the Human Spirit.* New York: Pantheon, 2005.

Lindberg, David C. "Galileo, the Church, and the Cosmos." In *When Science and Christianity Meet,* edited by David C. Lindberg and Ronald L. Numbers, 33–60. Chicago: University of Chicago Press, 2003.

Lindberg, David C., and Ronald L. Numbers, eds. *When Science and Christianity Meet.* Chicago: University of Chicago Press, 2003.

Livingstone, David N. "Re-placing Darwinism and Christianity." In *When Science and Christianity Meet,* edited by David C. Lindberg and Ronald L. Numbers, 183–202. Chicago: University of Chicago Press, 2003.

Long, Stephen D. "Radical Orthodoxy." In *The Cambridge Companion to Postmodern Theology,* edited by Kevin J. Vanhoozer, 126–45. Cambridge: Cambridge University Press, 2003.

Losch, Andreas. "On the Origins of Critical Realism." *Journal of Theology and Science* 7 (February 2009) 85–106.

MacIntyre, Alasdair. *Whose Justice? Whose Rationality?* Notre Dame, IN: University of Notre Dame Press, 1988.

McGrath, Alister. *The Science of God: An Introduction to Scientific Theology.* Grand Rapids: Eerdmans, 2004.

McKenny, Gerald P. *To Relieve the Human Condition.* Albany, NY: State University of New York Press, 1997.

Migliore, Daniel L. *Faith Seeking Understanding.* Grand Rapids: Eerdmans, 1991.

Moltmann, Jürgen. *Science and Wisdom.* Minneapolis: Fortress, 2003.

Murphy, Nancey. *Beyond Liberalism and Fundamentalism.* Valley Forge, PA: Trinity Press International, 1996.

Murphy, Nancey, and George F. R. Ellis. *On the Moral Nature of the Universe.* Minneapolis: Augsburg, 1996.

Neiman, Susan. *Evil in Modern Thought: An Alternative History of Philosophy.* Princeton, NJ: Princeton University Press, 2002.

Niekerk, Kees van Kooten. "A Critical Realist Perspective on the Dialogue between Theology and Science." In *Rethinking Theology and Science: Six Models for the Current Dialogue,* edited by Niels Henrik Gregersen and J. Wentzel van Huyssteen, 51–86. Grand Rapids: Eerdmans, 1998.

Numbers, Ronald L. "Science without God: Natural Laws and Christian Beliefs." In *When Science and Christianity Meet,* edited by David C. Lindberg and Ronald L. Numbers, 265–85. Chicago: University of Chicago Press, 2003.

Nygren, Anders. *Meaning and Method: Prolegomena to a Scientific Philosophy of Religion and a Scientific Theology.* Translated by Philip S. Watson. Philadelphia: Fortress, 1972.
Peacocke, Arthur. *Evolution: The Disguised Friend of Faith?* West Conshohocken, PA: Templeton Foundation, 2004.
———. *From DNA to Dean: Reflections and Explorations of a Priest-Scientist.* Harrisburg, PA: Canterbury, 1996.
———. *Intimations of Reality: Critical Realism in Science and Religion.* Notre Dame, IN: University of Notre Dame Press, 1984.
———. *Theology for a Scientific Age.* Minneapolis: Fortress, 1993.
Peters, Ted, ed. *Science and Theology: The New Consonance.* Boulder, CO: Westview, 1998.
Peters, Ted, Karen Lebacqz, and Gaymon Bennett. *Sacred Cells?: Why Christians Should Support Stem Cell Research.* Lanham, MD: Rowman & Littlefield, 2008.
Pinker, Steven. *The Better Angels of Our Nature.* New York: Viking, 2011.
———. *The Blank Slate: The Modern Denial of Human Nature.* New York: Viking, 2002.
———. *The Stuff of Thought: Language as a Window into Human Nature.* New York: Viking, 2007.
Placher, William. *Unapologetic Theology.* Philadelphia: Westminster John Knox, 1989.
Polkinghorne, John. *Belief in God in an Age of Science.* New Haven, CT: Yale University Press, 1998.
———. *Beyond Science: The Wider Human Context.* Cambridge: Cambridge University Press, 1996.
———. "Creation and the Structure of the Physical World. *Theology Today* XLIV (April 1987) 54–68.
———. *From Physicist to Priest: An Autobiography.* London: SPCK, 2007.
———. *Reason and Reality.* Philadelphia: Trinity Press International, 1991.
———. *Science and Christian Belief: Theological Reflections of a Bottom-Up Thinker.* London: SPCK, 1994.
———. *Science and the Trinity.* New Haven, CT: Yale University Press, 2004.
Polkinghorne, John, and Michael Welker. *Faith in the Living God.* Minneapolis: Fortress, 2001.
———. "Introduction: Science and Theology on the End of the World and the Ends of God." In *The End of the World and the Ends of God,* edited by John Polkinghorne and Michael Welker, 5–13. Harrisburg, PA: Trinity Press International, 2000.
Roberts, Jon H., and James Turner. *The Sacred and the Secular University.* Princeton, NJ: Princeton University Press, 2000.
Rolston, Holmes, "Does Nature Need to be Redeemed," *Zygon* 29 (June 1994) 205-29.
Rubenstein, Richard E. *Aristotle's Children.* Orlando, FL: Harcourt, 2003.
Russell, Robert J., ed. *Fifty Years in Science and Religion: Ian G. Barbour and His Legacy.* Burlington, VT: Ashgate, 2004.
Russell, R. J., N. Murphy, and A. Peacocke, eds. *Chaos and Complexity: Scientific Perspectives on Divine Action.* Notre Dame, IN: Vatican Observatory Foundation and The Center for Theology and the Natural Sciences, 1995.
———. "Theology and Science: Current Issues and Future Direction." http://ctns.org/russell_article.html.
Santmire. Paul. *The Travail of Nature: The Ambiguous Ecological Promise of Christian Theology.* Philadelphia: Fortress, 1985.

Shapin, Steven. *The Scientific Revolution*. Chicago: University of Chicago Press, 1996.
Sheets-Johnstone, Maxine. *The Roots of Morality*. University Park, PA: Pennsylvania State University Press, 2008.
Shermer, Michael. *How We Believe*. New York: Henry Holt and Company, 2000.
Schönborn, Christoph. "The Designs of Science." *First Things*, January 2006, 34–38.
———. "Reasonable Science, Reasonable Faith." *First Things*, April 2007, 21–24.
Sobel, Dava. *Longitude*. New York: Walker Publishing Co., 1995.
Steiner, George. *Real Presences*. Chicago: Chicago University Press, 1989
Stiver, Dan R. "Theological Method." In *The Cambridge Companion to Postmodern Theology*, edited by Kevin J. Vanhoozer, 170–85. Cambridge: Cambridge University Press, 2003.
Stout, Jeffrey. *The Flight from Authority*. Notre Dame, IN: University of Notre Dame Press, 1981.
Taylor, Charles. *A Secular Age*. Cambridge, MA: The Belknap Press of Harvard University Press, 2007.
———. *Sources of the Self: The Making of the Modern Identity*. Cambridge: Harvard University Press, 1989.
Thiemann, Ronald. *Revelation and Theology*. Notre Dame, IN: University of Notre Dame Press, 1994.
Thiselton, Anthony. *New Horizons on Hermeneutics*. Grand Rapids, Zondervan, 1992.
Torrance, Thomas F. *Theological Science*. Oxford: Oxford University Press, 1969.
Van Huyssteen, J. Wentzel. *Alone in the World? Human Uniqueness in Science and Theology*. The Gifford Lectures (2004). Grand Rapids: Eerdmans, 2006.
———. *Essays in Postfoundationalist Theology*. Grand Rapids: Eerdmans, 1997.
———. *The Shaping of Rationality: Toward Interdisciplinarity in Theology and Science*. Grand Rapids: Eerdmans, 1999.
Vanhoozer, Kevin J., ed. *The Cambridge Companion to Postmodern Theology*. Cambridge: Cambridge University Press, 2003.
Wasserman, Earl. *The Subtler Language*. Baltimore: Johns Hopkins University Press, 1959.
Weinberg, Steven. *Facing Up: Science and Its Cultural Adversaries*. Cambridge, MA: Harvard University Press, 2001.
———. "A Designer Universe?" In *Science and Religion: Are They Compatible?*, edited by Paul Kurtz, 31–40. Amherst, NY: Prometheus, 2003.
———. "Physics and History." In *The One Culture?*, edited by Jay A. Labinger and Harry Collins, 116–27. Chicago: University of Chicago Press, 2012.
Wilson, Edward O. *The Social Conquest of Earth*. New York: W. W. Norton, 2012.
Williams, Rowan. *Tokens of Trust*. Louisville: Westminster John Knox, 2007.
———. *Why Study the Past?* Grand Rapids: Eerdmans, 2005.
Witham, Larry. *The Measure of God: Our Century-Long Struggle to Reconcile Science and Religion*. San Francisco: HarperSanFrancisco, 2005.
Wolterstorff, Nicholas. *Divine Discourse: Philosophical Refection on the Claim that God Speaks*. Cambridge: Cambridge University Press, 1995.
Wright, N. T. *The Resurrection of the Son of God*. London: SPCK, 2003.

Author Index

Alder, Ken, 145–47
Aristotle, 4, 31–32, 37, 58, 179, 181, 203
Augustine, Thomas, 37, 42, 67, 191, 203–5

Bacon, Francis, 38, 41, 50, 55, 58–59, 84, 167 54, 236
Barbour, Ian, ix, 81–87, 94–96, 131, 132, 142, 206, 239, 255
Barr, Stephen M., 68–69, 93–94, 107
Barth, Karl, 22, 109, 112–14, 116, 117–18, 126, 177, 187–88, 200, 249
Berry, Wendell, 137, 173–74, 256–57
Bloom, Paul, 5, 8, 213
Boyle, Robert, 44, 51–55
Brooke, John Hedley, 30, 76, 111, 137
Brueggemann, Walter, 22, 195, 222, 257

Collins, Francis S., 12, 14, 20, 212, 226

Darwin, Charles, 8, 17, 24, 31, 33, 35, 38, 44, 45, 47, 145
  neo-Darwinism, 26 n.56, 39, 219
  On the Origin of Species, ix, 4, 28, 63, 70
  religious faith, 4, 49
Dennett, Daniel C., 4, 22, 42, 107, 181, 212, 259, 260 n.149
Descartes, René, 38, 50, 52, 83, 159, 222, 236, 237
Draper and White, 11, 30–31
Drees, George L. 217, 220–23
Dupré, Louis, 198, 202
Dyson, Freeman, 6, 150, 256, 258, 261

Eagleton, Terry, 181–82, 209
Ellul, Jacques, 23 n.49, 137–39, 190–95, 248–49, 257

Freeman, Charles, 37, 42

Galileo, Galilei, 15, 17, 31–41, 55, 56–58, 74, 99, 245
Geertz, Clifford, 92, 123, 162
Giberson, Karl W., 13 n.26, 14–15, 20
Gregersen, Niels Henrik, 81, 128, 257 n.136
Gould, Stephen Jay, 35, 47–48, 65, 217–20, 223

Harris, Sam, 3, 5, 19, 209
Hart, David Bentley, 34, 48, 57, 121, 173, 175, 178, 182, 190, 231, 254, 260
Hauerwas, Stanley, 23, 117–18, 186–87, 234–35
Haught, John F. 19, 80 n. 21, 97–98, 103–4, 109, 134, 227
Heller, Michael, 33, 251–52
Holton, Gerald, 36, 83
Hull, David L., 4, 45, 59, 64
Hunsinger, George, 200–202

James, William, 3, 117, 178, 187, 207
John Paul II (Pope), 16, 24–26, 74, 180, 184, 250

Kandel, Eric R., 149–50
Kehlmann, Daniel, 154–55
Kuhn, Thomas S., *92, 122, 123, 160, 163, 185*

269

Author Index

Küng, Hans, 109, 210, 239, 241
Lewis, C. S., 99, 105, 212
Lightman, Alan, 153–59
Lindberg, David C., 30, 34, 37, 58, 218
Livingstone, David N., 36 n.13, 62 n.75, 63
Luther, Martin, 9, 11, 38, 40, 41, 174–75, 187, 260

MacIntyre, Alasdair, 167, 203 n.82, 229, 238, 244, 245
McGrath, Alister, 111, 112, 118, 126–27, 209, 243
Moltmann, Jürgen, 102–4, 209, 210, 247
Murphy, Nancey, 72–73, 107, 125, 140

Neiman, Susan, 45–48, 237
Newton, Isaac, 31–32, 38, 44, 49–52, 59, 65–68, 137–38, 166, 219
Numbers, Ronald L., 34, 43, 70

Paul (Saint), 13, 17, 40, 100
Peacocke, Arthur, ix, 15, 80, 85–87, 107, 119, 125, 139–40, 206, 231–32, 255
Peters, Ted, 121, 123, 129, 136, 247, 250
Pinker, Steven, 7, 179, 194
Placher, William, 115
Polkinghorne, John, ix, 22, 82–87, 93, 95, 96, 99, 101, 104, 108, 117, 125–26, 130–32, 134, 138, 207–8, 223, 227, 232, 256
Rubenstein, Richard, 31–32, 227, 240
Russell, R. J., 86, 105, 128 n.57

Shapin, Steven, 51–52
Sheets-Johnstone, Maxine, 7, 27, 209 n.6
Schönborn, Christoph (Cardinal), 39, 67 n 88
Sobel, Dava, 144–45,
Stout, Jeffrey, 56, 115–17, 238, 257

Taylor, Charles, 6, 11, 40–42, 46, 63, 66, 67, 223, 236, 256, 261
Teilhard de Chardin, Pierre, ix, 2, 75, 77–80, 84
Torrance, Thomas F., 112–14, 126–27, 129

van Huyssteen, J. Wentzel, 92, 94, 97, 106, 109, 117, 119, 133–34, 140, 183, 225, 245, 251–52,

Warfield and Hodge, 36
Weinberg, Steven, 2, 92, 123–24, 133, 149, 162–64, 169, 243
Whitehead, Alfred, ix, 2, 76–82, 87, 108
Witham, Larry, 186
Wolterstorff, Nicholas, 201–2
Wright, N.T., 54, 100

Subject Index

atheism, atheistic, new atheism, 1, 2–9, 18–20, 28, 34, 36, 45, 63, 73, 75, 94, 97, 106, 137–39, 211, 259
Aristotelian science, 16, 31, 36, 51, 76, 177, 244 n.101
  renaissance, 32, 112 n.6
  apologetics, 39, 117, 171–77, 227

Center for Theology and the Natural Science, Berkley, CA, 89
Center of Theological Inquiry, Princeton, NJ, 210, 230
common ground, x, 19, 24, 28, 31, 74, 80, 90–94, 96, 110, 118–25, 141, 229, 230, 245, 246, 252
Creationists, 12, 19, 73, 135, 233. *See also* intelligent design, designers
critical realism, 94–96, 110, 113, 125–29, 133, 220, 221

dialogue, 25–29, 76, 86, 87, 90, 121, 127, 131–37, 142, 206–10, 229, 240, 248, 256
  asymmetrical, 129–31, 139, 206, 209
  interdisciplinary, 7, 97, 106, 109, 120, 129, 138, 140, 210, 226, 244–46, 252
dogmatics, 56, 113, 115, 171, 176–77, 227

existential, existentialism, 74, 186, 187
  ontological, 188
  seriousness, 174, 175, 181, 191, 197
  verification, 178

epistemology, 22, 31 n.3, 41, 52, 55, 58, 67, 72, 90, 115, 125, 142, 184, 198, 223. *See also* ontology
  crisis, 122 n.38, 244–45
  epistemic circle or fit, 50–61, 92, 129, 140
  epistemic scope, 133, 134
  isolation, 94, 140
  privilege, 91, 123, 133, 162, 235, 239 n.85
Evangelicals, 1, 18, 20–23, 28, 29, 67, 72, 113, 135 n.69, 175
  turnaround, 11–15
evil, 28, 45–49, 100, 102, 104, 136, 194 n.55, 237, 255, 260, 261

faith, x, 9, 18, 23, 25, 29, 39, 64, 112, 169
  faith and reason, 61, 105, 119, 125, 170–84, 205, 250, 260
  faith and revelation, 25, 126, 180, 197–99, 202, 215
  faith and science, 13, 14, 20, 58, 90, 207
fideism, 28, 86, 113

Gifford Lectures, 3, 53, 76, 85–87, 117, 136, 185–87, 207
grace, 26, 54, 103, 117, 201, 205

holism, holistic, 67, 76, 107–9, 115, 130, 170, 211, 224, 230, 235, 253

intelligent design (ID), 1, 4, 7, 9, 12, 22, 39, 64, 80, 107, 211, 233
  designers, Designer, 4, 7, 22, 47, 73, 93, 183, 227

271

Subject Index

irreconcilable differences, 30–69, 71, 139, 206, 207, 190

locutionary, illocutionary, 188, 201, 202

materialism, 25, 31, 50, 51, 67, 68, 81, 138–39, 206
methodology, 10, 20, 22, 33, 41, 44, 55–62, 82, 92, 110–18, 121, 171, 247
modernity, postmodern, 22, 34, 60, 67, 118–19, 260

natural law, 16–17, 26–27, 36, 44, 45, 64
natural theology, 48, 51–53, 185–88
naturalism, 31 n.3, 45–46, 71–73, 211, 217, 220–21
natural philosophy, 41, 49, 51–52, 72, 75, 111
non-foundational theology, 24, 92, 115, 117, 121, 133

objectivity, 33, 44, 65, 83, 95, 114–15, 122, 124, 148, 183, 203, 223
   subjectivity, 114, 115, 173, 183, 203, 204
ontology, 90–92, 129, 114, 235. *See also* epistemology
   ontological-epistemological fit, 61, 91, 92, 95, 129
   truth claims, 90, 117, 126, 128, 168, 185, 189
original sin, 14, 26, 54, 203, 225, 237

positivism, 71, 83, 86, 259
postmodern, x, 3, 6, 10, 24, 90–94, 110, 117–19, 122–25, 127, 168, 192
providence, 34, 35, 43–52, 64, 105

realism, 83, 95, 112, 119, 126–29, 136, 160, 221, 234
reason, rationality, 27, 28, 66, 94, 117, 120, 173, 229, 232, 244, 259
   disengaged, 11, 41, 236, 260–61
   mathematical, 151–51
reductionism, 24, 148–51, 169, 195, 210, 212

revolution, scientific, 32, 36, 50 n.50, 63, 66–68
revelation, see faith and revelation

secularism, 66–68, 208, 240
separate domains, ix, 25, 28, 36, 71, 76, 217–24, 247
self-authenticating, 40–42, 56, 90, 94, 127. *See also* fideism
sibling rivals, as theology and science, xi, 37, 139, 207, 220, 245
science
   collective enterprise, 91, 162, 165
   hard/soft, 20, 90, 123, 169
   history, xi, 30–38, 66, 83, 92, 109, 119, 123, 156, 162–63, 218–20
   modern, 1, 11, 18, 39, 41, 44, 62, 65, 66–69, 82, 130, 136, 147
   superior methodology, 20, 28, 64, 111, 140, 166, 240
   science and religion, 7–8, 9, 11, 31, 52, 62–63, 81, 207–14, 246, 250
sibling rivals,
soul, 8, 26, 74, 99, 205, 210–11, 222, 224
subjectivity, see objectivity
supernaturalism, 43–45, 71, 209

theology
   handmaiden, 37–39
   logic, 173, 178, 181, 188, 193, 202
   methodology, 116, 134, 171, 177, 197, 226, 229, 246
   queen of the sciences, 20, 33, 37–42, 49, 91, 140, 220, 239
   truth claims, 15, 80, 124, 127, 129, 165, 235, 181–84, 256–58
theology and science or religion and science, x, 133, 82, 142
teleology, teleological, 4, 51, 52, 64
thought experiment, 151–54, 72
Templeton Foundation, 89, 246, 255
truth, unity of, 16, 24–25, 136, 250

world view, 9, 21, 22, 33, 49–55, 63–65, 69, 76, 107, 224
word truth, 181, 185, 190–97
   public truth, 231–35, 237